Parties

A LITERARY COMPANION

SUSANNA JOHNSTON

Parties

A LITERARY COMPANION

Foreword by John Wells

M
MACMILLAN
LONDON

To Percy Weatherall

———◦◦◦———

First published 1994 by Macmillan London Limited

a division of Pan Macmillan Publishers Limited
Cavaye Place London SW10 9PG
and Basingstoke

Associated companies throughout the world

ISBN 0 333 59279 4

1 3 5 7 9 8 6 4 2

A CIP catalogue record for this book is available from
the British Library

Phototypeset by CentraCet Limited, Cambridge
Printed and bound in Great Britain by
Mackays of Chatham plc, Chatham, Kent

CONTENTS

PART FOUR: ENDINGS

FOREWORD

—————◦◦◦◦◦—————

The word 'party' comes from the French *partie*, and is to do with separateness, apartness, the part rather than the whole. Its primary sense in English since the eighteenth century has been in the political context of 'party strife', of one part or Party opposing another.

Used to mean a social gathering, the word turned up even earlier than that, but there has always been the sense, acknowledged or unacknowledged, of *apartheid* or exclusivity.

Being asked may be hell, but not being asked is far worse.

Those who go to parties in the so-called developed countries sometimes take a rather snooty attitude. They see pictures of people in the so-called developing countries stamping round in a circle, heads plastered with red ochre and ram's fat, yodelling and shrieking in the firelight, then look at the snaps in the social pages of people with double-barrelled names grinning into the camera in funny clothes and can't see any connection between them.

But parties, as we all know, are parties, wherever you go.

Manners, of course, vary: children in the Pacific are taught to eat an eel or a pigeon starting with the head; in England they are taught the right way to eat asparagus. Maoris press noses, Westerners press cheeks. In Vanuatu they stick biros through their noses; in the Isle of Wight they stick bits of polished stone and metal through their ears.

Sometimes, it is true, ways of life converge: Maori children learn Western dances, Western children unconsciously revert to a recognizably Maori style of dancing, quivering their fingers, popping their eyeballs and sticking out their tongues.

But parties are still parties.

The desire to celebrate is universal: the birth or naming of a child, its puberty, its circumcision, its election to Pop at Eton, its acceptance into the warrior class, its becoming a chieftain or managing director of ICI. So is the celebration of birthdays, betrothals and marriages.

More confusing to outside observers is the idea in Western culture of having a party apparently for the sake of having a party.

Scratch the surface, and the same universal urges are apparent.

Parties are always tribal, to do with membership of a group. They are also to do with the warding off of tribal terrors and the conjuring up of tribal pride and joy.

The Solomon Islanders bunch up and dance to frighten away the *dodore* or Giant Wandering Penis they fear will come to destroy their livelihood: executives in London and New York do the same to scare away the spectre of unemployment.

But the core of any good party is the core of the Voodoo dance: the summoning up of all the ancient powers of your tribe, the use of costume and rhythm and intoxicants to reach a state of ecstasy in which you can chew live coal or crunch glass between your teeth, apparently unharmed. You are immortal, inspired, inhabited by all the energy and magnificence of your ancestors.

It may involve, as it does in the South Seas, imitating enraged monkeys or snakes, 'weaving drunkards' or newborn babies, even smothering yourself all over in clay and pretending to be a ghost.

It can go wrong.

But, as you will discover as you turn the pages of this anthology, even Western parties can have thier own grisly anthropological fascination.

John Wells

INTRODUCTION

Parties, great shakers of the social kaleidoscope, provide a mechanism whereby mortals meet. They could be said to be a manifestation of the nature of humans; endemic to the essential gregariousness of our beings.

Parties romp through literature. When first I began to find material for this book I discovered sixty on the shelves of my bedroom alone. It made me wonder why I ever got out of bed. Since Roman times they have provided a popular subject for authors who, through social gatherings, have snatched at the opportunity to include serious and humorous conversations, exaggerated descriptions for satirical effect and much exposure of human frailty.

They are frequently linked with glamour, romance and courtship. When, in Jane Austen's *Pride and Prejudice*, Mr Bingley titillated Mrs Bennet's maternal ambitions by renting the nearby Netherfield estate, he also made it clear that he intended to be at the first Assembly with a large party. 'To be fond of dancing was a certain step towards falling in love; and very lively hopes of Mr Bingley's heart were entertained.'

None of this means, of course, that parties are necessarily going to be 'fun'. Guests can have a foul time and be made to feel hideously redundant – as did the thwarted performer in the song, much belted out by Gracie Fields, 'I took my harp to a party; but nobody asked me to play.'

The very mention of the word wallflower conjures up an image of rejection vivid enough to make the blood run cold. Hard though it is to imagine such an experience befalling Lady Diana Cooper, she tells us in her autobiography, *The Rainbow Comes and Goes*, that 'those of us who found the shame unendurable (and I was one) could only sneak downstairs to the cloakroom, ostensibly to have their dresses mended, and hope not to meet fellow wallflowers in the same predicament.'

I know of several party-goers who actually loathe them and consider each one a hurdle. None the less, year in year out, they continue – like any gambler – to accept the challenge of the lighted candle and to demonstrate, as did the future bridegroom (to quote Dr Johnson when speaking of a man who remarried immediately after the death of his wife with whom he had been very unhappy) 'the triumph of hope over experience'.

At parties it is the fittest who survive.

Miss Yeo, headmistress of Abbots Hill School for girls, where I boarded in the 1940s, proved herself to be thus fit. I think that it was thanks to Miss Yeo that I first became aware of veneration for rank. The war was over and she was summoned, as part of a teachers' convention, to a garden party at Buckingham Palace. It was announced with reverent excitement at prayers that the whole school might assemble in the courtyard to see her off. Although it was a weekday, those fortunate among us to possess a camera were given special dispensation to capture this moment of glory.

Miss Yeo smiled faintly, terrified that any movement might disarray her. Waving stiffly but gracefully, she was driven away by the garden boy in the school Austin.

In the evening the girls were invited to share her experience. So dense had been the crowds at Buckingham Palace that Miss Yeo never saw the King or the Queen but she found the overall spectacle 'interesting'. She said that she hoped that her pupils, as they embarked upon life after school, would realize that the monarchy was our most precious asset and that they would forbear to flirt with any ideology, alien or unpatriotic, such as 'Socialism, Communism or any other 'isms''. Miss Yeo didn't mention Conservatism.

Few parties can have been more harrowing than my own coming-out dance, held in the River Room of the Savoy Hotel in the summer of 1951.

An insurance tycoon and a friend of my parents who had more or less revived the skiing industry in Austria after the war, flew over a team of Tyrolean 'Schulplattner' musicians for the occasion. They arrived with zithers and guitars, leder-hosen, studded harness and feathers in their brimmed hats. All day they practised in the ballroom, looking out over the Embankment. Austerity was ending. The first postwar Conservative government was in power. Guests were agog. The moment came. The 'gimmick' of the Austrian players had been well publicized. They were announced by a major-domo who, in a deep voice, sonorously thanked the tycoon. Not a sound came from the instruments. The zithers and guitars had proved too much for the electrical supply and juices were cut off. The players struggled with bleeding fingers; tears rolling down their cheeks – knowing that the game was up. I don't remember much more about it but I recall my father saying, 'Let's get the hell out of here.'

Over the centuries parties, (and here I speak of almost all social gatherings: dances, balls, receptions and other contrived or spontaneous get-togethers), appear to have given as much pain as pleasure.

Olga, in Anton Chekhov's *The Party* didn't much enjoy herself.

Her arms and legs began to shake – the result, she supposed, of dejection, vexation, forced smiling and the discomfort that she felt all over her body. To conceal her trembling from the guests she tried to talk louder, to laugh, and to keep moving. 'If I suddenly burst into tears I'll say I've got toothache' she thought.

Mrs Hwfa Williams, however, in her wide-eyed autobiography of the 1930s, tells of dizzy happiness. 'It was such fun, that dance. The Ritz was at its zenith in those days, and they carried out all our plans and arrangements for the *cotillon* admirably. There was not a hitch of any kind and the food was excellent.'

For better for worse, we seem to have developed into party-going primates (as opposed to orang-utans who went in a different direction and became solitary creatures), along with chimpanzees who share our convivial tendencies and, although they do not necessarily agonize over guest lists, it is understood that they thoroughly delight in amusing an audience.

Household pets, dogs in particular, on the other hand, react pretty grumpily when their owners entertain. They feel threatened and invaded; not to mention neglected. F. Scott Fitzgerald describes such a situation in *The Great Gatsby*. 'The little dog was sitting on the table with blind eyes through the smoke, and from time to time groaning faintly.' Of course he may have been affecting this. All parties offer scope for showing off; for dressing up, flirting and making conquests.

Never can party exhibitionism have reached a higher peak than in the case of Lady Caroline Lamb. During her infatuation with Lord Byron, all hell broke loose.

Much chewed over, even today, is the story of the party at Devonshire House where she was reputed to have been carried in under a silver dish-cover from which, naked, she leapt on to the dinner table.

David Cecil, in his biography of her hapless husband, Lord Melbourne, describes Lady Caroline's attempt to unnerve her reluctant lover.

Wild with rage and resolved in revenge to bring him to public shame at whatever cost to herself, she rushed into the supper room and, breaking a glass, began to gash her naked arms with the pieces. Immediately the place was in tumult; women screamed. Only Lady Melbourne (Lady Caroline's mother-in-law), with her usual presence of mind, seized Caroline's hands and held her down. A few minutes later, still jabbing at herself with a pair of scissors, she was carried from the room.

The effects of excess of all types are regularly introduced through observation of party behaviour. Juvenal, in his satire on Roman society, jeers at the spectacle of feasting orgies.

What a mouth the man must have – to demolish whole boars – just the kind of animal to serve up at crowded dinner parties! But you'll pay for it in the end, when you remove your clothes and make your way into the bath with all that undigested peacock in your fat stomach.

Few of us, today, have problems with undigested peacock but party food and consciousness-altering drugs (the most usual of these, on account of the workings of the law, being alcohol) take their toll.

Man – a paradoxical creature; both solitary and gregarious – has since time immemorial deemed drugs a necessary route to the breaking down of barriers, self-consciousness and inhibitions.

Marriage, sex and ideas are sought and found in hand-picked crowds (turning parties into brokers of a sort) and there have always been an astonishing number of them; not least of a biblical nature (take the Last Supper), given for an astonishing number of reasons all over the world; in towns, in tents, in the country, in cities, in pubs, palaces or on the streets. Strings of occasions call for celebration and the word 'party' attaches itself euphoniously to most of them . . . birthday, anniversary, wedding, funeral, Hallowe'en, New Year's Eve or what you will.

For those with reasonably outgoing natures the first reaction on being invited to a party is excitement. It is, however, interesting to query many of the motives of hospitality. Some of them can be unappealing. It is tempting to surmise that, from time to time, parties are thrown to feed a power complex in those who instigate them. One of the by-products of this may be the intention of settling old scores by deliberately leaving rankling hopefuls off the guest list. Naturally there were other, more imaginative reasons for the throwing of the famous Devonshire House Ball in 1897, the year of Queen Victoria's Diamond Jubilee, but it did account for some devastating anguish. The invitations went out only a month before the great event – keeping those who were borderline cases in a state of unnatural anticipation. One society lady, it is believed, never made a total recovery from the pain she experienced as the day drew near and hope dwindled.

Another glittering ball was given by the present Duke and Duchess of Devonshire, just over a century later, at Chatsworth. As a matter of fact I went to it and so did an astonishing number of other people. I borrowed my Aunt's tiara and have never before witnessed so sublime a spectacle. On that occasion I don't believe that anyone was 'left out' but if, by chance, they were, I don't blame them for smarting.

In contrast to that Chatsworth Ball where the point of the party was, it seemed to me, to spread waves of pleasure, there are hosts and hostesses who wish to 'get on' or 'in' in society; who hope to be talked about and to stake out their places on the map. Parties are given for political advancement; for the promotion of business deals; for the launching of books, clothes or cars.

It goes without saying that there are thousands of wholesome parties; ones that are given for charity or for 'fun'. Not every female guest is going to be a wallflower and there are plenty of people who look forward to a 'jolly' in a straightforward way. Once there, some will exchange ideas, some will fall in love and some will tumble by the wayside.

Even Charity parties, set up for ostensibly high-minded reasons, can be dubious. The world-weary anti-hero of Frederick Forsyth's ironic short story 'No Comebacks' describes one during which his grizzly fate is sealed. 'It was at a party in aid of some charity – the sort of thing where a boring time is had by all and the tiny balance left from the ticket money is sent to provide a bowl of milk in Bangladesh.'

Children's parties, too, when looked back upon, often throw up negative emotions; unfair judgements of competitive games, terror of Punch and Judy, loathing of dressing up, burst balloons, mouldy presents and vomiting. This may be because they were not offered stimulants or sex.

There were some terrible parties in the 1960s. People lay in piles eating hash-cake and believing that they should be seen to be 'way out' as mature ladies danced naked with their teenage sons. It must have been agony for the truly conventional – trying so hard to be laid-back and speechless.

There are also dangers attached to arranging a party in order to introduce specific people to each other; parties where the, supposed, stars can remember nothing but pain. John Lehr, in his biography of Joe Orton describes just such a one.

Having befriended them, Monteith gave a party for Orton and Haliwell the next year. 'I realized that they had no friends whatsoever. The purpose of the party was to let them meet people who had an influence in the literary world. It was a big party. They sat on the sofa the whole evening and didn't speak to anybody. Haliwell and Orton were hopeless socially. The party was a total flop.'

The success of a party must depend largely on the party-giver. The renowned Sybil Colefax, hostess *extraordinaire* of the 1930s, would regularly tuck bills into the folded napkins of her guests at the start of a lunch party. People were happy to chip in for they knew that, at her house, they would meet celebrities with whom they would never have rubbed shoulders under any other circumstance. This can work both ways. Sometimes hosts and hostesses have paid their guests in order to put in an appearance. Soon after the last war there was a successful agency called 'Rent a Duchess'. It is rumoured that, at one time, there were ten dukes and thirty duchesses on their books.

I have come across other versions of this type of reciprocity. Recently my brother threw a party in Santo Domingo to honour both my visit and the quincentenary of Christopher Columbus. It took place in a sixteenth-century courtyard where a merenge group played in the background. As the guests took their leave, to my brother's surprise, two or three of them asked if he would refund their fares – pointing out that they had made a great sacrifice in coming. How, I wondered, does my brother differ from Sybil Colefax?

Perhaps individuals should be warned in the nursery that they take their lives into their own hands when they accept to go to anything but the cosiest of family parties (not that these are proof against complications). Marvellous things might happen but, equally, any guest might, unexpectedly, come face to face with a deadly enemy, a jealous rival, not to mention a livid ex-husband or wife. Nowadays revellers may be breathalysed on the way home from a gala; thus (if over the top) risking the loss of their driving licence, consequently their job and possibly their spouse. They should also be very careful not, by mistake, to rape anybody if invited in for a nightcap.

However easy it is to knock parties there is no doubt that, for many, there is something heady about being among a lot of people in a circumscribed space. Consciousness is heightened by the sporting of smart clothes; by the assistance of whichever drug is provided and by volume of noise; whether it emanates from a band, a discotheque or from a number of human larynxes.

Jeremy Taylor, that most sober of seventeenth-century clerics, saw parties as unenhancing and held them responsible for 'the perdition of precious hours', as did Milton when, in 'Paradise Lost', he chided at the degeneracy of 'Mixed dance, or wanton mask or midnight ball'. Notwithstanding the possibility that both Taylor and Milton may have been on to something, we have established that parties have their point.

In this collection, based on my own reading and on the suggestions of family and friends, I have tried, through the writings of favourite authors, to incorporate the main emotions engendered by parties and party-going.

To this end I have divided the book into sections, beginning with the 'concept' (thoughts, fears and beliefs behind an impending bash), and have followed it through with all manner of categories, culminating in the (often painful) aftermath. If any of these entries have tumbled into a section that seems a trifle inappropriate I must apologize and explain that, for instance, I have been presented with more than one glorious description of the beginning, middle and end of a party where drunkenness, chatter, loneliness, drama and aftermath have all played their part. In such cases I have popped them in where I decided they looked most at home.

Although I fear that, since I began to scrutinize the world of party-going, I may have emerged sounding slightly jaundiced, that is not the whole story. How would Cinderella ever have escaped from that rat-ridden kitchen without the opportunity of meeting her Prince at the ball? At such grand and glittering occasions enormous aesthetic pleasure can be gleaned and at intimate affairs there is a sense of belonging that can warm the cockles of any heart. I merely have to hum the ditty 'Knees up Mother Brown! Knees up Mother Brown! Knees up! Knees up! Don't get the breeze up. Knees up Mother Brown!' to come over completely slushy.

As this book goes to press I am lolling back and listening to a scratchy recording from 'Bells are Ringing':

'The Party's over. It's time to call it a day. No matter how we pretend; we knew it would end that way.'

ACKNOWLEDGEMENTS

I would like, in particular, to thank Felicity Rubinstein for suggesting that I should compile this anthology.

I would also like to thank the following friends and relations for their helpful suggestions:
Anne Allen-Stevens, Tessa Baring, James Barnard, Jasmine Blakeway, Jo Boothby, Simon Burne, Edward Chancellor, John Chancellor, Robin Chancellor, Fram Dinshaw, Victoria Faulkner, Catherine Gawne-Cain, Peter Halford-Thompson, Dorothy Heber-Percy, Rupert Hodson, Jonathon Hope, Rose Johnston, David Manson, Orlando Murrin, John Julius and Mollie Norwich, Roland Philipps, Hamish Robinson, Lorna Sage, James and Joy Skinner, Daniel and Lily Stevens, Benjamin and Silvy Weatherall, Percy and Clara Weatherall and Sophy Weatherall.

I owe a special thank-you to my editor, Katie Owen, for her patient encouragement, to Peta Nightingale in the final stages and, above all, to Nicholas Johnston.

Part One

BEGINNINGS

'Why does she give these parties?'

VIRGINIA WOOLF
Mrs Dalloway, 1922

'PETER! Peter!' cried Clarissa, following him out on to the landing. 'My party! Remember my party tonight!' she cried, having to raise her voice against the roar of the open air, and, overwhelmed by the traffic and the sound of all the clocks striking, her voice crying 'Remember my party tonight!' sounded frail and thin and very far away as Peter Walsh shut the door.

Remember my party, remember my party, said Peter Walsh as he stepped down the street, speaking to himself rhythmically, in time with the flow of the sound, the direct downright sound of Big Ben striking the half-hour. (The leaden circles dissolved in the air.) Oh these parties? he thought; Clarissa's parties. Why does she give these parties? he thought.

JAN STRUTHER
' – of a Party', 1938

GIVING a party is very like having a baby: its conception is more fun than its completion, and once you have begun it it is almost impossible to stop. How perfect it is, that first moment, when one of you says, 'It's about time we gave another party,' and suddenly the room is full of people, talking, laughing, drinking, the women all beautiful and the men witty. So rosy is the picture that you lose no time in setting the reality in train. To begin with, a date is chosen – not too near, lest the sought-after people should be already engaged, and not too far ahead, lest your own enthusiasm should flag. Next, the form of invitation has to be considered. It is desirable, you feel, to steer between the copper-plate formality of:

Mr and Mrs Moffat-Grimes At Home

and the self-conscious Bohemianism of 'Jane and Tommy are throwing a party on Thursday week – please come along.' Finally, you decide upon:

Mr and Mrs Moffat-Grimes invite you
to a Party on
....

And you fill in the date on the line below.

You have it printed on postcards (to save all that tedious tucking-in) in the chastest of 'sans' types; and on some of them, in one corner, you scribble 'Do come', and on others '*Do* come – J.' Then you go out to the post office and buy a complete sheet of halfpenny stamps, with a border of stamp-paper all round the edge. This is one of the cheapest ways I know of attaining the sensation of true lordliness. And lastly, sitting down with a saucer of water and a small piece of sponge, you stick on the first three hygienically and the rest with your tongue as God meant you to.

GEORGE SAVILE, MARQUESS OF HALIFAX

Advice to a Daughter, 1688

THE last thing I shall recommend to you is a wise and a safe method of using diversions. To be too eager in the pursuit of pleasure whilst you are young is dangerous, to catch at it in riper years is grasping a shadow; it will not be held. Besides that, by being less natural it groweth to be indecent. Diversions are the most properly applied to ease and relieve those who are oppressed by being too much employed. Those that are idle have no need of them, and yet they above all others give themselves up to them. To unbend our thoughts, when they are too much stretched by our cares, is not more natural than it is necessary, but to turn our whole life into a holiday is not only ridiculous but destroyeth pleasure instead of promoting it. The mind, like the body, is tired by being always in one posture; too serious breaketh it, and too diverting looseneth it.

It is variety that giveth the relish, so that diversions too frequently repeated grow first to be indifferent and at last tedious. Whilst they are well chosen and well timed they are never to be blamed, but when they are used to an excess, though very innocent at first they often grow to be criminal, and never fail to be impertinent.

Some ladies are bespoken for merry meetings, as Bessus was for duels. They are engaged in a circle of idleness, where they turn round for the whole year, without the interruption of a serious hour. They know all the players' names, and are intimately acquainted with all the booths in Bartholomew Fair. No soldier is more obedient to the sound of his captain's trumpet than they are to that which summoneth them to a puppet play or a monster. The spring that bringeth out flies and fools maketh them inhabitants in Hyde Park; in the winter they are an encumbrance to the play house and the ballast of the drawing room. The streets all this while are so weary of these daily faces, that men's eyes are over-laid with them. The sight is glutted with fine things, as the stomach with sweet ones, and when a fair lady will give too much of herself to the world she groweth luscious, and oppresseth instead of pleasing. These jolly ladies do so continually seek diversion that in a little time they grow into a jest, yet are unwilling to remember that if they were seldomer seen they would not be so often laughed at. Besides, they make themselves cheap, than which there cannot be an unkinder word bestowed upon your sex.

To play sometimes, to entertain company or to divert yourself, is not to be disallowed, but to do it so often as to be called a gamester is to be avoided, next to the things that are most criminal. It hath consequences of several kinds not to be endured; it will engage you into a habit of idleness and ill hours, draw you into ill-mixed company, make you neglect your civilities abroad and your business at home, and impose into your acquaintance such as will do you no credit.

To deep play there will be yet greater objections. It will give occasion to the world to ask spiteful questions. How you dare venture to lose, and what means you have to pay such great sums? If you pay exactly, it will be enquired from whence the money cometh? If you owe, and especially to a man, you must be so very civil to him for his forbearance that it layeth a ground of having it further improved if the gentleman is so disposed, who will be thought no unfair creditor, if where the estate faileth he seizeth upon the person. Besides, if a lady could see her own face upon an ill game, at a deep stake, she would certainly forswear anything that could put her looks under such a disadvantage.

To dance sometimes will not be imputed to you as a fault, but remember that the end of your learning it was, that you might the better know how to move gracefully. It is only an advantage so far. When it goeth beyond it one may call it excelling in a mistake, which is no very great commendation. It is better for a woman never to dance, because she hath no skill in it, than to do it too often because she doth it well. The easiest as well as the safest method of doing it is in private companies, amongst particular friends, and then carelessly, like a diversion, rather than with solemnity, as if it was a business, or had anything in it to deserve a month's preparation by serious conference with a dancing-master.

Much more might be said to all these heads, and many more might be added to them. But I must restrain my thoughts, which are full of my dear child, and would overflow into a volume, which would not be fit for a new year's gift.

COVENTRY PATMORE
The Angel in the House: 'Mary and Mildred', 1858

I LAUGH'D and sigh'd: for I confess
    I never went to Ball, or Fête,
Or Show, but in pursuit express
    Of my predestinated mate;
And thus to me, who had in sight
    The happy chance upon the cards,
Each beauty blossom'd in the light
    Of tender personal regards;
And, in the records of my breast,
    Red-letter'd, eminently fair,
Stood sixteen, who, beyond the rest,
    By turns till then had been my care:
At Berlin three, one at St Cloud,
    At Chatteris, near Cambridge, one,
At Ely four, in London two,
    Two at Bowness, in Paris none,
And, last and best, in Sarum three;
    But dearest of the whole fair troop,

In judgment of the moment, she
　　Whose daisy eyes had learn'd to droop.
Her very faults my fancy fired;
　　My loving will, so thwarted, grew;
And, bent on worship, I admired
　　Whate'er she was, with partial view.
And yet when, as to-day, her smile
　　Was prettiest I could not but note
Honoria, less admired the while,
　　Was lovelier, though from love remote.

JAMES LEES MILNE

People and Places, 1992

LACOCK Abbey may have been very down-at-heel like its saintly owner, Miss Matilda Talbot. Nothing could restrain her delight in entertaining. Miss Talbot's 'hops' in the great hall on winter evenings – *thés dansants* they may have been called – were not easily avoided without causing offence. Where she collected her young ladies from it is hard to say. All were exceedingly plain and utterly speechless. To an ancient gramophone which required winding every two minutes we danced the Roger de Coverley while the fog swirled against the Gothick windows and indoors a green yule log emitted such dense smoke that the guests were literally blinded and choking.

THOMAS HOBBES

De Cive, 1651

WE doe not therefore by nature seek Society for its own sake, but that we may receive some Honour or Profit from it; these we desire Primarily, that Secondarily: How by what advice Men doe meet, will be best known by observing those things which they doe when they are met: For if they meet for Traffique, it's plaine every man regards not his Fellow, but his Businesse; if to discharge some Office, a certain Market-friendship is begotten, which hath more Jealousie in it then True love, and when Factions sometimes may arise, but Good will never; if for Pleasure, and Recreation of mind, every man is wont to please himself most with those things which stirre up laughter, whence he may (according to the nature of that which is Ridiculous) by comparison of another mans Defects and Infirmities, passe the more currant in his owne opinion: and although this be sometimes innocent, and without offence; yet it is manifest they are not so much delighted with the Society, as their own Vain glory. But for the most part, in these kind of meetings, we wound the absent, their whole life, sayings, actions are examin'd, judg'd, condemn'd nay, it is very rare, but some present receive a fling before they part, so as his reason was not ill, who was wont alwayes at parting to goe out last. And these are indeed the true delights of Society, unto which we are carryed by nature, (i.e.) by those passions which are incident to all Creatures, untill either by sad experience, or good precepts, it so fall out (which in many never happens) that the Appetite, of present matters, be dul'd with the memory of things past, without which, the discourse of most quick and nimble men, on this subject, is but cold and hungry.

WILLIAM MAKEPEACE THACKERAY
Vanity Fair, 1847

IF Miss Rebecca Sharp had determined in her heart upon making the conquest of this big beau, I don't think, ladies, we have any right to blame her; for though the task of husband-hunting is generally, and with becoming modesty, entrusted by young persons to their mammas, recollect that Miss Sharp had no kind parent to arrange these delicate matters for her, and that if she did not get a husband for herself, there was no one else in the wide world who would take the trouble off her hands. What causes young people to 'come *out*', but the noble ambition of matrimony? What sends them trooping to watering-places? What keeps them dancing till five o'clock in the morning through a whole mortal season? What causes them to labour at pianoforte sonatas, and to learn four songs from a fashionable master at a guinea a lesson, and to play the harp if they have handsome arms and neat elbows, and to wear Lincoln Green toxophilite hats and feathers, but that they may bring down some 'desirable' young man with those killing bows and arrows of theirs? What causes respectable parents to take up their carpets, set their houses topsy-turvy, and spend a fifth of their year's income in ball suppers and iced champagne? Is it sheer love of their species, and an unadulterated wish to see young people happy and dancing? Psha! they want to marry their daughters; and, as honest Mrs Sedley has, in the depths of her kind heart, already arranged a score of little schemes for the settlement of her Amelia, so also had our beloved but unprotected Rebecca determined to do her very best to secure the husband, who was even more necessary for her than for her friend. She had a vivid imagination; she had, besides, read the *Arabian Nights* and *Guthrie's Geography*; and it is a fact, that while she was dressing for dinner, and after she had asked Amelia whether her brother was very rich, she had built for herself a most magnificent castle in the air, of which she was mistress, with a husband somewhere in the background (she had not seen him as yet, and his figure would not therefore be very distinct); she had arrayed herself in an infinity of shawls, turbans, and diamond necklaces, and had mounted upon an elephant to the sound of the march in 'Bluebeard', in order to pay a visit of ceremony to the Grand Mogul. Charming Alnaschar visions! it is the happy privilege of youth to construct you, and many a fanciful young creature besides Rebecca Sharp has indulged in these delightful day-dreams ere now!

MICHAEL ARLEN

Hell! Said the Duchess, 1934

MRS Nautigale had a pronounced gift for collecting the most intimate friendships possible with men and women who could never quite overcome their surprise at having been collected. They then found themselves subjected to the alarming process of being pinned down, exhibited and fed in groups of not fewer than twenty, at which it was taken for granted that a good time was being had by all, though no one knew exactly why.

BERNARD MANDEVILLE
A Search into the Nature of Society, 1714

BUT would not a Man, tho' he had seen no Mortal in a Fortnight, remain alone as much longer, rather than get into Company of Noisy Fellows that take delight in Contradiction, and place a Glory in picking a Quarrel? Would not one that has Books, Read for ever, or set himself to Write upon some Subject or other, rather than be every Night with Partymen who count the Island to be good for nothing whilst their Adversaries are suffer'd to live upon it? Would not a Man be by himself a Month, and go to Bed before Seven a Clock rather than mix with Fox Hunters, who having all Day long tried in vain to break their Necks, joyn at Night in a second Attempt upon their Lives by Drinking, and to express their Mirth, are louder in senseless Sounds within doors, than their Barking, and less Troublesome Companions are only without? I have no great value for a Man who would not rather tire himself with Walking, or if he was shut up, scatter Pins about the Room in order to pick them up again, than keep Company for six Hours with Half a Score Common Sailers the Day their Ship was paid off.

JOHN STEINBECK
Cannery Row, 1943

MORE than anything in the world Mary Talbot loved parties. She loved to give parties and she loved to go to parties. Since Tom didn't make much money Mary couldn't give parties all the time, so she tricked people into giving them. Sometimes she telephoned a friend and said bluntly, 'Isn't it about time you gave a party?'

Regularly, Mary had six birthdays a year, and she organized costume parties, surprise parties, holiday parties. Christmas Eve at her house was a very exciting thing. For Mary glowed with parties. She carried her husband along on the wave of her excitement.

In the afternoons when Tom was at work Mary sometimes gave tea-parties for the neighbourhood cats. She set a footstool with doll cups and saucers. She gathered the cats, and there were plenty of them, and then she held long and detailed conversations with them.

It was a kind of play she enjoyed very much – a kind of satiric game, and it covered and concealed from Mary the fact that she didn't have very nice clothes and the Talbots didn't have any money. They were pretty near absolute bottom most of the time, and when they really scraped, Mary managed to give some kind of a party.

She could do that. She could infect a whole house with gaiety and she used her gift as a weapon against the despondency that lurked always around outside the house waiting to get in at Tom. That was Mary's job as she saw it – to keep the despondency away from Tom because everyone knew he was going to be a great success some time. Mostly she was successful in keeping the dark things out of the house, but sometimes they got in at Tom and laid him out. Then he would sit and brood for hours, while Mary frantically built up a back-fire of gaiety.

One time when it was the first of the month and there were curt notes from the water company and the rent wasn't paid and a manuscript had come back from *Collier's* and the cartoons had come back from *The New Yorker* and pleurisy was hurting Tom pretty badly, he went into the bedroom and lay down on the bed.

Mary came softly in, for the blue-grey colour of his gloom had seeped out under the door and through the keyhole. She had a little bouquet of candytuft in a collar of paper lace.

'Smell,' she said and held the bouquet to his nose. He smelled the flowers and said nothing. 'Do you know what day this is?' she asked and thought wildly for something to make it a bright day.

Tom said, 'Why don't we face it for once? We're down. We're going under. What's the good kidding ourselves?'

'No we're not,' said Mary. 'We're magic people. We always have been. Remember that ten dollars you found in a book – remember when your cousin sent you five dollars? Nothing can happen to us.'

'Well, it has happened,' said Tom. 'I'm sorry,' he said. 'I just can't talk myself out of it this time. I'm sick of pretending everything. For once I'd like to have it real – just for once.'

'I thought of giving a little party tonight,' said Mary.

'On what? You're not going to cut out the baked ham picture from a magazine again and serve it on a platter, are you? I'm sick of that kind of kidding. It isn't funny any more. It's sad.'

'I could give a little party,' she insisted. 'Just a small affair. Nobody will dress. It's the anniversary of the founding of the Bloomer League – you didn't even remember that.'

'It's no use,' said Tom. 'I know it's mean, but I just can't rise to it.

Why don't you just go out and shut the door and leave me alone?
I'll get you down if you don't.'

She looked at him closely and saw that he meant it. Mary walked
quietly out and shut the door, and Tom turned over on the bed and
put his face down between his arms. He could hear her rustling
about in the other room.

ABRAHAM COWLEY

Essays: The Dangers of an Honest Man in Much Company, 1661

IF twenty thousand naked *Americans* were not able to resist the
assaults of but twenty well-armed *Spaniards*, I see little possibility
for one Honest man to defend himself against twenty thousand
Knaves who are all furnished *Cap a pe*, with the defensive arms of
worldly prudence, and the offensive loo of craft and malice He will
find no less than this against him, if he have much to do in humane
affairs. The only advice therefore which I can give him is to be sure
not to venture his person any longer in the open Campagn, to retreat
and entrench himself, to stop up all Avenues, and draw up all bridges
against so numerous an Enemy. The truth of it is that a man in much
business must either make himself a Knave, or else the world will
make him a Fool and if the injury went no farther than the being
laught at a wise man would content himself with the revenge of
retaliation but the case is much worse, for these civil *Cannibals* too,
as well as the wild ones, not only dance about a taken stranger, but
at last devour him. A sober man cannot get too soon out of drunken
company, though they be never so kind and merry among themselves, 'tis not unpleasant only, but dangerous to him. Do ye wonder
that a vertuous man should love to be alone?

ANTHONY TROLLOPE

Barchester Towers, 1857

THE trouble in civilized life of entertaining company, as it is
called too generally without much regard to strict veracity, is so
great that it cannot but be matter of wonder that people are so fond
of attempting it. It is difficult to ascertain what is the *quid pro quo*.

If they who give such laborious parties, and who endure such toil and turmoil in the vain hope of giving them successfully, really enjoyed the parties given by others the matter could be understood. A sense of justice would induce men and women to undergo, in behalf of others, those miseries which others had undergone in their behalf. But they all profess that going out is as great a bore as receiving; and to look at them when they are out, one cannot but believe them.

Entertain! Who shall have sufficient self-assurance, who shall feel sufficient confidence in his own powers to dare to boast that he can entertain his company? A clown can sometimes do so, and sometimes a dancer in short petticoats and stuffed pink legs; occasionally, perhaps, a singer. But beyond these, success in this art of entertaining is not often achieved. Young men and girls linking themselves kind with kind, pairing like birds in spring because nature wills it, they, after a simple fashion, do entertain each other. Few others even try.

Ladies, when they open their houses, modestly confessing, it may be presumed, their own incapacity, mainly trust to wax candles and upholstery. Gentlemen seem to rely on their white waistcoats. To these are added, for the delight of the more sensual, champagne and such good things of the table as fashion allows to be still considered as comestible. Even in this respect the world is deteriorating.

'Now just what is the situation about your invitation?'

<center>~~~◦◦◦◦~~~</center>

ROBERT KEE
Broadstrop in Season, 1959

IT was as much for mental as for physical comfort that he finally decided to board a bus, and seek sanctuary behind the driver's back from all eyes but his own.

An evening paper was lying on the seat beside him. He picked it up gingerly. The sight of it reminded him of the final enigmatic conversation he had had with the waiter.

'Look,' Broadstrop had said as he tucked the cardboard box a little awkwardly under his arm. 'There is one last thing you could help me with. I mean what sort of time should I get there actually?'

'What – not asked to dinner somewhere first?'

'No. Ought I to be?'

'No.' The waiter had swallowed trying to make an extraordinary situation seem very ordinary, as a good servant should. 'No; it's all right. Get there about eleven then. You got your invitation, though?'

'Well, yes and no. That is . . .'

'This isn't the Enfurnham ball by any chance?'

'Yes. Why?'

'Crumbs.'

'What do you mean?'

'Well, look.' The waiter had pulled the evening paper out from under his tails like an egg. The headlines still swam before Broadstrop's eyes:

PARTY OF THE DECADE
UNPRECEDENTED PRECAUTIONS AGAINST GATE-CRASHERS

'No; it's all right: first things first. Now just what is the situation about your invitation?'

Broadstrop had explained. All the time he had hoped to see an expression of relief break over the waiter's face, but none had come.

EVELYN WAUGH

Mr Loveday's Little Outing: Bella Fleace Gave a Party, 1936

I T struck eight. Bella waited. Nobody came.

She sat down on a gilt chair at the head of the stairs, looked steadily before her with her blank, blue eyes. In the hall, in the cloakroom, in the supper-room, the hired footmen looked at one another with knowing winks. 'What does the old girl expect? No one'll have finished dinner before ten.'

The linkmen on the steps stamped and chafed their hands.

At half-past twelve Bella rose from her chair. Her face gave no indication of what she was thinking.

'Riley, I think I will have some supper. I am not feeling altogether well.'

She hobbled slowly to the dining-room.

'Give me a stuffed quail and a glass of wine. Tell the band to start playing.'

The 'Blue Danube' waltz flooded the house. Bella smiled approval and swayed her head a little to the rhythm.

'Riley, I am really quite hungry. I've had nothing all day. Give me another quail and some more champagne.'

Alone among the candles and the hired footmen, Riley served his mistress with an immense supper. She enjoyed every mouthful.

Presently she rose. 'I am afraid there must be some mistake. No one seems to be coming to the ball. It is very disappointing after all our trouble. You may tell the band to go home.'

But just as she was leaving the dining-room there was a stir in the hall. Guests were arriving. With wild resolution Bella swung herself up the stairs. She must get to the top before the guests were announced. One hand on the banister, one on her stick, pounding heart, two steps at a time. At last she reached the landing and turned to face the company. There was a mist before her eyes and a singing in her ears. She breathed with effort, but dimly she saw four figures advancing and saw Riley meet them and heard him announce

'Lord and Lady Mockstock, Sir Samuel and Lady Gordon.'

Suddenly the daze in which she had been moving cleared. Here on the stairs were the two women she had not invited – Lady Mockstock the draper's daughter, Lady Gordon the American.

She drew herself up and fixed them with her blank, blue eyes.

'I had not expected this honour,' she said. 'Please forgive me if I am unable to entertain you.'

The Mockstocks and the Gordons stood aghast; saw the mad blue eyes of their hostess, her crimson dress; the ball-room beyond, looking immense in its emptiness; heard the dance music echoing through the empty house. The air was charged with the scent of chrysanthemums. And then the drama and unreality of the scene were dispelled. Miss Fleace suddenly sat down, and holding out her hands to her butler, said, 'I don't quite know what's happening.'

He and two of the hired footmen carried the old lady to a sofa. She spoke only once more. Her mind was still on the same subject. 'They came uninvited, those two . . . and nobody else.'

A day later she died.

Mr Banks arrived for the funeral and spent a week sorting out her effects. Among them he found in her escritoire, stamped, addressed, but unposted, the invitations to the ball.

ALFRED, LORD TENNYSON

from 'Come into the Garden, Maud', 1855

II

BUT to-morrow, if we live,
Our ponderous squire will give
A grand political dinner
To half the squirelings near;
And Maud will wear her jewels,
And the bird of prey will hover,
And the titmouse hope to win her
With his chirrup at her ear.

III

A grand political dinner
To the men of many acres,

A gathering of the Tory,
A dinner and then a dance
For the maids and marriage-makers,
And every eye but mine will glance
At Maud in all her glory.

IV

For I am not invited,
But, with the Sultan's pardon,
I am all as well delighted,
For I know her own rose-garden,
And mean to linger in it
Till the dancing will be over;
And then, oh then, come out to me
For a minute, but for a minute,
Come out to your own true lover,
That your true lover may see
Your glory also, and render
All homage to his own darling,
Queen Maud in all her splendour.

OLIVER GOLDSMITH

'Verses in reply to an invitation to dinner at Dr Baker's', 1837

YOUR mandate I got,
    You may all go to pot;
Had your senses been right,
You'd have sent before night;
As I hope to be saved,
I put off being shaved;
For I could not make bold,
While the matter was cold,
To meddle in suds;
Or to put on my duds;
So tell Horneck and Nesbitt,
And Baker and his bit,
And Kauffman beside,
And the Jessamy bride,
With the rest of the crew,

The Reynoldses two,
Little Comedy's face,
And the Captain in lace,
(By the bye you may tell him,
I have something to sell him;
Of use I insist,
When he comes to enlist.
Your worships must know
That a few days ago,
An order went out,
For the foot guards so stout
To wear tails in high taste,
Twelve inches at least;
Now I've got him a scale
To measure each tail,
To lengthen a short tail,
And a long one to curtail.)
   Yet how can I when vext,
Thus stray from my text?
Tell each other to rue
Your Devonshire crew,
For sending so late
To one of my state,
But 'tis Reynolds's way
From wisdom to stray
And Angelica's whim
To be frolick like him,
But, alas! your good worships, how could they be wiser,
When both have been spoil'd in today's Advertiser?

MIKE LEIGH

Abigail's Party, 1977

Rock music starts at Number 9, not especially loud.

BEVERLY: Aye aye! It's started, Sue.

ANGELA: They've got the record-player going, haven't they? They're going to have fun, aren't they?

BEVERLY: Sounds like it.

SUSAN: I hope so.

ANGELA: How old is she, your daughter?

SUSAN: Fifteen.

ANGELA: What does she look like? 'Cos I might have seen her.

SUSAN: Oh. Well, she's quite tall, and she's got fair hair, quite long fair hair.

ANGELA: She hasn't got a pink streak in her hair, has she?

SUSAN: Yes.

BEVERLY: Yeah, that's Abigail! And she wears those jeans, Ang, with patches on, and safety-pins right down the side, and scruffy bottoms.

ANGELA: Yes, I've seen her.

SUSAN: And plumber's overalls.

BEVERLY: Yeah, plumber's overalls. She makes me die, you know!

ANGELA: I've seen her: she was standing outside your gate with a friend. And you've seen her as well, haven't you? Getting off that motorbike.

TONY: Yeah.

ANGELA: How many people are coming to the party?

BEVERLY: About fifteen, isn't it, Sue?

SUSAN: Well, it was fifteen. Then it went up to twenty, and last night I gathered it was twenty-five.

BEVERLY: It's creeping up, Sue.

SUSAN: I've told her that's the limit. Well, I think that's enough. Don't you?

BEVERLY: Definitely, Sue, yeah, definitely.

ANGELA: Yeah.

BEVERLY: But, this is it with teenagers: okay, they tell you twenty-five, but a friend invites a friend: that friend invites another friend; and it creeps up till you end up with about seventy or eighty. This is it. This is the danger!

TONY: I've just seen a couple of people arriving, actually.

SUSAN: Yes. Nice of them to help you with the car.

TONY: Oh, no – not them: a couple of coloured chaps and a girl roared up in a Ford Capri.

SUSAN: Oh, really? [*Pause.*] Well, there were only half a dozen there when I left . . . When I was asked to leave.

BEVERLY: Yeah, this is it, isn't it? They don't want Mum sitting there, casting a beady eye on all the goings-on, do they?

ANGELA: No. Not when they get to fifteen. When I was fifteen I really wanted a party of my own, and my Dad, he'd never let me. You see, I've got four sisters. Haven't I, Tony?

TONY: Yeah.

ANGELA: And I think he was a little bit worried that I'd invite all my friends, and they'd bring along a few of theirs, and we'd end up with a houseful.

BEVERLY: This is it.

ANGELA: And he was worried about people pinching things, and things getting broken.

BEVERLY: Have you locked your silver away, Sue?

SUSAN: No, I haven't got any. Well, not much, anyway. I've put a few things upstairs; just in case of accidents.

ANGELA: Yes, well, it's better to, isn't it? 'Cos it can easily happen.

BEVERLY: Yeah.

ANGELA: Like that egg-timer. Tony was furious. It was a wedding present.

BEVERLY: Don't get me wrong, Sue: I wasn't meaning that any of Abigail's friends are thieves – please don't think that. But, you don't know who you get at a party. And let's face it: people are light-fingered.

ANGELA: Yes.

[Pause.]

BEVERLY: D'you leave your carpets down, Sue?

SUSAN: Er – yes.

ANGELA: Have you got fitted carpets?

SUSAN: Yes.

ANGELA: Yes ... we've got fitted carpets. The Macdonalds left them all. They were inclusive in the price of the house.

H. H. MUNRO

The Complete short Stories of 'Saki': 'The Boar-Pig', 1904

'THERE is a back way on to the lawn,' said Mrs Philidore Stossen to her daughter, 'through a small grass paddock and then through a walled fruit garden full of gooseberry bushes. I went all over the place last year when the family were away. There is a door that opens from the fruit garden into a shrubbery, and once we emerge from there we can mingle with the guests as if we had come in by the ordinary way. It's much safer than going in by the front entrance and running the risk of coming bang up against the hostess;

that would be so awkward when she doesn't happen to have invited us.'

'Isn't it a lot of trouble to take for getting admittance to a garden party?'

'To a garden party, yes; to *the* garden party of the season, certainly not. Every one of any consequence in the county, with the exception of ourselves, has been asked to meet the Princess, and it would be far more troublesome to invent explanations as to why we weren't there than to get in by a roundabout way. I stopped Mrs Cuvering in the road yesterday and talked very pointedly about the Princess. If she didn't choose to take the hint and send me an invitation it's not my fault, is it? Here we are: we just cut across the grass and through that little gate into the garden.'

Mrs Stossen and her daughter, suitably arrayed for a county garden party function with an infusion of Almanack de Gotha, sailed through the narrow grass paddock and the ensuing gooseberry garden with the air of state barges making an unofficial progress along a rural trout stream. There was a certain amount of furtive haste mingled with the stateliness of their advance as though hostile searchlights might be turned on them at any moment; and, as a matter of fact, they were not unobserved. Matilda Cuvering, with the alert eyes of thirteen years and the added advantage of an exalted position in the branches of a medlar tree, had enjoyed a good view of the Stossen flanking movement and had foreseen exactly where it would break down in execution.

'They'll find the door locked, and they'll jolly well have to go back the way they came,' she remarked to herself. 'Serves them right for not coming in by the proper entrance. What a pity Tarquin Superbus isn't loose in the paddock. After all, as every one else is enjoying themselves, I don't see why Tarquin shouldn't have an afternoon out.'

ELIZABETH GASKELL

Cranford, 1853

PERHAPS by this time Lady Glenmire had found out that Mrs Jamieson's was not the gayest, liveliest house in the world; perhaps Mrs Jamieson had found out that most of the county families were in London, and that those who remained in the country were not so alive as they might have been to the circumstance of Lady Glenmire being in their neighbourhood. Great events spring out of small causes; so I will not pretend to say what induced Mrs Jamieson to alter her determination of excluding the Cranford ladies, and send notes of invitation all round for a small party, on the following Tuesday. Mr Mulliner himself brought them round. He *would* always ignore the fact of there being a back-door to any house, and gave a louder rat-tat than his mistress, Mrs Jamieson. He had three little notes, which he carried in a large basket, in order to impress his mistress with an idea of their great weight, though they might easily have gone into his waistcoat pocket.

Miss Matty and I quietly decided we would have a previous engagement at home: – it was the evening on which Miss Matty usually made candle-lighters of all the notes and letters of the week; for on Mondays her accounts were always made straight – not a penny owing from the week before; so, by a natural arrangement, making candle-lighters fell upon a Tuesday evening, and gave us a legitimate excuse for declining Mrs Jamieson's invitation. But before our answer was written, in came Miss Pole, with an open note in her hand.

'So!' she said. 'Ah! I see you have got your note, too. Better late than never. I could have told my Lady Glenmire she would be glad enough of our society before a fortnight was over.'

'Yes,' said Miss Matty, 'we're asked for Tuesday evening. And perhaps you would just kindly bring your work across and drink tea with us that night. It is my usual regular time for looking over the last week's bills, and notes, and letters, and making candle-lighters of them; but that does not seem quite reason enough for saying I have a previous engagement at home, though I meant to make it do. Now, if you would come, my conscience would be quite at ease, and luckily the note is not written yet.'

I saw Miss Pole's countenance change while Miss Matty was speaking.

'Don't you mean to go then?' asked she.

'Oh no!' said Miss Matty quietly. 'You don't either, I suppose?'

'I don't know,' replied Miss Pole. 'Yes, I think I do,' said she rather briskly; and on seeing Miss Matty look surprised, she added, 'You see one would not like Mrs Jamieson to think that anything she could do, or say, was of consequence enough to give offence; it would be a kind of letting down of ourselves, that I, for one, should not like. It would be too flattering to Mrs Jamieson, if we allowed her to suppose that what she had said affected us a week, nay ten days afterwards.'

'Well! I suppose it is wrong to be hurt and annoyed so long about anything; and, perhaps, after all, she did not mean to vex us. But I must say, I could not have brought myself to say the things Mrs Jamieson did about our not calling. I really don't think I shall go.'

'Oh, come! Miss Matty, you must go; you know our friend Mrs Jamieson is much more phlegmatic than most people, and does not enter into the little delicacies of feeling which you possess in so remarkable a degree.'

'I thought you possessed them, too, that day Mrs Jamieson called to tell us not to go,' said Miss Matty innocently.

But Miss Pole, in addition to her delicacies of feeling, possessed a very smart cap, which she was anxious to show to an admiring world; and so she seemed to forget all her angry words uttered not a fortnight before, and to be ready to act on what she called the great Christian principle of 'Forgive and forget;' and she lectured dear Miss Matty so long on this head, that she absolutely ended by assuring her it was her duty, as a deceased rector's daughter, to buy a new cap, and go to the party at Mrs Jamieson's. So 'we were most happy to accept,' instead of 'regretting that we were obliged to decline.'

HENRY GREEN

Party Going, 1939

'I MUST say I can't see that makes the slightest difference. Anyway I did know about the Prince what d'you call him. You see, Angela, we were arguing about who could have sent the notice if Embassy Richard didn't sent it for himself. I can't see that it matters two hoots if the Prince Royal was cross.'

'I can,' said Julia, entering into it again. 'I think it's a score for Richard if the Ambassador's employer is cross with him for trying to score off Richard.'

'No,' and Alex was now speaking in his high voice he used when he was upset, 'that's not the point. The real point is that the Ambassador ticked off Embassy Richard in public by writing to the papers to say he had never invited him to his party. If the Prince

Royal told his Ambassador off for doing it, it doesn't make any difference to the fact that Richard was shown up in public.'

'But Alex, dear, it does,' Julia said. 'If the Prince Royal did not approve, and the party was being given for him, then it means that Embassy Richard should have been invited all the time.'

'I don't see that it does, Julia. He may not have approved of the way his Ambassador did it. My whole point is that the Prince Royal never made his Ambassador write another letter to the papers saying that Richard should have been invited after all. D'you see?'

Angela said 'No, Alex, I don't.'

'Well, what I mean is that you and I may know the Prince Royal was tremendously angry and threw fits, if you like, when he read his Ambassador's letter but the thousands of people in the street who read their newspapers every morning would not hear about it. All that they know is that Embassy Richard regretted not being able to attend a party he was not invited to.'

'Oh, if that's it,' said Angela, 'then who cares about the people in the street and what they think about it.'

GIUSEPPE DI LAMPEDUSA
The Leopard, 1960

SO frequent were the various and yet identical parties that the Prince and Princess of Salina had moved to their town palace for three weeks so as not to have to make the long drive from San Lorenzo almost every night. The ladies' dresses would arrive from Naples in long black cases like coffins, and there would be an hysterical coming and going of milliners, hairdressers and shoe-makers; of exasperated servants carrying excited notes to fitters. The Ponteleone ball was to be one of the most important of that short season; important for all concerned because of the standing of the family, the splendour of the palace and the number of guests; particularly important for the Salinas who would be presenting to 'society' Angelica, their nephew's lovely bride-to-be. It was still only half-past ten, rather early to appear at a ball if one is Prince of Salina, whose arrival should be timed for when a fête is at its height. But this time they had to be early if they wanted to be there for the entry of the Sedàra who were the sort of people ('they don't *know* yet, poor things') to take literally the times on the gleaming invitation card. It had taken a good deal of trouble to get one of those cards sent to them; no one knew them, and the Princess Maria Stella had been obliged to make a visit to Margherita Ponteleone ten days before; all had gone smoothly, of course, but even so it had been one of those little thorns that Tancredi's engagement had inserted into the Leopard's delicate paws.

BEN JONSON

Epigrams: 'Inviting a Friend to Supper', 1616

TONIGHT, grave Sir, both my poor house and I
    Do equally desire your company:
Not that we think us worthy such a guest.
    But that your worth will dignify our feast
With those that come; whose grace may make that seem
    Something, which else could hope for no esteem.
It is the fair acceptance, Sir, creates
    The entertainment perfect: not the eates.
Yet shall you have, to rectify your palate,
    An olive, capers, or some better salad,
Ushering the mutton; with a short-legged hen
    If we can get her, full of eggs, and then
Lemons, and wine for sauce; to these a cony
    Is not to be despaired of for our money;
And though fowl now be scarce, yet there are clerks,
    The sky not falling, think we may have larks.
I'll tell you of more, and lie, so you will come:
    Of partridge, pheasant, wood-cock, of which some
May yet be there; and godwit, if we can;
    Knot, rail and ruff too. How so ere, my man
Shall read a piece of Virgil, Tacitus,
    Livy, or of some better book to us,
Of which we'll speak our minds, amidst our meat;
    And I'll profess no verses to repeat:
To this, if ought appear which I not know of,
    That will the pastry, not my paper show of.
Digestive cheese and fruit there sure will be;
    But that which most doth take my Muse and me
Is a pure cup of rich Canary wine,

Which is the Mermaid's now, but shall be mine;
Of which had Horace or Anacreon tasted,
  Their lives, as do their lines, till now had lasted.
Tobacco, nectar, or the Thespian spring
  Are all but Luther's beer, to this I sing.
Of this we will sup free, but moderately,
  And we will have no Pooly or Parrot by;
Nor shall our cups make any guilty men,
  But at our parting we will be as when
We innocently met. No simple word
  That shall be uttered at our mirthful board
Shall make us sad next morning, or affright
The liberty that we'll enjoy tonight.

FYODOR DOSTOEVSKY
The Idiot, 1866

THE prince, in these circumstances, arrived at a most opportune moment. The announcement of his arrival caused some surprise and evoked a few strange smiles, especially when it became evident from Nastasya Filippovna's look of astonishment that she had never thought of inviting him. But after her initial surprise, Nastasya Filippovna suddenly looked so pleased that most of her guests at once prepared to welcome the unbidden visitor with mirth and laughter.

WILLIAM MAKEPEACE THACKERAY
The Newcomes, 1853

TO push on in the crowd, every male or female struggler must use his or her shoulders. If a better place than yours presents itself just beyond your neighbour, elbow him and take it. Look how a steadily-purposed man or woman at court, at a ball, or exhibition, wherever there is a competition and a squeeze, gets the best place; the nearest the sovereign, if bent on kissing the royal hand; the closest to the grand stand, if minded to go to Ascot; the best view and hearing of the Rev. Mr Thumpington, when all the town is rushing to hear that exciting divine; the largest quantity of ice, champagne, and seltzer, cold pâté, or other his or her favourite flesh-pot, if gluttonously minded, at a supper whence hundreds of people come empty away. A woman of the world will marry her daughter and have done with her, get her carriage, and be at home and asleep in bed; whilst a timid mamma has still her girl in the nursery, or is beseeching the servants in the cloak-room to look for her shawls, with which some one else has whisked away an hour ago. What a man has to do in society is to assert himself. Is there a good place at table? Take it. At the Treasury or the Home Office? Ask for it. Do you want to go to a party to which you are not invited? Ask to be asked. Ask A., ask B., ask Mrs C., ask everybody you know: you will be thought a bore; but you will have your way. What matters if you are considered obtrusive, provided that you obtrude? By pushing steadily, nine hundred and ninety-nine people in a thousand will yield to you. Only command persons, and you may be pretty sure that a good number will obey.

HORACE

Odes Book I: Ode XX, 'An Invitation to Maecenas', 19 BC

COME, drink with me – cheap Sabine, to be sure, and out of common tankards, yet wine that I with my own hand put up and sealed in a Grecian jar, on the day, dear Knight Maecenas, when such applause was paid thee in the Theatre that with one accord the banks of thy native stream and the sportive echo of Mount Vatican returned thy praises. Then thou shalt drink Caecuban and the juice of grapes crushed by Cales' presses; my cups are flavoured neither with the product of Falernum's vines nor of the Formian hills.

ANGELA HUTH

Invitation to the Married Life, 1991

THIS morning Rachel observed, with an excitement out of all proportion to the event, an expensive white envelope at the bottom of the brown ones. She pulled it out, examining it carefully. Black ink, large arrogant handwriting. Postmark: Northampton.

The Farthingoes, obviously. . . . Rachel slit open the envelope. In her exhilarated state she forgot that the noise of tearing paper would be bound to annoy Thomas; and suddenly she didn't care.

The thick white card, beautifully engraved, was indeed from the Farthingoes.

'Thomas,' said Rachel, fingering the card with all the reverence of a woman who once used to love parties and cannot quite discard the habit, 'Frances and Toby have asked us to a ball.'

There was a moment's terrible silence. Rachel could imagine her husband's eyes blazing to the end of a sentence. She could hear her own heart thumping very fast. Once again, in her foolish excitement, she had made an irretrievable mistake and would now have to bear the consequence.

'When?' asked Thomas at last.

The question, a chip of ice in the warmth of Rachel's expectancy, was devoid of all interest. Its single, tiny sound managed brilliantly to convey the uprising of his annoyance.

'September.'

Thomas put down the paper at last, folding it untidily. His reddish eyebrows, raised, scratched at the furrows on his brow – incredulous, scathing, bored.

'That's in four months' time, for heaven's sake.'

'You have to ask people very early if you want to be sure of their coming.'

'Ridiculous system.'

MARCEL PROUST

Selected Letters, Volume Two, To Madame Straus

Friday [21 June 1907]
Madame,

Forgive me for bothering you yet again: have you any idea now how you will be placed on Monday the 1st; do you think you could come to dinner or could you only come after? I feel that it's odious of me to pester you. But you see, *six* people have replied to me as you did! So if I'm left in uncertainty until the last moment, I'm threatened either – if I count on people who then don't come – with being left more or less alone with Madame d'Haussonville without her husband and Madame de Clermont-Tonnerre who are definitely coming, which will be very disagreeable for me for their sakes, as I know them only very slightly, or else – if to guard against that I invite more people now and at the last moment the six others come – with having ladies whom I won't know where to seat or at any rate will seat badly. And if you tell me at seven o'clock on the 1st of July that you're coming to dinner, I shall be mad with joy but I'll seat you very badly if the six come and I invite more people now. I invited Mme Aimery de La Rochefoucauld whom I haven't seen for years but whom I'd like you to be friends with because I'm sure it could have beneficial consequences as regards the Princesse de Monaco who is in the process of *killing* her daughter. But unfortunately she wasn't free. My other guests will all be people you know (no Gabriel de La Rochefoucauld). I invited Dufeuille, by the way, telling him the truth, that I was afraid you would only come after dinner. He too sent me a reply making it clear that he wouldn't know until the last minute whether he would be free. But I had to stop there and not tell him that I'd keep a place for him because I needed men and didn't want to have to place him at the last minute if he came.

I already have Fauré who isn't young, Calmette for whom I'm giving the dinner, Béraud who is very touchy, M. de Clermont-Tonnerre who is young but descended from Charlemagne, and some strangers. As it kills me to write and I do it all by telephone, which kills me just as much although I don't do the telephoning myself, I tell them to do it while I'm sleeping, so that a second one is asked when the first has already accepted. In case you should find that you're too tired to come to dinner I've taken pains to ensure that there's something later on that you'll enjoy and that will avoid your having to talk. That's why I got Fauré. They'll play things you like, I think Fauré will play (alas, Reynaldo will be in London), and as we shall be only about twenty, I can still enjoy you a little, your eyes during the music

> Music at times transports me like the sea
> And I set sail . . . towards my sombre star.

But naturally I shall enjoy you more if you come to dinner. I intend to invite Robert Dreyfus after dinner but I shall beg him not to talk about it as I don't even know whether I'll invite my sister-in-law. I want no one to know about it except those invited and I shall send someone round to all the newspapers to make sure they don't mention it. Because of that and also because it would be so tiring for me to have my flat put in order (it's still in the state it was in when I arrived with nothing installed) and to have people smoking there, I think I shall try to find, at the Ritz or rather the Madrid or Armenonville, a private room where one could feel at home; I think I'd find it less suffocating. I had thought of asking M. Reinach whom I haven't seen for a long time. But as M. de Clermont-Tonnerre has accepted which I didn't expect and as it appears that he's very anti-Dreyfusard and very violent, and as M. Reinach is the very incarnation of Dreyfusism, I thought it might be better at such a small dinner party to avoid a collision the first time I was having M. de Clermont-Tonnerre who has invited me so often while M. Reinach never has. If however you would like it, I think it would be possible. I still have three pathetic and hideous little Japanese trees for you. Having seen them advertised in a sale I sent my pseudo-secretary to buy them. What a disappointment when I saw them! But still, they'll grow to be nice, and they're so old and so tiny. It's like when one looks at Mont Blanc framed in an opera-glass and has to tell oneself that it's 4,810 metres high. I wanted to have all this explained to you by the so-called secretary who will bring them round to you one of these days, because writing tires me so and I like writing to you. Mme de Chevigné in accordance with the usual formula asked me to keep a place for her just in case! But since then she has refused. As a matter of fact I'm very sorry; she is so nice. Madame Lemaire doesn't know whether she'll be back from London, Mme de Brantes whether she won't have lost a cousin, Mme d'Eyragues whether she won't be on the banks of the Loire, M. Dufeuille whether his friends from Lower Normandy will have returned (word for word).

My dear little Madame Straus, don't forget this date, the 1st of July. If you decide only belatedly to come, don't blame me if I seat you badly, and if the worst happens and you don't come to dinner, make sure you come as soon as possible afterwards to hear Fauré and see me. I shall let you know the place.

Your respectful friend who would write to you at greater length if he were not so tired

Marcel Proust

I forgot to say that Mme de Noailles is in London and will probably not be back until the 2nd, and Mme de Chimay in Holland and doesn't know whether she'll be back before the 3rd.

No need to remind you that my invitation, either to dinner or after, applies, *with the strongest desire to have him*, to *Monsieur* Straus.

'With social blood pressure so high. . .'

E. F. BENSON
Lucia's Progress, 1935

WITH social blood pressure so high, with such embryos of plots and counterplots darkly developing, with, generally, an atmosphere so charged with electricity, Susan Wyse's party to-night was likely (to change the metaphor once more) to prove a scene of carnage. These stimulating expectations were amply fulfilled.

CANDIA McWILLIAM
A Case of Knives, 1988

BY the Thursday of Lucas Salik's dinner party, I was blown with thoughts of him. I had so little information, most of it from glancing reference or tabloid newspaper, the one too sketchy, the other too heavy-handed. But I could sit for hours turning my head like a sunflower to thoughts of him. He was a continent to me; I could have made charts of his eyes, maps of his hands. My perceptions were distorted by pregnancy and by obsession. I felt like Alice, so extremely did the scale of things swell, or shrink. In my dreams, I was walking over terrain which was Lucas, he was carrying me safe in his hand, he was wearing me in his buttonhole. In the day, I seemed suddenly to grow, to knock things over with my monstrous limbs, to have such heightened senses that the powder of another girl on the tube would nauseate me, the smell of flowers make me weak with maudlin grief. I could not read newspapers without crying. Every tale of gallantry or misery made me shake.

The simpler the story, the deeper was my response. I was becoming the perfect tabloid reader. I left Tertius's chambers drunk on the delicious raspberry smell of Windolene, arrived home weeping after seeing the headline 'PLUCKY LITTLE AHMED – MOTHER'S VIGIL'. Moreover, I could not stop myself.

I was possessed.

LADY ELIZABETH ANSON

Party Planners Book, 1986

Nose bleeds
Do not panic: they always stop in the end. Sit him down with his head bent a little forwards. Put a cork between his teeth; let the blood dribble into a bowl. Ask him not to sniff or swallow. Leave for ten minutes, by which time all should be well.
Suicide attempts
People who stage suicide attempts hysterically or as a means of emotional blackmail will, unhappily, often choose a party for the gesture, as it ensures a huge audience and plenty of excitement. Always treat dramatic announcements at face value: if your guest says he has taken two hundred of your sleeping tablets, believe him and act promptly. Almost any prescribed drug and many agents used in house or garden are poisonous in sufficient quantity.

If you find your guest with a half-empty bottle of weedkiller or sitting amongst scattered pills, do not panic.

GEORGE ELIOT

Adam Bede, 1859

THE thirtieth of July was come, and it was one of those half-dozen warm days which sometimes occur in the middle of a rainy English summer. No rain had fallen for the last three or four days, and the weather was perfect for that time of the year: there was less dust than usual on the dark-green hedgerows, and on the wild camomile that starred the roadside, yet the grass was dry enough for the little children to roll on it, and there was no cloud but a long dash of light, downy ripple, high, high up in the far-off blue sky. Perfect weather for an outdoor July merrymaking, yet surely not the best time of year to be born in. Nature seems to make a hot pause just then – all the loveliest flowers are gone; the sweet time of early growth and vague hopes is past; and yet the time of harvest and ingathering is not come, and we tremble at the possible storms that may ruin the precious fruit in the moment of its ripeness. The woods are all one dark monotonous green; the waggon-loads of hay no longer creep along the lanes, scattering their sweet-smelling fragments on the blackberry branches; the pastures are often a little tanned, yet the corn has not got its last splendour of red and gold; the lambs and calves have lost all traces of their innocent frisky prettiness, and have become stupid young sheep and cows. But it is a time of leisure on the farm – that pause between hay and corn harvest, and so the farmers and labourers in Hayslope and Broxton thought the Captain did well to come of age just then, when they could give their undivided minds to the flavour of the great cask of ale which had been brewed the autumn after 'the heir' was born, and was to be tapped on his twenty-first birthday. The air had been merry with the ringing of church bells very early this morning, and every one had made haste to get through the needful work before twelve, when it would be time to think of getting ready to go to the Chase.

The mid-day sun was streaming into Hetty's bed-chamber, and there was no blind to temper the heat with which it fell on her head as she looked at herself in the old speckled glass. Still, that was the only glass she had in which she could see her neck and arms, for the small hanging glass she had fetched out of the next room – the room that had been Dinah's – would show her nothing below her little chin, and that beautiful bit of neck where the roundness of her cheek melted into another roundness shadowed by dark delicate curls. And to-day she thought more than usual about her neck and arms; for at the dance this evening she was not to wear any neckerchief, and she had been busy yesterday with her spotted pink-and-white frock, that she might make the sleeves either long or short at will. She was dressed now just as she was to be in the evening, with a tucker made of 'real' lace, which her aunt had lent her for this unparalleled occasion, but with no ornaments besides; she had even taken out her small round ear-rings which she wore every day. But there was something more to be done, apparently, before she put on her neckerchief and long sleeves, which she was to wear in the day-time, for now she unlocked the drawer that held her private treasures. It is more than a month since we saw her unlock that drawer before, and now it holds new treasures, so much more precious than the old ones that these are thrust into the corner. Hetty would not care to put the large coloured glass ear-rings into her ears now; for see! she has got a beautiful pair of gold and pearls and garnet, lying snugly in a pretty little box lined with white satin. Oh the delight of taking out that little box and looking at the ear-rings! Do not reason about it, my philosophical reader, and say that Hetty, being very pretty, must have known that it did not signify whether she had on any ornaments or not; and that, moreover, to look at ear-rings which she could not possibly wear out of her bedroom could hardly be a satisfaction, the essence of vanity being a reference to the impressions produced on others; you will never understand women's natures if you are so excessively rational.

DYLAN THOMAS
Under Milk Wood, 1954

CAPTAIN CAT: *That's* Polly Garter. (*Softly*) Hullo, Polly my love, can you hear the dumb goose-hiss of the wives as they huddle and peck or flounce at a waddle away? Who cuddled you when? Which of their gandering hubbies moaned in Milk Wood for your naughty mothering arms and body like a wardrobe, love? Scrub the floors of the Welfare Hall for the Mothers' Union Social Dance, you're one mother won't wriggle her roly poly bum or pat her fat little buttery feet in that wedding-ringed holy to-night though the waltzing breadwinners snatched from the cosy smoke of the Sailors Arms will grizzle and mope.

LEO TOLSTOY
Anna Karenina, 1875

DURING the interval between dinner and the beginning of the evening party, Kitty experienced something resembling a young man's feelings before a battle. Her heart was beating violently and she could not fix her thoughts on anything.

She felt that this evening, when those two men were to meet for the first time, would decide her fate; and she kept picturing them to herself, now individually and now together. When she thought of the past, she dwelt with pleasure and tenderness on her former relations with Levin. Memories of childhood and of Levin's friendship with her dead brother lent a peculiar poetic charm to her relations with him. His love for her, of which she felt sure, flattered and rejoiced her, and she could think of him with a light heart. With her thought of Vronsky was mingled some uneasiness, though he was an extremely well-bred and quiet-mannered man; a sense of something false, not in him, for he was very simple and kindly, but in herself; whereas in relation to Levin she felt herself quite simple and clear. On the other hand when she pictured to herself a future with Vronsky a brilliant vision of happiness rose up before her, while a future with Levin appeared wrapped in mist.

On going upstairs to dress for the evening and looking in the glass, she noticed with pleasure that this was one of her best days, and that she was in full possession of all her forces, which would be so much wanted for what lay before her. She was conscious of external calmness and of freedom and grace in her movements.

VITA SACKVILLE-WEST
The Edwardians, 1930

YES, she was indeed a beautiful woman, she decided, catching sight of herself in a long mirror as she came out of the cloakroom at Buckingham Palace. She was alone in the passage, but for the beef-eaters, and they affected her no more than so many pieces of furniture. She could take stock of herself in the mirror without any consciousness of men watching her; beef-eaters were not men, they were effigies stuck down at intervals; no more men than sentries, or dummies in suits of armour. So she loitered, having come out of the cloak-room only to face an unexpected mirror that returned to her, full-length, the image of the complete woman she might have postulated from the head-and-shoulders revealed to her in the mirror propped on the cloak-room table. There, she had scrutinized a lovely head, something after the manner of Lely, she thought – having been told so innumerable times – and the bare shoulders, oyster satin, and pearls of Lely, all of which she affected on state occasions because she knew they accorded with her type of beauty. Here, in the long mirror, she saw herself not only as a kit-cat, but full-length: oyster satin flowing out at her feet, pearls vanishing into the valley between her breasts, pearls looped round her wrists, a rosy scarf tossed round her shoulders. She wore no tiara. The fact that Lady Roehampton wore no tiara at Court balls made other women say, with a half-deprecatory, half-envious laugh, that Lady Roehampton was an unconventional woman. Such daring was almost insolent. It was almost rude. But the Order of St John of Jerusalem caught and held her rosy scarf.

ROSAMOND LEHMANN

Invitation to the Waltz, 1932

SHE experienced a sudden distress of spirit, thinking in a half-conscious way that she hadn't – hadn't yet found herself ... couldn't – *could* not put herself together, all of a piece. During a period of insanity she had accepted, with alacrity, with excitement, an invitation to a dance. Now, this moment having recovered her wits, she saw what she was in for.

Why go? It was unthinkable. Why suffer so much? Wrenched from one's foundations; neglected, ignored, curiously stared at; partnerless, watching Kate move serenely from partner to partner, pretending not to watch; pretending not to see one's hostess wondering: must she do something about one again? – (but really one couldn't go on and on introducing these people); pretending not to care; slipping off to the ladies' cloakroom, fiddling with unnecessary pins and powder, ears strained for the music to stop; wandering forth again to stand by oneself against the wall, hope struggling with despair beneath a mask of smiling indifference. ... The band strikes up again, the first couple link and glide away. Kate sails past once more. ... Back to the cloakroom, the pins, the cold scrutiny or (worse) the pitying small talk of the attendant maid.

Oh, horrible images! Solitude in the midst of crowds! Feast from which, sole non-participator, one would return empty!

MAUREEN FREELY
The Life of the Party, 1984

THIS evening she and Margaret were watching the sunset from a bench on the college terrace. They were already dressed for the Ashes' party, their hair carefully arranged, their highheeled shoes well polished, their stockings fresh from the haberdasher's, their clothes a poor but respectable imitation of the French fashions sported by the wealthy Turkish girls they went to school with at the American College for Girls. They had taken the precaution of dressing early so that Chloe's mother would not have the chance to tell Chloe that she really would prefer it if Chloe did not attend adult parties.

Chloe thought her mother unfair. For God's sake, she was going on seventeen. Margaret had been attending her parents' parties all her life, and she was still in one piece, wasn't she? Year after year she had been reporting the scandals she had witnessed in minute detail. There was no immoral act that Chloe was not prepared to witness.

ELIZABETH BOWEN
The Death of the Heart, 1938

THIS was to be her first party. Tonight, the ceiling rose higher, the lounge extended tense and mysterious. Columns of translucent tawny shadow stood between the orange shades of the lamps. The gramophone stood open, a record on it, the arm with the needle bent back like an arm ready to strike. Doris not seeing Portia, Doris elate and ghostly in a large winged cap passed through the lounge with trays. Out there at sea they might take this house for another lighted ship – and soon this magnetic room would be drawing people down the dark esplanade. Portia saw her partners with no faces: whoever she danced with, it would always be Eddie.

LOUIS SIMPSON
'Tonight the Famous Psychiatrist', 1966

TONIGHT the famous psychiatrist
Is giving a party.
There are figures from the sporting world
And flesh-coloured girls
Arriving straight from the theatre.

And many other celebrities . . .
The Jew looks serious,
Questioning, always questioning, his liberal error;
The Negro laughs
Three times, like a trumpet.

The wife of the host enters slowly,
Poor woman!
She thinks she is still in Hungary,
And clings to her knitting needles,
For her the time passes slowly.

RADCLYFFE HALL
The Well of Loneliness, 1928

IT can safely be said that Stephen at eighteen had in no way
outgrown her dread of the Antrims; there was only one member
of that family who liked her, she knew, and that was the small, henpecked Colonel. He liked her because, a fine horseman himself, he
admired her skill and her courage out hunting.

'It's a pity she's so tall, of course—' he would grumble, 'but she
does know a horse and how to stick on one. Now my children might
have been brought up at Margate, they're just about fitted to ride
the beach donkeys!'

But Colonel Antrim would not count at the dance; indeed in his
own house he very seldom counted. Stephen would have to endure
Mrs Antrim and Violet – and then Roger was home from Sandhurst.
Their antagonism had never quite died, perhaps because it was too
fundamental. Now they covered it up with a cloak of good manners,
but these two were still enemies at heart, and they knew it. No,

Stephen did not want to go to that dance, though she went in order to please her mother. Nervous, awkward and apprehensive, Stephen arrived at the Antrims that night, little thinking that Fate, the most expert of tricksters, was waiting to catch her just round the corner.

CHRISTOPHER MARLOWE

Ovid's Elegies Book 1, 1597

THY husband to a banquet goes with me,
Pray God it may his latest supper be.
Shall I sit gazing as a bashful guest.
While others touch the damsel I love best?
Will lying under him, his bosom clip
About thy neck shall he at pleasure skip?
Marvel not, though the fair bride did incite
The drunken Centaurs to a sudden fight;
I am no half-horse, nor in woods I dwell,
Yet scarce my hands from thee contain I well.
But how thou shouldst behave thyself now know,
Nor let the winds away my warnings blow.
Before thy husband come, though I not see
What may be done, yet there before him be.
Lie with him gently, when his limbs he spread
Upon the bed, but on my foot first tread.
View me, my becks and speaking countenance;
Take and receive each secret amorous glance.
Words without voice shall on my eyebrows sit,
Lines thou shalt read in wine by my hand writ.
When our lascivious toys come in thy mind,
Thy rosy cheeks be to thy thumb inclined.
If aught of me thou speak'st in inward thought,
Let thy soft finger to thy ear be brought.
When I (my light) do or say aught that please thee,
Turn round thy gold ring, as it were to ease thee.
Strike on the board like them that pray for evil,
When thou dost wish thy husband at the devil.
What wine he fills thee, wisely will him drink;
Ask thou the boy what thou enough dost think.
When thou hast tasted, I will take the cup,

And where thou drink'st, on that part I will sup.
If he gives thee what first himself did taste,
Even in his face his offered gobbets cast.
Let not thy neck by his vile arms be pressed,
Nor lean thy soft head on his boist'rous breast.
Thy bosom's roseate buds let him not finger,
Chiefly on thy lips let not his lips linger.
If thou givest kisses, I shall all disclose,
Say they are mine and hands on thee impose.
Yet this I'll see, but if thy gown aught cover,
Suspicious fear in all my veins will hover.
Mingle not thighs nor to his leg join thine,
Nor thy soft foot with his hard foot combine.
I have been wanton, therefore am perplexed,
And with mistrust of the like measure vexed.
I and my wench oft under clothes did lurk,
When pleasure moved us to our sweetest work.
Do not thou so, but throw thy mantle hence,
Lest I should think thee guilty of offence.
Entreat thy husband drink, but do not kiss,
And while he drinks, to add more do not miss;
If he lies down with wine and sleep oppressed,
The thing and place shall counsel us the rest.
When to go homewards we rise all along,
Have care to walk in middle of the throng;
There will I find thee or be found by thee,
There touch whatever thou canst touch of me.
Aye me, I warn what profits some few hours,
But we must part when heav'n with black night lours.
At night thy husband clips thee: I will weep
And to the doors sight of thyself keep.
Then will he kiss thee, and not only kiss,
But force thee give him my stol'n honey bliss.
Constrained against thy will, give it the peasant;
Forbear sweet words, and be your sport unpleasant.
To him I pray it no delight may bring,
Or if it do, to thee no joy thence spring;
But though this night thy fortune be to try it,
To me tomorrow constantly deny it.

MARGARET DRABBLE

The Middle Ground, 1980

THERE she sits, Kate Armstrong, in her black Marks and
Spencer petticoat, her feet dangling in their emerald Arabian
slippers, wondering what to wear, and wondering what will happen
at her party. Will Hunt stay reasonably sober and refrain from
insulting people, will Marylou turn up and if so what on earth will
people make of her, will Stuart be civil to Ted, will Ted make a pass
at Rosamund Stacey, will Evelyn find the whole thing too exhausting,
will Hugo's mother find it too much of a squash, will the neighbours
object to the noise? Will she abandon all hesitation and agree to fly
out to Baghdad with Hugo, will she find a voice in which to speak,
at last, to Ted, there, amongst so many people? will she fall in love
with Ruth's Rastaman?

. . . It is all in the future. Excitement fills her, excitement, joy,
anticipation, apprehension. Something will happen.

LESLIE JULIAN JONES

'The Borgia Orgy', date unknown

THE Borgias are giving an orgy,
   There's a Borgia Orgy tonight.
And isn't it sickening, we've run out of strychnine,
The gravy will have to have ground glass for thickening.
The poisoned Chianti is terribly scanty,
But everything else is all right.
I've hidden an asp in the iced canteloupe,
There's arsenic mixed in the mock turtle soup,
And straight benzedrine in the apricot *coupe*
At the Borgia Orgy tonight.

Our guests are exclusively chosen
From the people who give us a pain;
And the cream of the joke is the knowledge
That they won't come here again . . .

The Borgias are giving an orgy,
There's a Borgia Orgy tonight;

We have poison ptomaine that will rack them with pain,
We've nothing to lose and a whole lot to gain;
We're pushing some people we know off a steeple,
It should be a wonderful sight.
We've bricked up some cousins of ours in a wall,
Their agonised cries won't disturb us at all
As we sit here sipping our wormwood and gall –
At the Borgia Orgy tonight.

We revel in giving a party,
A fete or a fancy dress ball;
There's always a regular beano
And a good time had by all . . .

The Borgias are giving an orgy,
There's a Borgia Orgy tonight.
For the Duke's eldest son there's a monstrous Bath bun
Soaked in hot Prussic acid, it's all good clean fun.
The tank in the Ladies will blow them to Hades
If anyone turns on the light.
The bodies will fall through a trapdoor below
To the Tiber, and drift out to sea on the flow –
We think we can promise a jolly good show
At the Borgia Orgy tonight.

We've got all the nobles from Naples
At the Borgia Orgy tonight.
The soup minestrone is frightfully phoney
And laudanum reeks in the stewed macaroni;
We'll laugh like a drain when they eat the henbane
In the third tangerine from the right.
When the butler flings open the dining-room door
There's a cunning contraption concealed in the floor;
We wonder who'll sit on the circular saw. . .
At the Borgia Orgy tonight.

'The preparations meanwhile went on ...'

JANE AUSTEN
Mansfield Park, 1814

THE preparations meanwhile went on, and Lady Bertram continued to sit on her sofa without any inconvenience from them. She had some extra visits from the housekeeper, and her maid was rather hurried in making up a new dress for her: Sir Thomas gave orders, and Mrs Norris ran about; but all this gave *her* no trouble, and as she had foreseen, 'there was, in fact, no trouble in the business.'

F. SCOTT FITZGERALD
The Great Gatsby, 1925

THERE was music from my neighbour's house through the summer nights. In his blue gardens men and girls came and went like moths among the whisperings and the champagne and the stars. At high tide in the afternoon I watched his guests diving from the tower of his raft, or taking the sun on the hot sand of his beach while his two motor-boats slit the waters of the Sound, drawing aquaplanes over cataracts of foam. On weekends his Rolls-Royce became an omnibus, bearing parties to and from the city between nine in the morning and long past midnight, while his station wagon scampered like a brisk yellow bug to meet all trains. And on Mondays eight servants, including an extra gardener, toiled all day with mops and scrubbing-brushes and hammers and garden-shears, repairing the ravages of the night before.

Every Friday five crates of oranges and lemons arrived from a fruiterer in New York – every Monday these same oranges and lemons left his back door in a pyramid of pulpless halves. There was a machine in the kitchen which could extract the juice of two hundred oranges in half an hour if a little button was pressed two hundred times by a butler's thumb.

At least once a fortnight a corps of caterers came down with several hundred feet of canvas and enough coloured lights to make a Christmas tree of Gatsby's enormous garden. On buffet tables, garnished with glistening hors-d'œuvre, spiced baked hams crowded against salads of harlequin designs and pastry pigs and turkeys bewitched to a dark gold. In the main hall a bar with a real brass rail was set up, and stocked with gins and liquors and with cordials so long forgotten that most of his female guests were too young to know one from another.

By seven o'clock the orchestra has arrived, no thin five-piece affair, but a whole pitful of oboes and trombones and saxophones and viols and cornets and piccolos, and low and high drums. The last swimmers have come in from the beach now and are dressing upstairs; the cars from New York are parked five deep in the drive, and already the halls and salons and verandas are gaudy with primary colours, and hair bobbed in strange new ways, and shawls beyond the dreams of Castile.

SOMERSET MAUGHAM

Before the Party, 1926

MRS Skinner liked to be in good time. She was already dressed, in black silk as befitted her age and the mourning she wore for her son-in-law, and now she put on her toque. She was a little uncertain about it, since the egrets' feathers which adorned it might very well arouse in some of the friends she would certainly meet at the party acid expostulations; and of course it was shocking to kill those beautiful white birds, in the mating season too, for the sake of their feathers; but there they were, so pretty and stylish, and it would have been silly to refuse them, and it would have hurt her son-in-law's feelings. He had brought them all the way from Borneo and he expected her to be so pleased with them. Kathleen had made herself rather unpleasant about them, she must wish she hadn't now, after what had happened, but Kathleen had never really liked Harold. Mrs Skinner, standing at her dressing-table, placed the toque on her head, it was after all the only nice hat she had, and put in a pin with a large jet knob. If anybody spoke to her about the ospreys she had her answer.

'I know it's dreadful,' she would say, 'and I wouldn't dream of buying them, but my poor son-in-law brought them back the last time he was home on leave.'

That would explain her possession of them and excuse their use. Everyone had been very kind. Mrs Skinner took a clean handkerchief from a drawer and sprinkled a little *Eau de Cologne* on it. She never used scent, and she had always thought it rather fast, but *Eau de Cologne* was so refreshing. She was very nearly ready now, and her eyes wandered out of the window behind her looking-glass. Canon Heywood had a beautiful day for his garden-party. It was warm and the sky was blue; the trees had not yet lost the fresh green of the spring.

ARNOLD BENNETT
The Card, 1911

ON the evening of the ball, Denry spent at least two hours in the operation which was necessary before he could give the Countess the pleasure of his company. This operation took place in his minute bedroom at the back of the cottage in Brougham Street, and it was of a complex nature. Three weeks ago he had innocently thought that you had only to order a dress-suit and there you were! He now knew that a dress-suit is merely the beginning of anxiety. Shirt! Collar! Tie! Studs! Cuff-links! Gloves! Handkerchief! (He was very glad to learn authoritatively from Shillitoe that handkerchiefs were no longer worn in the waistcoat opening, and that men who so wore them were barbarians and the truth was not in them. Thus, an everyday handkerchief would do.) Boots! . . . Boots were the rock on which he had struck. Shillitoe, in addition to being a tailor was a hosier, but by some flaw in the scheme of the universe hosiers do not sell boots. Except boots, Denry could get all he needed on credit; boots he could not get on credit, and he could not pay cash for them. Eventually he decided that his church boots must be dazzled up to the level for this great secular occasion. The pity was that he forgot

– not that he was of a forgetful disposition in great matters; he was simply over-excited – he forgot to dazzle them up until after he had fairly put his collar on and his necktie in a bow. It is imprudent to touch blacking in a dress-shirt, so Denry had to undo the past and begin again. This hurried him. He was not afraid of being late for the first waltz with Miss Ruth Earp, but he was afraid of not being out of the house before his mother returned. Mrs Machin had been making up a lady's own materials all day, naturally – the day being what it was! If she had had twelve hands instead of two, she might have made up the own materials of half-a-dozen ladies instead of one, and earned twenty-four shillings instead of four. Denry did not want his mother to see him ere he departed. He had lavished an enormous amount of brains and energy to the end of displaying himself in this refined and novel attire to the gaze of two hundred persons, and yet his secret wish was to deprive his mother of the beautiful spectacle.

MARGARET MITCHELL

Gone With the Wind, 1936

WHAT dress would best set off her charms and make her most irresistible to Ashley? Since eight o'clock she had been trying on and rejecting dresses, and now she stood dejected and irritable in lace pantalets, linen corset cover and three billowing lace and linen petticoats. Discarded garments lay about her on the floor, the bed, the chairs, in bright heaps of colour and straying ribbons.

The rose organdie with long pink sash was becoming, but she had worn it last summer when Melanie visited Twelve Oaks and she'd be sure to remember it. And might be catty enough to mention it. The black bombazine, with its puffed sleeves and princess lace collar, set off her white skin superbly, but it did make her look a trifle elderly. Scarlett peered anxiously in the mirror at her sixteen-year-old face as if expecting to see wrinkles and sagging chin muscles. It would never do to appear sedate and elderly before Melanie's sweet youthfulness. The lavender-barred muslin was beautiful with those wide insets of lace and net about the hem, but it had never suited her type. It would suit Carreen's delicate profile and wishy-washy expression perfectly, but Scarlett felt that it made her look like a schoolgirl. It would never do to appear schoolgirlish beside Melanie's poised self. The green plaid taffeta, frothing with flounces and each flounce edged in green velvet ribbon, was most becoming, in fact her favourite dress, for it darkened her eyes to emerald. But there was unmistakably a grease spot on the front of the basque. Of course, her brooch could be pinned over the spot, but perhaps Melanie had sharp eyes. There remained varicoloured cotton dresses which Scarlet felt were not festive enough for the occasion, ball dresses and the green sprigged muslin she had worn yesterday. But it was an afternoon dress. It was not suitable for a barbecue, for it had only tiny puffed sleeves and the neck was low enough for a dancing dress. But there was nothing else to do but wear it. After all, she was not ashamed of her neck and arms and bosom, even if it was not correct to show them in the morning.

As she stood before the mirror and twisted herself about to get a side view, she thought that there was absolutely nothing about her figure to cause her shame. Her neck was short but rounded and her arms plump and enticing. Her breasts, pushed high by her stays, were very nice breasts. She had never had to sew tiny rows of silk ruffles in the lining of her basques, as most sixteen-year-old girls did, to give their figures the desired curves and fullness. She was glad she had inherited Ellen's slender white hands and tiny feet, and she wished she had Ellen's height, too, but her own height pleased her very well. What a pity legs could not be shown, she thought, pulling up her petticoats and regretfully viewing them, plump and neat under pantalets. She had such nice legs. Even the girls at the Fayetteville Academy had admitted as much. And as for her waist – there was no one in Fayetteville, Jonesboro or in three counties, for that matter, who had so small a waist.

The thought of her waist brought her back to practical matters. The green muslin measured seventeen inches about the waist, and Mammy had laced her for the eighteen-inch bombazine. Mammy would have to lace her tighter. She pushed open the door, listened and heard Mammy's heavy tread in the downstairs hall. She shouted for her impatiently, knowing she could raise her voice with impunity, as Ellen was in the smokehouse, measuring out the day's food to Cookie.

THE BIBLE
St Luke, Chapter 15

BUT the father said to his servants, Bring forth the best robe, and put *it* on him; and put a ring on his hand, and shoes on *his* feet:

And bring hither the fatted calf, and kill *it*; and let us eat, and be merry:

For this my son was dead, and is alive again; he was lost, and is found. And they began to be merry.

Now his elder son was in the field: and as he came and drew nigh to the house, he heard musick and dancing.

And he called one of the servants, and asked what these things meant.

And he said unto him, Thy brother is come; and thy father hath killed the fatted calf, because he hath received him safe and sound.

And he was angry, and would not go in: therefore came his father out, and intreated him.

And he answering said to *his* father, Lo, these many years do I serve thee, neither transgressed I at any time thy commandment: and yet thou never gavest me a kid, that I might make merry with my friends:

But as soon as this thy son was come, which hath devoured thy living with harlots, thou hast killed for him the fatted calf.

And he said unto him, Son, thou art ever with me, and all that I have is thine.

It was meet that we should make merry, and be glad: for this thy brother was dead, and is alive again; and was lost, and is found.

NANCY MITFORD
The Pursuit of Love, 1945

BUT, in spite of the fact that the preparations seemed to be going forward without a single hitch, Aunt Sadie's brow was still furrowed with anxiety, because she had collected a large house-party of girls and their mammas, but not one single young man. The fact was that those of her own contemporaries who had daughters were glad to bring them, but sons were another matter. Dancing partners, sated with invitations at this time of year, knew better than to go all the way down to Gloucestershire to a house as yet untried, where they were by no means certain of finding the warmth, the luxury and fine wines which they looked upon as their due, where there was no known female charmer to tempt them, where they had not been offered a mount, and where no mention had been made of a shoot, not even a day with the cocks.

Uncle Matthew had far too much respect for his horses and his pheasants to offer them up to be messed about by any callow unknown boy.

So here was a horrible situation. Ten females, four mothers and six girls, were advancing from various parts of England, to arrive at a household consisting of four more females (not that Linda and I counted, still, we wore skirts and not trousers, and were really too old to be kept all the time in the school-room) and only two males, one of whom was not yet in tails.

The telephone now became red-hot, telegrams flew in every direction. Aunt Sadie abandoned all pride, all pretence that things were as they should be, that people were asked for themselves alone, and launched a series of desperate appeals. Mr Wills, the vicar, consented to leave Mrs Wills at home, and dine, *en garçon*, at Alconleigh. It would be the first time they had been separated for forty years. Mrs Aster, the agent's wife, also made the same sacrifice, and Master Aster, the agent's son, aged not quite seventeen, was hurried off to Oxford to get himself a ready-made dress suit.

Davey Warbeck was ordered to leave Aunt Emily and come. He said he would, but unwillingly, and only after the full extent of the crisis had been divulged. Elderly cousins, and uncles who had been for many years forgotten as ghosts, were recalled from oblivion and urged to materialize. They nearly all refused, some of them quite rudely – they had, nearly all, at one time or another, been so deeply and bitterly insulted by Uncle Matthew that forgiveness was impossible.

At last Uncle Matthew saw that the situation would have to be taken in hand. He did not care two hoots about the ball, he felt no particular responsibility for the amusement of his guests, whom he seemed to regard as an onrushing horde of barbarians who could not be kept out, rather than as a group of delightful friends summoned for mutual entertainment and joyous revelry. But he did care for Aunt Sadie's peace of mind, he could not bear to see her looking so worried, and he decided to take steps. He went up to London and attended the last sitting of the House of Lords before the recess. His journey was entirely fruitful.

'Stromboli, Paddington, Fort William and Curtley have accepted,' he told Aunt Sadie, with the air of a conjuror producing four wonderful fat rabbits out of one small wineglass.

'But I had to promise them a shoot – Bob, go and tell Craven I want to see him in the morning.'

LEO TOLSTOY
War and Peace, 1865

NATASHA was going to her first grand ball. She had got up at eight that morning and had been in a fever of excitement and energy all day. All her energies from the moment she woke had been directed to the one aim of ensuring that they all – herself, mamma and Sonya – should look their very best. Sonya and the countess put themselves entirely in her hands. The countess was to wear a dark red velvet gown; the two girls, white tulle dresses over pink silk slips, with roses on their bodices. Their hair was to be arranged *à la grecque.*

All the essentials had been done: feet, hands, neck and ears most carefully washed, perfumed and powdered, as befits a ball. The open-work silk stockings and white satin slippers with ribbons were already on; their hair was almost finished. Sonya was nearly ready, so was the countess; but Natasha, who had bustled about helping everyone, was less advanced. She was still sitting before the looking-glass with a *peignoir* thrown over her thin shoulders. Sonya, on the last stage, stood in the middle of the room fastening on a final bow and hurting her dainty finger as she pressed the pin that squeaked as it went through the ribbon.

'Not like that, Sonya, not like that!' cried Natasha, turning her head and clutching with both hands at her hair which the maid, who was dressing it, had not time to let go. 'That bow isn't right. Come here!'

Sonya sat down and Natasha pinned the ribbon differently.

'If you please, miss, I can't get on like this,' said the maid, still holding Natasha's hair.

'Oh, goodness gracious, wait then! There, that's better, Sonya.'

'Will you soon be ready?' came the countess's voice. 'It is nearly ten.'

'Coming, coming! What about you, mamma?'

'I have only my cap to pin on.'

'Don't do it without me!' cried Natasha. 'You won't do it right.'

'Yes, but it's ten o'clock.'

It had been agreed that they should arrive at the ball at half past ten, but Natasha had still to get her dress on before they called for Madame Peronsky.

When her hair was done, Natasha, in a short petticoat from under which her dancing-slippers showed, and her mother's dressing-jacket, ran up to Sonya, inspected her critically, and then flew on to her mother. Turning the countess's head this way and that, she fastened on the cap, gave the grey hair a hasty kiss and scurried back to the maids who were shortening her skirt.

The cause of the delay was Natasha's skirt, which was too long. Two maids were at work turning up the hem and hurriedly biting off the threads. A third, with her mouth full of pins, was running backwards and forwards between the countess and Sonya, while a fourth held the gossamer garment high on one uplifted hand.

'Hurry up, Mavra, darling!'

'Hand me that thimble, please, miss.'

'Aren't you ever going to be ready?' asked the count, coming to the door. 'Here are you still perfuming yourselves. Madame Peronsky must be tired of waiting.'

HARVEY ALLEN
Anthony Adverse, 1934

THE dinner for the Jorhams was to be an unusual feast; one not for business alone. Indeed, McNab had been instructed to return to the brig and to arrange for Anthony's passage on the captain's terms. He had done so. He and Philadelphia had returned with the turtle which was killed in the courtyard amidst immense curiosity. Dinner was to be a memorable, final feast.

Mr Bonnyfeather had planned it with a double motive. As a farewell to Anthony it was to be a merry one. He would spare Anthony the sadness of a sorrowful parting and he would also spare himself the lonely, private agony of a good-bye that he scarce dared to face. 'The last, the dear last of us all,' he thought looking at the boy's golden head. They sat in his room together talking, making last arrangements, pausing, and reverting to familiar topics as one goes back to look at something for the last time.

Faith was very busy outside packing Anthony's chests. They could hear her moving about in the hall.

'I suppose you will be taking the madonna with you, Mr Anthony,' she said coming in suddenly.

'Oh,' said he getting up. He had almost forgotten her. '*Yes*, wrap her up carefully. Put her in the big chest.'

Faith nodded. So she would see the last of *that*, she thought. She turned the thing face downward and closed the lid. 'Farewell to the bad luck of a Paleologus!'

In the room Anthony and Mr Bonnyfeather sounded very merry. But it seemed to both of them at times that the misty landscapes on the wall were hazier than usual. The old man lighted his candles. He wiped his spectacles and put them on again several times. Thus they both talked through the long twilight as if they would always be able to do so till evenings were no more. At eight o'clock the guests arrived.

THOMAS HARDY

Under the Greenwood Tree, 1872

DURING the afternoon unusual activity was seen to prevail about the precincts of tranter Dewy's house. The flagstone floor was swept of dust, and a sprinkling of the finest yellow sand from the innermost stratum of the adjoining sand-pit lightly scattered thereupon. Then were produced large knives and forks, which had been shrouded in darkness and grease since the last occasion of the kind, and bearing upon their sides, 'Shear-steel, warranted,' in such emphatic letters of assurance, that the warranter's name was not required as further proof, and not given. The key was left in the tap of the cider-barrel, instead of being carried in a pocket. And finally the tranter had to stand up in the room and let his wife wheel him round like a turnstile, to see if anything discreditable was visible in his appearance.

'Come, open the door to us, let us come in.'

———✦———

HILAIRE BELLOC

'Drinking Song on the Excellence of Burgundy Wine',
date unknown

MY jolly fat host with your face all a-grin,
Come, open the door to us, let us come in.
A score of stout fellows who think it no sin
If they toast till they're hoarse, and they drink till they spin,
    Hoofed it amain,
    Rain or no rain,
To crack your old jokes, and your bottle to drain.

JOHANN WOLFGANG VON GOETHE

Italian Journey, 1792

IN order to get to the whimsical little Princess on time, and not to miss the right house, I hired a servant, who conducted me to the gates of a large palazzo. Since I did not credit her with living in such a magnificent residence, I spelled out her name once more, letter by letter, but he assured me that this was the right place. I entered a spacious empty courtyard, enclosed by the main building and several annexes – all in the gay Neapolitan style of architecture – and faced an enormous portal and a wide though not very long staircase, on either side of which servants in splendid livery were lined up, who bowed deeply as I passed. I felt like the sultan in Wieland's Fairy Tale and, following his example, took my courage in both hands. At the head of the staircase, I was received by the upper servants and,

in due course, the grandest of them opened a door and I was
confronted by a magnificent but perfectly empty salon. As I paced
up and down I caught a glimpse of a side gallery where a table was
laid for about forty persons on the same scale of splendour as
everything else. A secular priest entered: without asking who I was
or where I came from, he took my presence for granted and made
polite conversation.

Double doors were thrown open to admit an elderly man, and
immediately closed behind him. The priest advanced to meet him, so
I did the same. We greeted him with a few polite words to which he
replied with some barking and stammering noises. For all that I
could make of them, he might have been speaking Hottentot. When
he had taken up a position by the fireplace, the priest stepped back
and I followed his example. Now an imposing Benedictine entered,
accompanied by a younger brother. He, too, greeted our host and,
after being barked at, withdrew and joined us by the window. The
members of religious orders, especially the more elegantly dressed
ones, are at a great advantage in society: their habit, though it
indicates humility and renunciation, at the same time lends them a
decided dignity. They can appear submissive without abasing themselves, and when they draw themselves up to their full height, they
are invested with a certain self-complacency which would be intol-
erable in any other profession but becomes them rather well. The
Benedictine was this kind of man. I asked him about Monte Cassino:
he invited me to come there and promised me the warmest reception.
In the meantime, officers, courtiers, secular priests, even some
Capuchins had arrived, and the salon was full of people.

I looked in vain for a lady. At last, the double doors opened and
closed again and a lady entered who looked even older than the
master of the house. The presence of the lady of the house – for that
is what I took her to be – convinced me that I was in the wrong
palazzo and a total stranger to its owners.

Dinner was announced and I stuck close to the ecclesiastics,
hoping to sneak in with them into the paradise of the dining room.
At this moment Filangieri and his wife entered hurriedly, apologizing
for being late; and a moment later the little Princess came running
into the salon, curtsying, bowing, and nodding to all the guests
as she passed, and made straight for me. 'How nice of you to keep
your promise!' she cried. 'Sit next to me at table, and you shall
have all the titbits. But wait a moment! First I have to find my
place.'

CECIL BEATON

Diaries: The Parting Years, 1978

BECAUSE I was still in hospital after an operation I wondered if I would be prevented from going to the Ball. As it happened I was given permission by the doctors.

It was one of the most beautiful moonlit nights of a wonderful summer. Windsor looked lively at this hour of the evening with crowds coming out of the theatre and the pubs. The castle was floodlit. Little posses of people stood around watching the guests arrive. Policemen and yeomen of the guard were at every point.

Surprisingly informal in a rather cavernous light, the Queen received her guests at the top of a small flight of stairs. As I got nearer I could see the marvellous sheen on the Queen's skin, her teeth, her lips, her hair. She was dressed in white with some sparklets round the neck and her hair a bit stiff. I have never in my life seen such a marvellous regard or such a look of interest and compassion. I was thrilled.

The silence after 'Good evening' was broken by 'Are you better?' Prince Philip asked: 'What's all this about?' I explained that I had left hospital to come here. He laughed, as much as to say: 'You must be mad' or 'What else is new?' He would have liked to bully me but I moved on. Patrick Plunket told me to go to the long Gothic gallery where the guests were gathering and a buffet stretched the length of one wall. The party was to celebrate the seventieth birthdays of the Queen Mother, the Duke of Gloucester (he's too old to appear), the Duke of Beaufort and Lord Mountbatten.

Prince and Princess Paul of Yugoslavia were there, and a lot of German royals, and all sorts of young, including several long-haired young men. Ava Waverley looked like a drawing of an old woman by Dürer, her mouth fallen open and her eyes popping. Her hair was like the fluff of a five-day-old chick. Diana Cooper was a *tour-de-force* of aristocratic beauty in white.

The Queen Mother was wearing pale moth-coloured chiffon with pelisses covered with solid sequins, a big pearl and diamond necklace and tiara. Princess Alexandra looked ravishing, long tendril curls, a dark red satin dress and a sheen on her skin: the most adorable of human beings, she exuded beauty.

ADA LEVERSON
The Limit, 1911

ON the evening of the Ritz dinner party Harry was not in a particularly good temper, and thought to himself he was rather like a Barnum as he introduced his guests one by one to the modest millionaire, who said to them all, 'Pleased to meet you', and fixed his admiring glance with a sentimental respect on Daphne, an undisguised admiration on Valentia, and an almost morbid curiosity on Miss Luscombe, the first actress he had ever met.

Miss Luscombe was a conventional, rather untidy-looking creature, very handsome, with loose hair parted and waved over her ears, and with apparently no design or general idea either in her dress or manner. She varied from minute to minute from being what she thought theatrical to appearing what she supposed to be social. She evidently hadn't settled on her pose, always a disastrous moment for a natural woman who wishes to be artificial. Practically she always wore evening dress except in the evening, so while at her own flat in the afternoon she was photographed in a *décolletée* tea-gown, this evening she was dressed as if for Ascot, except for the hat, with an emaciated feather boa and a tired embroidered *crêpe de Chine* scarf thrown over her shoulders, also a fan, long gloves, and a rose in her hair by way of hedging. To these ornaments she added a cold, of which she complained as soon as she saw the other guests. But no one listened. No one ever listened to Miss Luscombe, no one ever could, and yet in a way she was popular – a kind of pet among a rather large circle of people. Women never disliked her because she created no jealousy and always unconsciously put herself at a disadvantage; men did not mind her prattle and coquettish airs, being well aware that nothing was expected of them. For Miss Luscombe, though vain, was a pessimist, and quite good-natured. She was also a standing joke.

The other guests besides Valentia in yellow and Daphne in pink – both looking as fresh as daisies and as civilized as orchids – consisted of Lady Walmer, a smart, good-looking, commonplace woman, rather fatter than she wished to be, but very straight-fronted, straightforward, and sporting, with dark red hair and splendid jewels; a faded yet powerful beauty who had been admired in the eighties, but had only had real success since she turned forty-six.

LOUIS AUCHINCHLOSS
The Rector of Justin, 1964

MY naïveté in this case let me in for an appalling scene. One night I went to the duplex to find myself the only guest. Cordelia, reclining in a pink negligee before a pitcher of martinis, in which she had obviously been imbibing prior to my arrival, might have scared me to instant flight had not her voice been so gruff and matter-of-fact.

'Yes, sweetie, we're all alone,' she said as she took in my apprehensive glance at the table set cosily for two by the window. 'After dinner I'll play soft music and show you my etchings. Don't look so scared. It won't hurt. Here, give yourself a drink.' But when she abruptly changed the subject, I decided in a flutter of relief that she must be joking. 'This damn war,' she continued. 'I'm sick of it already. The last one was bad enough, but at least there was all that Wilsonian idealism. Oh, I grant you, it nauseated me at the time, but now I find it's worse without it. All you young people are so terrified that anyone will think *you* think you're making the world safe for democracy that of course you won't. Not a chance of it.'

She continued morosely in this vein all during a lengthy cocktail period and a much shorter dinner. I wondered hopefully if the amount of gin that she was consuming might not end by disposing of my problem, but her capacity seemed unlimited. Only her temper was affected, for it grew shorter and shorter. After the meal she blew up at me for suggesting that we listen to *The Magic Flute*.

KATHERINE MANSFIELD
Collected Stories: 'Her First Ball', 1945

EXACTLY when the ball began Leila would have found it hard to say. Perhaps her first real partner was the cab. It did not matter that she shared the cab with the Sheridan girls and their brother. She sat back in her own little corner of it, and the bolster on which her hand rested felt like the sleeve of an unknown young man's dress suit; and away they bowled, past waltzing lamp-posts and houses and fences and trees.

'Have you really never been to a ball before, Leila? But, my child, how too weird—' cried the Sheridan girls.

'Our nearest neighbour was fifteen miles,' said Leila softly, gently opening and shutting her fan.

Oh dear, how hard it was to be indifferent like the others! She tried not to smile too much; she tried not to care. But every single thing was so new and exciting . . . Meg's tuberoses, Jose's long loop of amber, Laura's little dark head, pushing above her white fur like a flower through snow. She would remember for ever. It even gave her a pang to see her cousin Laurie throw away the wisps of tissue paper he pulled from the fastenings of his new gloves. She would like to have kept those wisps as a keepsake, as a remembrance. Laurie leaned forward and put his hand on Laura's knee.

'Look here, darling,' he said. 'The third and the ninth as usual, Twig?'

Oh, how marvellous to have a brother! In her excitement Leila felt that if there had been time, if it hadn't been impossible, she couldn't have helped crying because she was an only child and no brother had ever said 'Twig?' to her; no sister would ever say, as Meg said to Jose that moment, 'I've never known your hair go up more successfully than it has tonight!'

But of course, there was not time. They were at the drill hall already; there were cabs in front of them and cabs behind. The road was bright on either side with moving fan-like lights, and on the pavement gay couples seemed to float through the air; little satin shoes chased each other like birds.

'Hold on to me, Leila; you'll get lost,' said Laura.

'Come on, girls, let's make a dash for it,' said Laurie.

Leila put two fingers on Laura's pink velvet cloak, and they were somehow lifted past the big golden lantern, carried along the passage, and pushed into the little room marked 'Ladies'. Here the crowd was so great there was hardly space to take off their things; the noise was deafening. Two benches on either side were stacked high with wraps. Two old women in white aprons ran up and down tossing fresh armfuls. And everybody was pressing forward trying to get at the little dressing-table and mirror at the far end.

A great quivering jet of gas lighted the ladies' room. It couldn't wait; it was dancing already. When the door opened again and there came a burst of tuning from the drill hall, it leaped almost to the ceiling.

Dark girls, fair girls were patting their hair, tying ribbons again,

tucking handkerchiefs down the fronts of their bodices, smoothing
marble-white gloves. And because they were all laughing it seemed
to Leila that they were all lovely.

'Aren't there any invisible hairpins?' cried a voice. 'How most
extraordinary! I can't see a single invisible hairpin.'

'Powder my back, there's a darling,' cried someone else.

'But I must have a needle and cotton. I've torn simply miles and
miles of the frill,' wailed a third.

HENRY JAMES
The Wings of a Dove, 1902

THE beginning – to which she often went back – had been a
scene, for our young woman, of supreme brilliancy; a party
given at a 'gallery' hired by a hostess who fished with big nets. A
Spanish dancer, understood to be at that moment the delight of the
town, an American reciter, the joy of a kindred people, an Hungarian
fiddler, the wonder of the world at large – in the name of these and
other attractions the company in which Kate, by a rare privilege,
found herself had been freely convoked. She lived under her mother's
roof, as she considered, obscurely, and was acquainted with few
persons who entertained on that scale; but she had had dealings
with two or three connected, as appeared, with such – two or three
through whom the stream of hospitality, filtered or diffused, could
thus now and then spread to outlying receptacles. A good-natured
lady in fine, a friend of her mother and a relative of the lady of the
gallery, had offered to take her to the party in question and had
there fortified her, further, with two or three of those introductions
that, at large parties, lead to other things – that had at any rate on
this occasion culminated for her in conversation with a tall fair, a
slightly unbrushed and rather awkward, but on the whole a not
dreary, young man. The young man had affected her as detached, as
– it was indeed what he called himself – awfully at sea, as much
more distinct from what surrounded them than any one else
appeared to be, and even as probably quite disposed to be making
his escape when pulled up to be placed in relation with her. He gave
her his word for it indeed, this same evening, that only their meeting
had prevented his flight, but that now he saw how sorry he should
have been to miss it.

GRAHAM GREENE

Travels with my Aunt, 1969

THE party was larger than I had conceived possible after seeing my aunt alone in the empty unfurnished house, and I could only explain it by the fact that not one real friend was present among all the hundred guests, unless one could call O'Toole a friend. As more and more guests assembled I wondered from what highways and hedges Mr Visconti had drummed them up. The street was lined with cars, among them two armoured ones, for the Chief of Police had arrived as promised bringing with him a very fat and ugly wife and a beautiful daughter called Camilla. Even the young officer who had arrested me was there, and he gave me a hearty slap on the back to show that there was no ill feeling on his part. (I had still a piece of plaster on my ear where he had struck me on the earlier occasion.) I think Mr Visconti must have visited every hotel bar in town, and the most passing acquaintances had been invited to bring their friends. The party was to be his apotheosis. After it no one would ever care to remember the former Mr Visconti who had lain sick and impoverished in a mean hotel by the yellow Victorian station.

The great gates had been cleaned of rust and flung open; the chandeliers sparkled in the *sala*, lights were turned on in even the empty rooms, while coloured globes had been strung from tree to tree and over the boards of the dance-floor laid on the grass. On the terrace two musicians tuned a guitar and a harp. O'Toole was there, the Czech who had failed to sell two million plastic straws had brought his wife from the Hotel Guarani, and suddenly I saw moving inconspicuously through the crowd and disappearing again as though into some warren in the garden the export-import merchant who had shared our table on the boat, grey and thin, twitching his rabbit nose. On the lawn the ox steamed and crackled on its iron frame, and the smell of roasting meat chased away the perfume of orange and jasmine.

JANE AUSTEN

Mansfield Park, 1814

WHEN the carriages were really heard, when the guests began really to assemble, her own gaiety of heart was much subdued: the sight of so many strangers threw her back into herself; and besides the gravity and formality of the first great circle, which the manners of neither Sir Thomas nor Lady Bertram were of a kind to do away, she found herself occasionally called on to endure something worse. She was introduced here and there by her uncle, and forced to be spoken to, and to courtesy, and speak again. This was a hard duty, and she was never summoned to it without looking at William, as he walked about at his ease in the background of the scene, and longing to be with him.

The entrance of the Grants and Crawfords was a favourable epoch. The stiffness of the meeting soon gave way before their popular manners and more diffused intimacies: little groups were formed, and everybody grew comfortable. Fanny felt the advantage; and, drawing back from the toils of civility, would have been again most happy, could she have kept her eyes from wandering between Edmund and Mary Crawford. *She* looked all loveliness – and what might not be the end of it? Her own musings were brought to an end on perceiving Mr Crawford before her, and her thoughts were put into another channel by his engaging her almost instantly for the two first dances. Her happiness on this occasion was very much à-la-mortal, finely chequered. To be secure of a partner at first was a most essential good – for the moment of beginning was now growing seriously near; and she so little understood her own claims as to think that if Mr Crawford had not asked her, she must have been the last to be sought after, and should have received a partner only through a series of enquiry, and bustle, and interference, which would have been terrible; but at the same time there was a pointedness in his manner of asking her which she did not like, and she saw his eye glancing for a moment at her necklace, with a smile – she thought there was a smile – which made her blush and feel wretched. And though there was no second glance to disturb her, though his object seemed then to be only quietly agreeable, she could not get the better of her embarrassment, heightened as it was by the idea of his perceiving it, and had no composure till he turned away to some one else. Then she could gradually rise up to the genuine satisfaction of having a partner, a voluntary partner, secured against the dancing began.

PATRICK WHITE

The Eye of the Storm, 1973

TO allow them to share in her triumph and pay homage, Mrs Cheeseman led her guests on a somewhat uncertain course towards the objective. They tottered, or stomped, or titttuped, or swayed past: the blue and the pink, the pink and the blue, the double-barrels and the knights, Rotarians who squeezed your glove till they had practically emptied it, those op deceivers whose naked faces and mermaid hair disguised ambivalence as innocence, the lissom younger men, who might have been longing to take you to their ruffles.

'And this is Zillah. She's an actress.'

'How is Sir *Basil*?' the actress whispered in professional tones out of an expert mouth; a hairless kangaroo-rat of a woman, she vibrated in basso from deep down amongst the Iceland poppies stencilled on her velvet shift.

Mrs Cheeseman explained that Zillah Puttuck was dedicated to serious drama, and had played all the major Chekov roles – in North Sydney.

The hostess was entranced to reveal her own artistic connections. 'And Brian Learmonth.' She gave her wheezy giggle. 'If you're not careful, Brian will write you up for his paper.'

The princess saw she had been written up already.

When suddenly Mrs Cheeseman reverted to more important matters, and spun round, a topheavy top. 'Is there time for her, Doug, to knock back a teensy one? Or will that bloody woman walk out if we keep dinner waiting any longer?'

To which her husband replied, 'Don't work yourself up, Treasure. If a crash comes, it comes. To start expecting one, gives a person blood pressure.'

The princess was persuaded to accept a drink they did not want to give her, and which she did not want. As nothing would have moistened her by now, she slid her glass behind the lavishly inscribed photograph of somebody in tights called 'Bobby'.

At dinner she was sat between her host, and, she was alarmed to discover, an Australian Writer she hadn't heard of. It was perhaps his increasing awareness of this which made him slash at the wings of his Dickens hairdo, while glancing in the mirror opposite at the woman who continued to exist in spite of her incredible deficiency.

'Don't you read?' he inquired, when he could no longer leave her unmasked.

'Not adventurously,' she admitted. 'I'm reading *La Chartreuse de Parme* for I think probably the seventh time.'

'The who?' The Australian Writer could not have sounded more disgusted.

'*The Charterhouse of Parma.*' Repetition made her throat swell as though forced to confess a secret love to someone who might defile its purity simply by knowing about it.

'Oh – *Stendhal!*' He gave her a rather literary smile; and slashed at his Dickens wings; and turned to his other neighbour to explain – again a waste of intellect – how he was adapting the Gothic novel to local conditions.

ISABEL COLEGATE

The Shooting Party, 1980

SIR Randolph wondered why Harry Stamp always greeted him as if he were a dog. He did not feel like a dog, least of all the friendly sort of trusting retriever Harry Stamp seemed to be addressing.

'My dear Mildred,' Sir Randolph turned instead to greet Mrs Stamp, taller and stouter than her stocky, weatherbeaten little husband, daughter of a Leicestershire landowner, Boadicea in the Corston village pageant since time immemorial, *bête noire* of Minnie. She was wearing a dress of heavy purple brocade with a curiously asymmetrical neckline.

'How charming you look my dear,' said Minnie, putting an arm in hers and leading her over to be introduced to the other guests.

'It is rather nice, isn't it? It's this wonderful little woman in the village.'

'Fascinating,' breathed Minnie, rolling her eyes at Sir Reuben Hergesheimer as she introduced him. Minnie's scarcely concealed insincerity in all of her encounters with Mildred Stamp deterred the latter not in the least; she considered Minnie Nettleby one of her oldest friends, and a wonderful woman if a little on the worldly side.

So, studded, jewelled, feathered, draped, they went in procession to dinner, and there was not one of them that did not feel some slight, however brief, lifting of the heart as they did so, for even in a ceremonious age to prepare for and then to undertake the opening movements of one more ceremonial the perfection of whose design you did not question, was pleasant. After the opening movements there did for some lurk the spectre of boredom, leading to dread, leading in the end perhaps to that questioning of purposes which had been at the beginning absent; but that was only for some, for Sir Randolph, who had been brought up to a simpler life, for Lionel Stephens, who could not altogether control that capacity to think about anything which Olivia Lilburn so admired in him and who was anyway unsettled by the overwhelming nature of his feeling for Olivia, and for Olivia herself, in whom the whole thing was tentative, the questions half-formed and the answers, though guessed at, unspoken, because she was young, ill-educated and wished to be a good wife. The spectre, though, was altogether absent from Cicely's view of things.

GUSTAVE FLAUBERT

Madame Bovary, 1857

AS she went in, Emma felt herself plunged into a warm atmosphere compounded of the scent of flowers and of fine linen, of the savour of meat and the smell of truffles. The candles in the chandeliers glowed on the silver dish-covers with elongated flames. The pieces of cut glass had steamed over, and reflected a dull glimmer from one to the other. Bunches of flowers were set in a row down the whole length of the table, and on the wide-rimmed plates stood serviettes folded in the form of a bishop's mitre, each with an oval-shaped roll inside the fold. The red claws of the lobsters lay over the edge of the dishes. Luscious fruits were piled on moss in open baskets. The quails still had their feathers on them. The fumes rose. Solemn as a judge in his silk stockings and knee-breeches, his white cravat and frilled shirt, the major-domo handed the dishes, ready carved, between the guests' shoulders, and flicked the piece

you chose on to your plate with his spoon. On the big porcelain
stove with its copper rod, a statue of a woman draped to the chin
stared fixedly at the roomful of people.

Madame Bovary noticed that several of the ladies had not put
their gloves in their glasses.

At the top end of the table, alone among all these women, sat one
aged man, crouched over his plate, with his serviette tied round his
neck like a bib, dribbling gravy as he ate. His eyes were bloodshot,
and he wore a little pigtail wound round with black ribbon. This
was the Marquis's father-in-law, the old Duc de Laverdière, once
favourite of the Comte d'Artois, in the days of the Marquis de
Conflans's hunting-parties at La Vaudreuil; he was said to have been
the lover of Marie Antoinette, between Messieurs de Coigny and de
Lauzun. He had filled his life with riot and debauch, with duels,
wagers and abductions; had squandered his wealth and been the
terror of his family. He pointed to the dishes, mumbling, and a
footman stationed behind him named them aloud in his ear. Emma's
eyes kept turning in spite of themselves towards that old man with
the drooping lips, as though to some august curiosity. He had lived
at Court, had lain in the Queen's bed!

Iced champagne was served. Emma shivered all over at the cold
taste of it in her mouth. She had never seen pomegranates before, or
tasted a pineapple. Even the castor sugar looked finer and whiter
than elsewhere.

Part Two

ALL MANNER OF PARTIES

'This isn't a funeral, it's a christening.'

THOMAS MANN
Buddenbrooks, 1901

THREE minutes later, the guests have disposed themselves in salon and living-room, and the sweets are passed. Even Pastor Pringsheim, the toes of his broad, shiny boots showing under his black vestments, sits and sips the cool whipped cream off his hot chocolate, chatting easily the while, and wearing his serene expression, which is most effective by way of contrast with his sermon. His manner says, as plainly as words: 'See how I can lay aside the priest and become the jolly ordinary guest!' He is a versatile, an accommodating sort of man. To the Frau Consul he speaks rather unctuously, to Thomas and Gerda like a man of the world, and with Frau Permaneder he is downright jocose, making jokes and gesturing fluently. Now and then, whenever he thinks of it, he folds his hands in his lap, tips back his head, glooms his brows, and makes a long face. When he laughs he draws the air in through his teeth in little jerks.

Suddenly there is a stir in the corridor, the servants are heard laughing, and in the doorway appears a singular figure, come to offer congratulations. It is Grobleben: Grobleben, from whose thin nose, no matter what the time of year, there ever hangs a drop, which never falls. Grobleben is a workman in one of the Consul's granaries, and he has an extra job, too, at the house, as boots. Every morning early he appears in Broad Street, takes the boots from before the door, and cleans them below in the court. At family feasts he always appears in holiday attire, presents flowers, and makes a speech, in a whining, unctuous voice, with the drop pendant from his nose. For this, he always gets a piece of money – but that is *not* why he does it!

He wears a black coat – an old one of the Consul's – greased leather top-boots, and a blue woollen scarf round his neck. In his wizened red hand he holds a bunch of pale-coloured roses, which are a little past their best, and slowly shed their petals on the carpet. He blinks with his small red eyes, but apparently sees nothing. He stands still in the doorway, with his flowers held out in front of him, and begins straightway to speak. The old Frau Consul nods to him encouragingly and makes soothing little noises, the Consul regards him with one eyebrow lifted, and some of the family – Frau Permaneder, for instance – put their handkerchiefs to their mouths.

'I be a poor man, yer honour 'n' ladies 'n' gentlemen, but I've a feelin' hairt: 'n' the happiness of my master comes home to me, it do, seein's he's allus been so good t'me; 'n' so I've come, yer honour 'n' ladies 'n' gentlemen, to congratulate the Herr Consul 'n' the Frau Consul, 'n' the whole respected family, from a full hairt, 'n' that the child may prosper, for that they desarve fr'm God'n' man, for such a master as Consul Buddenbrook there aren't so many, he's a noble gentleman, 'n' our Lord will record him for all . . .'

'Splendid, Grobleben! That was a beautiful speech. Thank you very much, Grobleben. What are the roses for?'

But Grobleben has not nearly done. He strains his whining voice and drowns the Consul out.

'. . . 'n' I say th' Lord will reward him, him and the whole respected family; 'n' when his time has come to stan' before His throne, for stan' we all must, rich *and* poor, 'n' one'll have a fine polished hard-wood coffin 'n' 'tother 'n' old box, yet all on us must come to mother earth at th' last, yes, we must all come to her at th' last – to mother earth – to mother—'

'Oh, come, come, Grobleben! This isn't a funeral, it's a christening. Get along with your mother earth!'

'. . . 'n' these be a few flowers,' concludes Grobleben.

'Thank you, Grobleben, thank you. This is too much – what did you pay for them, man? But I haven't heard such a speech as that for a long time! Wait a minute – here, go out and give yourself a treat, in honour of the day!' And the Consul puts his hand on the old man's shoulder and gives him a thaler.

'Here, my good man,' says the Frau Consul. 'And I hope you love our blessed Lord?'

'I be lovin' him from my hairt, Frau Consul, thet's the holy truth!' And Grobleben gets another thaler from her, and a third from

Frau Permaneder, and retires with a bow and a scrape, taking the roses with him by mistake, except for those already fallen on the carpet.

STEELE RUDD

Baptizing Bartholomew, 1903

B UT the ceremony was soon over, and everybody was radiant with joy, everybody but Bartholomew. He had been asleep until the parson dropped the water on his face, when he woke suddenly. He glared at the strange assemblage a moment, then whined and cried hard. Mother shushed him and danced him up and down, saying, 'Did they frigh–ten 'im?' Mrs McDoolan took him and shushed him and jumped him about and said, 'There now, there now.'

But Bartholomew resented it all and squealed till it seemed that some part of him must burst. Mrs Todd and Mrs Anderson and Judy Jubb each had a go at him. 'Must have the wind,' murmured Mrs Ryan feelingly, and Mrs Johnson agreed with her by nodding her head. Mother took him again and showed him the dog, but he didn't care for dogs. Then Sal ran out with him and put him on the gee-gee, the parson's old moke that stood buried in thought at the fence, and he was quiet.

A long table erected in the barn was laden with provisions, and Dad invited the company to come along and make a start. They crowded in and stared about. Green boughs and corn-cobs hung on the walls, some bags of shelled corn stood in one corner, and from a beam dangled a set of useless old cart-harness that Dad used to lend anyone wanting to borrow. Dad and Paddy Maloney took up the carving. Dad stood at one end of the table, Paddy at the other. Both brandished long knives. Dad proceeded silently, Paddy with joyous volubility. 'Fowl or pig?' he shouted, and rattled the knife, and piled the provender on their plates, and told them to 'back in their carts' when they wanted more; and he called the minister 'Boss'. Paddy was in his element.

It was a magnificent feast and went off most successfully. It went off until only the ruins remained. Then the party returned to the house and danced. Through the afternoon, and far into the night, the concertina screeched its cracked refrain, while the forms of weary

females, with muffled infants in their arms, hovered about the drays
in the yard, and dog-tired men, soaked to the knees with dew-wet
grass, bailing and blocking horses in a paddock corner, took strange,
shadowy shape. It wasn't until all was bright and the sun seemed
near that the last dray rolled heavily away from the christening of
Bartholomew.

F. SCOTT FITZGERALD

Glamour and Disillusionment: 'The Baby Party', 1926

THE baby party started at half past four, but Edith Andros,
calculating shrewdly that the new dress would stand out more
sensationally against vestments already rumpled, planned the arrival
of herself and little Ede for five. When they appeared it was already
a flourishing affair. Four baby girls and nine baby boys, each one
curled and washed and dressed with all the care of a proud and
jealous heart, were dancing to the music of a phonograph. Never
more than two or three were dancing at once, but as all were
continually in motion running to and from their mothers for
encouragement, the general effect was the same.

As Edith and her daughter entered, the music was temporarily
drowned out by a sustained chorus, consisting largely of the word
cute and directed towards little Ede, who stood looking timidly
about and fingering the edges of her pink dress. She was not kissed
– this is the sanitary age – but she was passed along a row of mamas
each one of whom said 'cu-u-ute' to her and held her pink little hand
before passing her on to the next. After some encouragement and a
few mild pushes she was absorbed into the dance, and became an
active member of the party.

Edith stood near the door talking to Mrs Markey, and keeping
one eye on the tiny figure in the pink dress. She did not care for Mrs
Markey; she considered her both snippy and common, but John and
Joe Markey were congenial and went in together on the commuting
train every morning, so the two women kept up an elaborate
pretence of warm amity. They were always reproaching each other
for 'not coming to see me,' and they were always planning the kind
of parties that began with 'You'll have to come to dinner with us
soon, and we'll go to the theatre,' but never matured further.

'Little Ede looks perfectly darling,' said Mrs Markey, smiling and moistening her lips in a way that Edith found particularly repulsive. 'So *grown-up* – I can't *believe* it!'

Edith wondered if 'little Ede' referred to the fact that Billy Markey, though several months younger, weighed almost five pounds more. Accepting a cup of tea she took a seat with two other ladies on a divan and launched into the real business of the afternoon, which of course lay in relating the recent accomplishments and insouciances of her child.

DAISY ASHFORD
The Young Visitors, 1919

THE sumshious room was packed with men of noble nature dressed like the earl in satin knickerboccers etc and with ladies of every hue with long trains and jewels by the dozen. You could hardly moove in the gay throng. Dukes were as nought as there were a good lot of princes and Arch Dukes as it was a very superier levie indeed. The earl and Mr Salteena struggled through the crowd till they came to a platform draped with white velvit. Here on a golden chair was seated the prince of Wales in a lovely ermine cloak and a small but costly crown. He was chatting quite genially with some of the crowd.

Up clambered the earl followed at top speed by Mr Salteena.

Hullo Clincham cried the Prince quite homely and not at all grand so glad you turned up – quite a squash eh.

A bit over powering your Highness said the earl who was quite used to all this may I introduce my friend Lord Hyssops he is staying with me so I thought I would bring him along if you don't mind Prince.

Not at all cried the genial prince looking rarther supprised. Mr Salteena bowed so low he nearly fell off the platform and as the prince put out a hand Mr Salteena thought he had better kiss it. the Prince smiled kindly I am pleased to see you Lord Hyssops he said in a regal voice.

Then the Earl chipped in and how is the dear Queen he said reveruntly.

Not up to much said his Highness she feels the heat poor soul and he waved to a placard which said in large letters The Queen is indisposed.

Presently his Highness rose I think I will have a quiet glass of
champagne he said you come too Clincham and bring your friend
the Diplomats are arriving and I am not much in the mood for deep
talk I have already signed a dozen documents so I have done my
duty.

They all went out by a private door and found thenselves in a
smaller but gorgous room. The Prince tapped on the table and
instantly two menials in red tunics appeared. Bring three glasses of
champaigne commanded the prince and some ices he added majesti-
kally. the goods appeared as if by majic and the prince drew out a
cigar case and passed it round.

One grows weary of Court Life he remarked.

FRANCES HODGSON BURNETT
Little Lord Fauntleroy, 1886

WHAT a grand day it was when little Lord Fauntleroy's
birthday arrived, and how his young lordship enjoyed it! How
beautiful the park looked filled with the thronging people dressed in
their gayest and best, and with the flags flying from the tents and the
top of the Castle! Nobody had stayed away who could possibly
come, because everybody was really glad that little Lord Fauntleroy
was to be little Lord Fauntleroy still, and some day was to be the
master of everything. Everyone wanted to have a look at him, and at
his pretty, kind mother, who had made so many friends. And
positively every one liked the Earl rather better, and felt more
amiably toward him because the little boy loved and trusted him so,
and because, also, he had now made friends with and behaved
respectfully to his heir's mother. It was said that he was even
beginning to be fond of her too, and that between his young lordship
and his young lordship's mother, the Earl might be changed in time
into quite a well-behaved old nobleman, and everybody might be
happier and better off.

What scores and scores of people there were under the trees, and
in the tents, and on the lawns! Farmers and farmers' wives in their
Sunday suits and bonnets and shawls; girls and their sweethearts;
children frolicking and chasing about; and old dames in red cloaks
gossiping together.

SERGE NABOKOV

Lolita, 1955

A ND as soon as she was well again, I threw a Party with Boys.
Perhaps I had drunk a little too much in preparation for the
ordeal. Perhaps I made a fool of myself. The girls had decorated and
plugged in a small fir tree – German custom, except that coloured
bulbs had superseded wax candles. Records were chosen and fed
into my landlord's phonograph. Chic Dolly wore a nice grey dress
with fitted bodice and flared skirt. Humming, I retired to my study
upstairs – and then every ten or twenty minutes I would come down
like an idiot just for a few seconds; to pick up ostensibly my pipe
from the mantelpiece or hunt for the newspaper; and with every new
visit these simple actions became harder to perform, and I was
reminded of the dreadfully distant days when I used to brace myself
to casually enter a room in the Ramsdale house where Little Carmen
was on.

The party was not a success. Of the three girls invited, one did not
come at all, and one of the boys brought his cousin Roy, so there
was a superfluity of two boys, and the cousins knew all the steps,
and the other fellows could hardly dance at all, and most of the
evening was spent in messing up the kitchen, and then endlessly
jabbering about what card game to play, and sometime later, two
girls and four boys sat on the floor of the living-room, with all
windows open, and played a word game which Opal could not be
made to understand while Mona and Roy, a lean handsome lad,
drank ginger ale in the kitchen, sitting on the table and dangling
their legs, and hotly discussing Predestination and the Law of
Averages. After they had all gone my Lo said ugh, closed her eyes,
and dropped into a chair with all four limbs starfished to express the
utmost disgust and exhaustion and swore it was the most revolting
bunch of boys she had ever seen. I bought her a new tennis racket
for that remark.

JOHN BETJEMAN
'Indoor Games Near Newbury', 1948

IN among the silver birches winding ways of tarmac wander
 And the signs to Bussock Bottom, Tussock Wood, and Windy
   Brake,
Gabled lodges, tile-hung churches, catch the lights of our Lagonda
 As we drive to Wendy's party, lemon curd and Christmas cake.
   Rich the makes of motor whirring,
   Past the pine-plantation purring
     Come up, Hupmobile, Delage!
   Short the way your chauffeurs travel,
   Crunching over private gravel
     Each from out his warm garáge.

Oh but Wendy, when the carpet yielded to my indoor pumps
   There you stood, your gold hair streaming,
   Handsome in the hall-light gleaming
There you looked and there you led me off into the game of clumps
   Then the new Victrola playing
   And your funny uncle saying
   'Choose your partners for a fox-trot! Dance until its *tea* o'clock!
     'Come on, young 'uns, foot it featly!'
     Was it chance that paired us neatly,
     I, who loved you so completely,
You, who pressed me closely to you, hard against your party frock?

'Meet me when you've finished eating!' So we met and no one found
   us.
 Oh that dark and furry cupboard while the rest played hide and
   seek!
Holding hands our two hearts beating in the bedroom silence round
   us,
 Holding hands and hardly hearing sudden footstep, thud and
   shriek.
   Love that lay too deep for kissing –
   'Where *is* Wendy? Wendy's missing!'
     Love so pure it *had* to end,
   Love so strong that I was frighten'd
   When you gripped my fingers tight and
Hugging, whispered 'I'm your friend.'

Good-bye Wendy! Send the fairies, pinewood elf and larch tree
    gnome,
    Spingle-spangled stars are peeping
    At the lush Lagonda creeping
Down the winding ways of tarmac to the leaded lights of home.
    There, among the silver birches,
    All the bells of all the churches
Sounded in the bath-waste running out into the frosty air.
    Wendy speeded my undressing,
    Wendy is the sheet's caressing
    Wendy bending gives a blessing,
Holds me as I drift to dreamland, safe inside my slumberwear.

ALEXANDER REID

'A Zoo Party', 1947

I'D like to give a party
And ask them all to tea:
The alligator, antelope,
The owl and chimpanzee;
The elephant and eagle;
The fox and the gazelle;
The tiger and the llama;
The octopus and snail;
The python and the pelican.
I'd ask them all to come,
And, of course, I'd have the penguins
Or it wouldn't be such fun.

I'd have the lion cubs for sure.
I must have polar bears.
I'd like to have a walrus,
And the wild cat – if she cares;
I'd have – but, when I think of it,
What would we have to eat?
And I wouldn't like the tiger
To come and share *my* seat.
It scarcely would be pleasant,
To say the very least,

To give the Zoo a party
And find *I* was the feast.

SUSAN COOLIDGE

What Katy Did Next, 1887

MABEL and Mary Matilda, with their two doll visitors, sat
gravely round the table, in the laps of their little mistresses;
and Katy, putting on an apron and an improvised cap, and speaking
Irish very fast, served them with a repast of rolls and cocoa,
raspberry jam, and delicious little almond cakes. The fun waxed fast
and furious; and Lieutenant Worthington, coming in with his hands
full of parcels for the Christmas-tree, was just in time to hear Katy
remark in a strong County Kerry brogue,

'Och, thin indade, Miss Amy, and it's no more cake you'll be
getting out of me the night. That's four pieces you've ate, and it's
little slape your poor mother 'll git with you a tossin' and tumblin'
forenenst her all night long because of your big appetite.'

F. E. WEATHERLEY

The Cats' Tea-Party, date unknown

FIVE little pussy-cats, invited out to tea,
Cried: 'Mother, let us go – Oh, do! for good we'll surely be.
We'll wear our bibs and hold our things as you have shown us
        how –
Spoon in right paws, cups in left – and make a pretty bow;
We'll always say "Yes, if you please," and "Only half of that." '
'Then go, my darling children,' said the happy Mother Cat.
The five little pussy-cats went out that night to tea,
Their heads were smooth and glossy, their tails were swinging free;
They held their things as they had learned, and tried to be polite; –
With snowy bibs beneath their chins they were a pretty sight.
But, alas, for manners beautiful, and coats as soft as silk!
The moment that the little kits were asked to take some milk,
They dropped their spoons, forgot to bow, and – oh, what do you
        think?

They put their noses in the cups and all began to drink!
Yes, every naughty little kit set up a miou for more,
Then knocked the tea-cups over, and scampered through the door.

KENNETH GRAHAME

The Wind in the Willows, 1908

THE Badger had ordered everything of the best, and the banquet was a great success. There was much talking and laughter and chaff among the animals, but through it all Toad, who of course was in the chair, looked down his nose and murmured pleasant nothings to the animals on either side of him. At intervals he stole a glance at the Badger and the Rat, and always when he looked they were staring at each other with their mouths open; and this gave him the greatest satisfaction. Some of the younger and livelier animals, as the evening wore on, got whispering to each other that things were not so amusing as they used to be in the good old days; and there were some knockings on the table and cries of 'Toad! Speech! Speech from Toad! Song! Mr Toad's Song!' But Toad only shook his head gently, raised one paw in mild protest, and, by pressing delicacies on his guests, by topical small-talk, and by earnest inquiries after members of their families not yet old enough to appear at social functions, managed to convey to them that this dinner was being run on strictly conventional lines.

He was indeed an altered Toad!

BEATRIX POTTER

The Tale of Tom Kitten, 1907

QUITE the contrary; they were not in bed: *not* in the least.
Somehow there were very extraordinary noises over-head, which disturbed the dignity and repose of the tea party.

JAMES JOYCE

A Portrait of the Artist as a Young Man, 1914

HE was sitting in the midst of a children's party at Harold's Cross. His silent watchful manner had grown upon him and he took little part in the games. The children, wearing the spoils of their crackers, danced and romped noisily and, though he tried to share their merriment, he felt himself a gloomy figure amid the gay cocked hats and sunbonnets.

But when he had sung his song and withdrawn into a snug corner of the room he began to taste the joy of his loneliness. The mirth, which in the beginning of the evening had seemed to him false and trivial, was like a soothing air to him, passing gaily by his senses, hiding from other eyes the feverish agitation of his blood while through the circling of the dancers and amid the music and laughter her glance travelled to his corner, flattering, taunting, searching, exciting his heart.

In the hall the children who had stayed latest were putting on their things: the party was over. She had thrown a shawl about her and, as they went together towards the tram, sprays of her fresh warm breath flew gaily above her cowled head and her shoes tapped blithely on the glassy road.

WILLIAM MAKEPEACE THACKERAY

The Book of Snobs, 1847

SIR – As your publication finds its way to almost every drawing-room table in this metropolis, and is read by the young and old in every family, I beseech you to give admission to the remonstrance of an unhappy parent, and to endeavour to put a stop to a practice which appears to me to be increasing daily, and is likely to operate most injuriously upon the health, morals and comfort of society in general.

The awful spread of Juvenile Parties, sir, is the fact to which I would draw your attention. There is no end to those entertainments, and if the custom be not speedily checked, people will be obliged to fly from London at Christmas, and hide their children during the holidays. I gave mine warning in a speech at breakfast this day, and said with tears in my eyes that if the Juvenile Party system went on, I would take a house at Margate next winter, for that, by heavens! I could not bear another Juvenile Season in London.

If they would but transfer Innocents' Day to the summer holidays, and let the children have their pleasures in May or June, we might get on. But now in this most ruthless and cut-throat season of sleet, thaw, frost, wind, snow, mud, and sore throats, it is quite a tempting of fate to be going much abroad; and this is the time of all others that is selected for the amusement of our little darlings.

As the first step towards the remedying of the evil of which I complain, I am obliged to look *Mr Punch* himself in his venerable beard, and say, 'You sir, have, by your agents, caused not a little of the mischief. I desire that, during Christmas time at least, Mr Leech should be abolished, or sent to take a holiday. Judging from his sketches, I should say that he must be endowed with a perfectly monstrous organ of philoprogenitiveness; he revels in the delineation of the dearest and most beautiful little boys and girls in turn-down collars and broad sashes, and produces in your *Almanack* a picture of a child's costume ball, in which he has made the little wretches in the dresses of every age, and looking so happy, beautiful, and charming, that I have carefully kept the picture from the sight of the women and children of my own household, and – I will not say burned it, for I had not the heart to do that – but locked it away privately, lest they should conspire to have a costume ball themselves, and little Polly should insist upon appearing in the dress of Anne Boleyne, or little Jacky upon turning out as an Ancient Briton.'

An odious, revolting and disagreeable practice, sir, I say, ought not to be described in a manner so atrociously pleasing. The real satirist has no right to lead the public astray about the Juvenile *Fête* nuisance, and to describe a child's ball as if it was a sort of Paradise, and the little imps engaged as happy and pretty as so many cherubs. They should be drawn, one and all, as hideous – disagreeable – distorted – affected – jealous of each other – dancing awkwardly – with shoes too tight for them – over-eating themselves at supper – very unwell (and deservedly so) the next morning, with Mamma administering a mixture made after the Doctor's prescription, and which should be painted awfully black, in an immense large teacup, and (as might be shown by the horrible expression on the little patient's face) of the most disgusting flavour. Banish, I say, that Mr Leech during Christmas time, at least; for, by a misplaced kindness and absurd fondness for children, he is likely to do them and their parents an incalculable quantity of harm.

RICHMAL CROMPTON
William Carries on, 1942

IT was Mrs Monks' idea that the children whose fathers were not serving in the forces should give a party to the children whose fathers were serving in the forces. 'Such a nice gesture,' she said, adding vaguely: 'Of course, it will take a little organizing.' It took more organizing than she had realized, for evacuees had swollen the child population of the village to many times its pre-war figure. It was finally decided that, though all the children of men serving in the forces must attend the party, it would be impossible to find room for all the others. They, therefore, as hosts and hostesses, must provide the tea and entertainment, but only half a dozen of them must actually attend the party, and the half-dozen must be chosen by lot. Excitement rose high as the time for the drawing of the lots came near. They were drawn by Mrs Monks herself, looking like a composite incarnation of Fate and Justice. The names were William, Ginger, a boy called Ralph, and three little girls of the type who are seen and not heard and give no trouble. There was, of course, a good deal of disappointment; but, on the whole, people were sporting about it. Even if their children were not to be at the party, they promised to give what help they could.

All except Mrs Lane. And Mrs Lane was furious. If darling Hubie were not to be at the party, she said, she wouldn't raise a finger to help. On the contrary, she would do all she could to hinder. It was a shame, it was a scandal, it was a conspiracy. Hubie was heartbroken. She would never forgive them for it. She went to Mrs Monks and made a scene. She went to Mrs Brown's and made a scene. She went to Ginger's home and made a scene. She went to the homes of the three little girls and made scenes. She told them all that it was a shame and a scandal and a conspiracy, and that Hubert had more right than any of them to go to the party and that they wouldn't get a crumb or a penny out of her, so they needn't waste their time trying. She added that Hubert's father was just as angry as she was about it and that no one need think they were going to take an insult like this lying down, because they weren't.

HORACE WALPOLE

Correspondence with the Countess of Upper Ossary, 3 April 1773

I WAS not quite so sober last night at Monsieur de Guines's, where the evening began with a ball of children from eighteen to four years old. They danced amazingly well, yet disappointed me, so many of them were ugly – but Lord Delawar's two eldest daughters and the Ancaster infanta performed a *pas de trois* as well as Mlle Heinel, and the two eldest were pretty: yet I promise you, Madam, the next age will be a thousand degrees below the present in beauty. The most interesting part was to observe the anxiety of the mothers while their children danced or supped. They supped at ten in three rooms – I should not omit telling you that the Vernons, especially the eldest, were not the homeliest part of the show. The former quadrilles then came again upon the stage, and Harry Conway the younger was so astonished at the agility of Mrs Hobart's bulk, that he said he was sure she must be hollow.

OSCAR WILDE

The Birthday of the Infanta, 1889

IT was the birthday of the Infanta. She was just twelve years of age, and the sun was shining brightly in the gardens of the palace.

Although she was a real Princess and the Infanta of Spain, she had only one birthday every year, just like the children of quite poor people, so it was naturally a matter of great importance to the whole country that she should have a really fine day for the occasion. And a really fine day it certainly was. The tall striped tulips stood straight up upon their stalks, like long rows of soldiers, and looked defiantly across the grass at the roses, and said: 'We are quite as splendid as you are now.' The purple butterflies fluttered about with gold dust on their wings, visiting each flower in turn; the little lizards crept out of the crevices of the wall, and lay basking in the white glare; and the pomegranates split and cracked with the heat, and showed their bleeding red hearts. Even the pale yellow lemons, that hung in such profusion from the mouldering trellis and along the dim arcades, seemed to have caught a richer colour from the wonderful sunlight, and the magnolia trees opened their great glove-like blossoms of folded ivory, and filled the air with a sweet heavy perfume.

The little Princess herself walked up and down the terrace with her companions, and played at hide and seek round the stone vases and the old moss-grown statues. On ordinary days she was only allowed to play with children of her own rank, so she had always to play alone, but her birthday was an exception, and the King had given orders that she was to invite any of her young friends whom she liked to come and amuse themselves with her. There was a stately grace about these slim Spanish children as they glided about, the boys with their large-plumed hats and short fluttering cloaks, the girls holding up the trains of their long brocade gowns, and shielding the sun from their eyes with huge fans of black and silver. But the Infanta was the most graceful of all, and the most tastefully attired, after the somewhat cumbrous fashion of the day. Her robe was of grey satin, the skirt and the wide puffed sleeves heavily embroidered with silver, and the stiff corset studded with rows of fine pearls. Two tiny slippers with big pink rosettes peeped out beneath her dress as she walked. Pink and pearl was her great gauze fan, and in her hair, which like an aureole of faded gold stood out stiffly round her pale little face, she had a beautiful white rose.

WILLIAM PLOMER

'A Basuto Coming of Age', 1960

THE winter sun, a distant roar of light,
  Immensely sets, and far below this place
Cold on the plains the vast blue tides of night
Press on, and darken as they race.
Out of retreat, with dancing and with dirges,
Men bring a boy in whom a man emerges.

The new man sees anew the twisted aloes,
His father's house, his cattle in the shallows,
And up the hill a crowd of girls advancing
To carry him to drinking and to dancing –
His heart leaps up as he descends the steep,
For, where the boy slept, now the man shall sleep.

WILLIAM BECKFORD

from his Introduction to *Vathek*, 1786

IMMURED we were 'au pied de la lettre' for three days following – doors and windows so strictly closed that neither common day light nor common place visitors could get in or even peep in – careworn visages were ordered to keep aloof – no sunk-in mouths or furroughed foreheads were permitted to meet our eye. Our société was extremely youthful and lovely to look upon. . . . The solid Egyptian Hall looked as if hewn out of a living rock – the line of apartments and apparently endless passages extending from it on either side were all vaulted – an interminable stair case, which when you looked down it – appeared as deep as the well in the pyramid – and when you looked up – was lost in vapour, led to suites of stately apartments gleaming with marble pavements – as polished as glass – and gawdy ceilings. . . . Through all these suites – through all these galleries – did we roam and wander – too often hand in hand – strains of music swelling forth at intervals. . . . Sometimes a chaunt was heard – issuing, no one could devine from whence – innocent affecting sounds – that stole into the heart with a bewitching languour and melted the most beloved the most susceptible of my fair companions into tears. Delightful indeed were these romantic wanderings – delightful the straying about this little interior world of exclusive happiness surrounded by lovely beings, in all the freshness of their early bloom, so fitted to enjoy it. Here, nothing was dull or vapid – here, nothing ressembled in the least the common forms and usages, the 'train-train' and routine of fashionable existence – all was essence – the slightest approach to sameness was here untolerated – monotony of every kind was banished. Even the uniform splendour of gilded roofs – was partially obscured by the vapour of wood aloes ascending in wreaths from cassolettes placed low on the silken carpets in porcelain salvers of the richest japan. The delirium of delight into which our young and fervid bosoms were cast by such a combination of seductive influences may be conceived but too easily. Even at this long, sad distance from these days and nights of exquisite refinements, chilled by age, still more by the coarse unpoetic tenor of the present disenchanting period – I still feel warmed and irradiated by the recollections of that strange, necromantic light which Loutherbourg had thrown over what absolutely appeared a realm of Fairy, or rather, perhaps, a Demon Temple deep beneath the earth set apart for tremendous mysteries – and yet how soft, how genial was this quiet light. Whilst the wretched world without lay dark, and bleak, and howling, whilst the storm was raging against our massive walls and the snow drifting in clouds, the very air of summer seemed playing around us – the choir of low-toned melodious voices continued to sooth our ear, and that every sense might in turn receive its blandishment tables covered with delicious viands and fragrant flowers – glided forth, by the aid of mechanism at stated intervals, from the richly draped, and amply curtained recesses of the enchanted precincts. The glowing haze investing every object, the mystic look, the vastness, the intricacy of this vaulted labyrinth occasioned so bewildering an effect that it became impossible for any one to define – at the moment – where he stood, where he had been, or to whither he was wandering – such was the confusion – the perplexity so many illuminated storys of infinitely varied apartments gave rise to.

ELIZABETH von ARNIM

The Pastor's Wife, 1914

ON the following afternoon there was a party at the Palace, arranged by Mrs Bullivant in the confident days before she knew what Ingeborg was really like. It was a congratulatory party for Judith, and all Redchester and all the county had been invited. Nothing could stop this party but a death in the household – any death, even Richards' might do, but nothing short of death, thought the afflicted lady, wondering how she was to get through the afternoon; and as she crept on to her sofa at a quarter to four to be put by Richards' into the final folds and knew that as four struck a great surge of friends would pour in over her and that for three hours she would have to be bright and happy about Judith, and sympathetically explanatory about Ingeborg – who looked altogether too odd to be explained only by a long past dentist – she felt so very low that she was unable to stop herself from thinking it was a pity people didn't die a little oftener. Especially maids. Especially maids who were being so clumsy with the cushions. . . .

HONORÉ DE BALZAC
Cousin Bette, 1847

EVERYONE has attended a wedding ball at least once in his life, and can hardly fail to smile as he recalls all those wedding guests in their Sunday best with expressions to match. Of all ceremonial social occasions, this is the one that most effectively demonstrates the influence of atmosphere, afflicting even habitually well-dressed people with the self-consciousness of those dressed up for a red-letter day in their lives. Then one thinks of the unfestive guests: the old men so indifferent to all the fuss that they have not changed their everyday black suits, and the men, many years married, whose faces proclaim their sad experience of the life that the young are just beginning. Do you remember the effervescing gaiety, like the bubbles in the champagne, and the envious girls, and the women with their minds preoccupied with the success of their toilettes, and the poor relations in their skimped finery, and the smart people *in fiocchi* – in their smartest – and the greedy thinking only of supper, and the gamblers only of the game? There they all are, as one remembers them, rich and poor, envious and envied, the cynics and the dazzled dreamers, all clustered like the flowers in a bouquet around one rare flower, the bride. A wedding ball is a miniature world.

COLETTE
My Mother's House, 1922

MY white frock with the purple sash, my hair hanging loose and making me hot, my bronze shoes – far too small, alas! – and my white stockings, everything has been ready since the evening before. In fact my hair, plaited to give it a wave, has been torturing my temples for forty-eight hours.

It is a fine day, indeed scorching, just the weather for pastoral weddings. The Mass has not been unduly long. In the procession the Follet boy has offered me his arm, but once the procession is over, what should he do with a partner of thirteen years? ... Madame Follet drives the cart that overflows with us and our laughter, with her four daughters dressed alike in blue, with Julie David in shot pink and mauve alpaca. The carts rattle along the road and we are coming to the moment that I like best of all.

Where did I get my violent passion for rustic wedding breakfasts? What ancestor bequeathed to me, via my frugal parents, a positively religious fervour for stewed rabbit, leg of mutton with garlic, soft-boiled eggs in red wine, all served between barn walls draped with buff sheets decorated with branches of red June roses? I am only thirteen, and the familiar menu of these four-o'clock repasts does not appal me. Glass basins filled with loaf sugar are strewn about the table: everyone knows that they are so placed in order that the guests, between courses, may suck lumps of sugar soaked in wine, an infallible method of loosening the tongue and of renewing the appetite. Bouilloux and Labbé, gargantuan freaks, indulge in a guzzling match here as at all weddings. Labbé drinks white wine from a pail used for milking the cows, and Bouilloux is offered an entire leg of mutton, which he consumes unaided, leaving nothing but the bare bone.

What with songs, feasting and carousing, Adrienne's wedding is a lovely wedding. Five meat courses, three sweets, and the tiered wedding cake surmounted by a trembling plaster rose. Since four o'clock the open doorway of the barn has framed the green pond shaded by elms, and a patch of sky now gradually flushing with the evening glow. Adrienne Septmance, dark and unfamiliar in her cloud of tulle, leans languorously against her husband's shoulder and wipes the sweat from a shining face. A tall, bony peasant bellows patriotic songs, 'Paris must be saved! Paris must be saved!' and he encounters looks of awe, because his voice is powerful and sad, and he himself comes from so great a distance: 'Just think! A man from Dampierre-sous-Bouhy! At least thirty miles from here!' The swallows dart and scream above the drinking cattle. The bride's mother is weeping for no particular reason. Julie David has stained her dress; the dresses of the four Follet girls are as blue as phosphorus in the gathering gloom. The candles will not be lighted until the ball begins. A happiness in advance of any years, a subtle happiness of satiated greed, keeps me sitting there peacefully gorged with rabbit stew, boiled chicken, and sweetened wine.

EMILE ZOLA

L'Assommoir, 1876

NONE of the guests evinced the slightest doubt. They had reached the dessert stage, and the waiters were clearing the table with much clattering of plates. And then Madame Lorilleux, who up to then had been most genteel and ladylike, let out a 'bloody fool!' because one of the waiters as he moved a plate had tipped something wet down her neck. Her silk dress would be stained for certain. Monsieur Madinier had to inspect her back, but he swore there was nothing there. Now there were set out in the middle of the tablecloth a salad bowl containing *œufs à la neige*, flanked on each side by two plates of cheese and two of fruit. The pudding, with the egg-whites overcooked and floating on the yellow custard, caused a respectful pause; it was unexpected and considered rather grand. Mes-Bottes was still eating non-stop. He had asked for another loaf. He had finished off both cheeses and as some of the custard was left he got the bowl passed to him, and into it he cut large slices of bread as though it were soup.

'The gentleman really is remarkable,' said Monsieur Madinier, once again lost in admiration.

Then the men rose to get their pipes, pausing for a moment behind Mes-Bottes to slap him on the back and ask if he felt better now. Bibi-la-Grillade lifted him, chair and all, and by God the blighter weighed twice what he did before! Coupeau, always one for a joke, pointed out that their mate was only just beginning to get under way, and that he was all set now for eating bread just like that all through the night. The waiters had vanished, appalled. Boche, who had retired downstairs for a moment, came back describing the face of the proprietor down there. He was deathly pale behind his counter, and his good lady had just sent out to see if the bakers were still open. Even the cat looked woebegone. It really was a scream, and was well worth the cost of the dinner. You couldn't go out for a meal without that guzzler Mes-Bottes! The men sat smoking their pipes and looking at him with envy, for a bloke must have the hell of a body to be able to eat like that!

'I shouldn't like the job of feeding you!' said Madame Gaudron. 'No, that I shouldn't!'

'Look here, Mum, none of your kidding,' answered Mes-Bottes, casting a sidelong glance at his neighbour's belly. 'You've swallowed more than what I have!'

There was general applause: bravo! well answered! By now it was quite dark, and three gas-jets had been lit in the room and cast great moving patches of light amid the clouds of pipe-smoke. The waiters had served coffee and brandy and taken away the last piles of dirty plates. Down below under the three acacias dancing had begun, and the sound of a cornet and two violins, playing very loud and mingled with shrill feminine laughter, filled the hot night air.

'Now we could do with a burnt brandy,' yelled Mes-Bottes. 'Two bottles of fire-water, lots of lemon and not too much sugar.'

But Coupeau, conscious of Gervaise's anxious face opposite him, rose and declared that they weren't going to drink any more. They had killed twenty-five bottles – one and a half per person, counting the kids as grown-ups, and that was already more than enough. They had had a friendly bite together, without a lot of fuss and feathers, because they all liked one another and wanted to celebrate a family occasion among themselves. It was all very nice and they were all happy, and they shouldn't start getting beastly drunk now if they had any respect for the ladies. In fact, and this was all he had to say, they had met together to drink the health of a spliced couple and not to get sozzled.

LEWIS GLYN COTHI or TUDUR PENLLYN
The English Wedding, date unknown

LAST Sunday I came – a man whom the Lord God made – to the town of Flint, with its great double walls and rounded bastions; may I see it all aflame! An obscure English wedding was there, with but little mead – an English feast! and I meant to earn a shining solid reward for my harper's art. So I began with ready speed, to sing an ode to the kinsmen; but all I got was mockery, spurning of my song, and grief. It was easy for hucksters of barley and corn to dismiss all my skill, and they laughed at my artistry, my well-prepared panegyric which they did not value; John of the Long Smock began to jabber of peas, and another about dung for his land. They all called for William the Piper to come to the table, a low fellow he must be. He came forward as though claiming his usual rights, though he did not look like a privileged man, with a groaning bag, a paunch of heavy guts, at the end of a stick between chest and arm. He rasped away, making startling grimaces, a horrid noise, from the swollen belly, bulging his eyes; he twisted his body here and there, and puffed his two cheeks out, playing with his fingers on a bell of hide – unsavoury conduct, fit for the unsavoury banqueters. He hunched his shoulders, amid the rout, under his cloak, like a worthless balladmonger; he snorted away, and bowed his head until it was on his breast, the very image of a kite with skilful zeal preening its feathers. The pigmy puffed, making an outlandish cry, blowing out the bag with a loud howl; it sang like the buzzing of a hornet, that devilish bag with the stick in its head, like a nightmare howl, fit to kill a mangy goose, like a sad bitch's hoarse howl in its hollow kennel; a harsh paunch with monotonous cry, throat-muscles squeezing out a song, with a neck like a crane's where he plays, like a stabbed goose screeching aloud. There are voices in that hollow bag like the ravings of a thousand cats: a monotonous, wounded, ailing, pregnant goat – no pay for its hire. After it ended its wheezing note, that cold songstress whom love would shun, Will got his fee, namely bean-soup and pennies (if they paid) and sometimes small halfpennies, not the largesse of a princely hand; while *I* was sent away in high vexation from the silly feast all empty-handed! I solemnly vow, I do forswear wretched Flint and all its children, and its wide, hellish furnace, and its English people and its piper! That they should be slaughtered is all my prayer, my curse in their midst and on their children; sure, if I go there again, may I never return alive!

TREVOR FISHLOCK
Out of Red Darkness, 1993

WE drove back to the city and I visited the university. As we were leaving we encountered a young couple, she in her bridal gown, he in his best suit. She was Russian and he a Yakut. They had just been married in the register office and, both being students, had gone into the university to brush their hair and tidy up before going on to their wedding party. 'It would be good luck to have a foreigner,' they said, 'so why don't you come?'

In a few minutes I found myself in a restaurant filled with a hundred wedding guests. I was installed at the top table next to the bride's mother, with Nadia on my left. 'Wonderful,' said Nadia, 'I hardly ever go to a party.'

The tables were filled with cold meats, chicken, mare's blood sausage, dumplings, pickles, vegetables and salads and bottles of wine, Russian champagne and vodka. The toasts began at once and the newly-weds were called on to stand and kiss each other to a count of eight. An old leathery man sang a Yakut wedding song and more toasts were drunk and the couple stood and kissed again to a count of ten. A man played a sentimental tune on an accordion. There were speeches in praise of the couple's fathers, more songs and more toasts, more kisses, then a song saluting the Yakut troops who won fame in the Second World War for their bravery. A young man twanged a Jew's harp, one of the favourite instruments of the region, so popular that Yakutsk was host to the world Jew's Harp Congress some months later. A flame was lit in a lamp to signify the warmth of hearth and home. More toasts. Just when I thought there might be a respite from the non-stop entertainment a group of young men rushed forward, gently kidnapped the bride and kept her hidden behind a screen at the end of the room until money was raised around the table for her return.

It was soon my turn to make a toast in halting Russian, at the urging of the guests. 'Very good,' said Nadia loyally. 'I understood every word.' I gave her another packet of cigarettes.

A band struck up 'In the mood' and everyone rushed to the floor to dance. During a break in the dancing I was surrounded by men demanding to know how they could take part in a market economy. 'Please', they said, 'tell us how to start joint ventures – we want to go into business.' One young man asked, 'What is your sport?' I thought for a second and said 'Sailing'. 'Hugh!' he said. 'My sport is Thailand kick-boxing.' And he leant back and kicked his leg straight out so that his reindeer-boot foot came within two inches of my nose, which everyone thought a good joke.

The eating and toasts resumed, followed by another bout of dancing. At eleven o'clock, when we were all dizzy, buses came to take us away, for in weather that severe no one walks home. The short walk from the restaurant to the bus provided a sobering cold slap. 'Leaving at this time means that you did not see one of our old wedding party traditions,' said Nadia, 'the fight between young men who have had too much to drink.'

JORIS KARL HUYSMAN
Against Nature, 1884

ONE of these meals, modelled on an eighteenth-century original, had been a funeral feast to mark the most ludicrous of personal misfortunes. The dining-room, draped in black, opened out on to a garden metamorphosed for the occasion, the paths being strewn with charcoal, the ornamental pond edged with black basalt and filled with ink, and the shrubberies replanted with cypresses and pines. The dinner itself was served on a black cloth adorned with baskets of violets and scabious; candelabra shed an eerie green light over the table and tapers flickered in the chandeliers.

While a hidden orchestra played funeral marches, the guests were waited on by naked negresses wearing only slippers and stockings in cloth of silver embroidered with tears.

Dining off black-bordered plates, the company had enjoyed turtle soup, Russian rye bread, ripe olives from Turkey, caviare, muiler botargo, black puddings from Frankfurt, game served in sauces the colour of liquorice and boot-polish, truffle jellies, chocolate creams, plum-puddings, nectarines, pears in grape-juice syrup, mulberries and black heart-cherries. From dark-tinted glasses they had drunk the wines of Limagne and Roussillon, of Tenedos, Valdepenas and Oporto. And after coffee and walnut cordial, they had rounded off the evening with kvass, porter and stout.

On the invitations, which were similar to those sent out before more solemn obsequies, this dinner was described as a funeral banquet in memory of the host's virility, lately but only temporarily deceased.

SYBILLE BEDFORD
A Legacy, 1956

AS they came up the stairs the number 50 large and round greeted them from everywhere. Festooned with paper garlands, framed by leaves of extraordinary deadness, gloss and durability, in icing, in marzipan, in electric candles, in candied fruit; 5 and o cut out in tin foil and wired between the antlers of the nineteen-ender stag sent, not shot, by Max from his Silesian estate, a trophy that reclined on the carpet in the antechamber at the foot of an altar of offerings, attentions to Merz from Merz connections – poultry in their feathers, hares in fur, strings of partridge, a dozen brace of this and a dozen brace of that, cray-fish clambering weakly through damp seaweed. Westphalia hams, snake-lengths of smoked eel, great glistening lumps of sheer boned goose flesh sewn into its own faultless skin, five-pound tins of caviare afloat in silver coolers, Strasbourg terrines large as band-boxes, hot-house asparagus thick as pillars, fifty plover's eggs in a nest of bronze twigs, and rising Pelion upon Ossa, tier on tier, crested at the apex by the plumes of massed heads of pineapple, corbeille upon box on box on case on satined case, Port and Havanas, Arabian Mocha, Smyrna figs, grapes in cotton-wool, Turkish delight, Marrons glacés, Sacher cake and Karlsbad plums. The presents proper were laid out in the ball-room; and through the salons to the dining-room there stretched a buffet displaying the substances of the antechamber at a stage nearer to, indeed already surpassing, the customary degrees of commestibility. Supremes and Fondants, Velours and Claires, Masques and Glazes, en Bellevue, en Chartreuse, en Savarin, en Bouquetière, Surelévés and Richelieus, Figaros and Maintenons, Niagaras and Metternichs and Miroités – en Grenadin; en Favorite; en Chambertin; en Financière; en Chassé, en Croisé, en Frappé, en Triple-Eau, en Glissade, en Diadème; en Sainte-Alliance, en Belvedère, en Ballonné, en Demi-Deuil and Demidoff; Gramouts, Chimays, Souvaroffs, Albufera and Tivoli.

THOMAS LOVE PEACOCK

Headlong Hall, 1816

IN his last binn SIR PETER lies,
   Who knew not what it was to frown:
Death took him mellow, by surprise,
   And in his cellar stopped him down.
Through all our land we could not boast
   A knight more gay, more prompt than he,
To rise and fill a bumper toast,
   And pass it round with THREE TIMES THREE.

None better knew the feast to sway,
  Or keep Mirth's boat in better trim;
For Nature had but little clay
  Like that of which she moulded him.
The meanest guest that graced his board
  Was there the freest of the free.
His bumper toast when PETER poured.
  And passed it round with THREE TIMES THREE.

He kept at true good humour's mark
  The social flow of pleasure's tide:
He never made a brow look dark,
  Nor caused a tear, but when he died.
No sorrow round his tomb should dwell:
  More pleased his gay old ghost would be,
For funeral song, and passing bell,
  To hear no sound but THREE TIMES THREE.

H. G. WELLS
The History of Mr Polly, 1910

EVERYBODY was in profound mourning, of course – mourning in the modern English style, with the dyer's handiwork only too apparent, and hats and jackets of the current cut. There was very little crape, and the costumes had none of the goodness and specialization and genuine enjoyment of mourning for mourning's sake that a similar Continental gathering would have displayed. Still that congestion of strangers in black sufficed to stun and confuse Mr Polly's impressionable mind. It seemed to him much more extraordinary than anything he had expected.

'Now, gals,' said Mrs Larkins, 'see if you can help,' and the three daughters became confusingly active between the front room and the back.

'I hope every one'll take a glass of sherry and a biscuit,' said Mrs Johnson. 'We don't stand on ceremony,' and a decanter appeared in the place of Uncle Pentstemon's vegetables.

Uncle Pentstemon had refused to be relieved of his hat; he sat stiffly down on a chair against the wall, with that venerable head-

dress between his feet, watching the approach of any one jealously.
'Don't you go squashing my hat,' he said. Conversation became
confused and general. Uncle Pentstemon addressed himself to Mr
Polly.

'You're a little chap,' he said, 'a puny little chap. I never did agree
to Lizzie marrying him, but I suppose bygones must be bygones
now. I suppose they made you a clerk or something.'

'Outfitter,' said Mr Polly.

'I remember. Them girls pretend to be dressmakers.'

'They *are* dressmakers,' said Mrs Larkins across the room.

'I *will* take a glass of sherry,' he remarked; and then mildly to Mr
Polly, 'They 'old to it, you see.'

He took the glass Mrs Johnson handed him, and poised it critically
between a horny finger and thumb. 'You'll be paying for this,' he
said to Mr Polly. 'Here's *to* you. . . . Don't you go treading on my
hat, young woman. You brush your skirts against it and you take a
shillin' off its value. It ain't the sort of 'at you see nowadays.'

He drank noisily.

The sherry presently loosened everybody's tongue, and the opening coldness passed.

'There ought to have been a *post-mortem*,' Polly heard Mrs Punt
remarking to one of Mrs Johnson's friends, and Miriam and another
were lost in admiration of Mrs Johnson's decorations. 'So very nice
and refined,' they were both repeating at intervals.

The sherry and biscuits were still being discussed when Mr Podger,
the undertaker, arrived, a broad, cheerfully sorrowful, clean-shaven,
little man, accompanied by a melancholy faced assistant. He conversed for a time with Johnson in the passage outside. The sense
of his business stilled the rising waves of chatter and carried off
every one's attention in the wake of his heavy footsteps to the room
above.

JAMES JOYCE

Finnegans Wake, 1939

SHIZE? I should shee! Macool, Macool, orra whyi deed ye diie?
of a trying thirstay mournin? Sobs they sighdid at Fillagain's
chrissormiss wake, all the hoolivans of the nation, prostrated in their
consternation and their duodisimally profusive plethora of ululation.

There was plumbs and grumes and cheriffs and citherers and raiders and cinemen too. And the all gianed in with the shout-most shoviality. Agog and magog and the round of them agrog. To the continuation of that celebration until Hanandhunigan's extermination! Some in kinkin corass, more, kankan keening. Belling him up and filling him down. He's stiff but he's steady is Priam Olim! 'Twas he was the dacent gaylabouring youth. Sharpen his pillowscone, tap up his bier! E'erawhere in this whorl would ye hear sich a din again? With their deepbrow fundigs and the dusty fidelios. They laid him brawdawn alanglast bed. With a bockalips of finisky fore his feet. And a barrowload of guenesis hoer his head. Tee the tootal of the fluid hang the twoddle of the fuddled, O!

OLIVER GOLDSMITH
The Vicar of Wakefield, 1766

MICHAELMAS-EVE happening on the next day, we were invited to burn nuts and play tricks at neighbour Flamborough's. Our late mortifications had humbled us a little, or it is probable we might have rejected such an invitation with contempt: however, we suffered ourselves to be happy. Our honest neighbour's goose and dumplings were fine; and the lamb's wool, even in the opinion of my wife, who was a connoisseur, was excellent. It is true, his manner of telling stories was not quite so well: they were very long and very dull, and all about himself, and we had laughed at them ten times before: however, we were kind enough to laugh at them once more.

Mr Burchell, who was of the party, was always fond of seeing some innocent amusement going forward, and set the boys and girls to blindman's buff: my wife too was persuaded to join in the diversion, and it gave me pleasure to think she was not yet too old. In the mean time, my neighbour and I looked on, laughed at every feat, and praised our own dexterity when we were young: hot cockles succeeded next, questions and commands followed that, and, last of all, they sat down to hunt the slipper. As every person may not be acquainted with this primeval pastime, it may be necessary to observe, that the company, in this play, plant themselves in a ring upon the ground, all except one, who stands in the middle, whose business it is to catch the shoe, which the company shove about under their hams from one to another, something like a weaver's shuttle. As it is impossible, in this case, for the lady who is up to face all the company at once, the great beauty of the play lies in hitting her a thump with the heel of the shoe on that side least capable of making defence. It was in this manner that my eldest daughter was hemmed in and thumped about, all blowzed, in spirits, and bawling for fair play with a voice that might deafen a ballad-singer, when, confusion on confusion! who should enter the room, but our two great acquaintances from town, Lady Blarney, and Miss Carolina Wilelmina Amelia Skeggs? Description would but beggar, therefore it is unnecessary to describe this new mortification. Death! to be seen by ladies of such high breeding in such vulgar attitudes! Nothing better could ensue from such a vulgar play of Mr Flamborough's proposing. We seemed struck to the ground for some time, as if actually petrified with amazement.

THE BIBLE

St Matthew, Chapter 26

NOW the first *day* of the *feast of* unleavened bread the disciples came to Jesus, saying unto him, Where wilt thou that we prepare for thee to eat the passover?

And he said, Go into the city to such a man, and say unto him, The Master saith, My time is at hand; I will keep the passover at thy house with my disciples.

And the disciples did as Jesus had appointed them; and they made ready the passover.

Now when the even was come, he sat down with the twelve.

And as they did eat, he said, Verily I say unto you, that one of you shall betray me.

And they were exceeding sorrowful, and began every one of them to say unto him, Lord, is it I?

And he answered and said, He that dippeth *his* hand with me in the dish, the same shall betray me.

The Son of man goeth as it is written of him: but woe unto that man by whom the Son of man is betrayed! it had been good for that man if he had not been born.

Then Judas, which betrayed him, answered and said, Master, is it I? He said unto him, Thou hast said.

And as they were eating, Jesus took bread, and blessed *it*, and brake *it*, and gave *it* to the disciples, and said, Take, eat; this is my body.

And he took the cup, and gave thanks, and gave *it* to them, saying, Drink ye all of it;

For this is my blood of the new testament, which is shed for many for the remission of sins.

But I say unto you, I will not drink henceforth of this fruit of the vine, until that day when I drink it new with you in my Father's kingdom.

And when they had sung an hymn, they went out into the mount of Olives.

ROBERT HERRICK

'Hesperides', 1648

1. GIVE way, give way ye Gates, and win
   An easie blessing to your Bin,
   And Basket, by our entring in.

2. May both with manchet stand repleat;
   Your Larders too so hung with meat,
   That though a thousand, thousand eat;

3. Yet, ere twelve *Moones* shall whirl about
   Their silv'rie Spheres, ther's none may doubt,
   But more's sent in, then was serv'd out.

4. Next, may your Dairies Prosper so,
   As that your pans no Ebbe may know;
   But if they do, the more to flow.

5. Like to a solemne sober Stream
   Bankt all with Lillies, and the Cream
   Of sweetest *Cow-slips* filling Them.

6. Then, may your Plants be prest with Fruit,
   Nor Bee, or Hive you have be mute;
   But sweetly sounding like a Lute.

7. Next may your Duck and teeming Hen
   Both to the Cocks-tread say *Amen*;
   And for their two egs render ten.

8. Last, may your Harrows, Shares and Ploughes,
   Your Stacks, your Stocks, your sweetest Mowes,
   All prosper by your Virgin-vowes.

9. Alas! we blesse, but see none here,
   That brings us either Ale or Beere;
   In a drie-house all things are neere.

10. Let's leave a longer time to wait,
    Where Rust and Cobwebs bind the gate;
    And all live here with *needy Fate.*

11. Where Chimneys do for ever weepe,
    For want of warmth, and Stomachs keepe
    With noise, the servants eyes from sleep.

12. It is in vain to sing, or stay
    Our free-feet here; but we'l away:
    Yet to the Lares this we'l say.

13. The time will come, when you'l be sad,
    And reckon this for fortune bad,
    T'ave lost the good ye might have had.

GEORGE MEREDITH

Diana of the Crossways, 1885

IN the Assembly Rooms of the capital city of the Sister Island there
was a public ball, to celebrate the return to Erin of a British hero
of Irish blood, after his victorious Indian campaign; a mighty
struggle splendidly ended; and truly could it be said that all Erin
danced to meet him; but this was the pick of the dancing, past
dispute the pick of the supping. Outside those halls the supping was
done in Lazarus fashion, mainly through an excessive straining of
the organs of hearing and vision, which imparted the readiness for
more, declared by physicians to be the state inducing to sound
digestion. Some one spied the figure of the hero at a window and
was fed; some only to hear the tale chewed the cud of it; some told

of having seen him mount the steps; and sure it was that at an hour of the night, no matter when, and never mind a drop or two of cloud, he would come down them again, and have an Irish cheer to freshen his pillow. For 'tis Ireland gives England her soldiers, her generals too. Further away, over field and bogland, the whiskies did their excellent ancient service of watering the dry and drying the damp, to the toast of 'Lord Larrian, God bless him; he's an honour to the old country!' and a bit of a sigh to follow, hints of a story, and loud laughter, a drink, a deeper sigh, settling into conversation upon the brave Lord Larrian's deeds, and an Irish regiment he favoured – had no taste for the enemy without the backing of his 'boys'. Not he. Why, he'd never march to battle and they not handy; because when he struck he struck hard he said.

AMANDA M. ROSS

Delina Delaney, 1935

THE joyful news of the innocence of his betrothed was nowhere more welcomed than in the home of his youth, and those on his estate. The great grief shown by his tenants at the result of the trial was now transformed into greatest joy, as they assembled in hundreds in front of Columba Castle to further aid in welcoming their respected landlord, under such auspices, once more amongst them. Hurrahs, loud and long, burst forth as the carriage drove up the broad and winding avenue, increasing a hundredfold as Lord Gifford alighted. Men, young and old, shook him by both hands, and, in gleeful moments of excitement, grasped the tail of his coat. Young girls, women, middle-aged and infirm, wept for joy at the nature of his presence amongst them again, echoing prayers, with uplifted hands, for the forthcoming freedom of the meek little orphan who sat, undergoing the penalty of a false imprisonment, in Mountjoy Prison, Dublin, whither she had been transferred.

PHYLLIS McGINLEY

'Office Party', 1948

THIS holy night in open forum
    Miss McIntosh, who handles Files,
Has lost one shoe and her decorum.
    Stately, the frozen chairman smiles

On Media, desperately vocal.
    Credit, though they have lost their hopes
Of edging toward an early Local,
    Finger their bonus envelopes.

The glassy boys, the bursting girls
    Of Copy, start a Conga clatter
To a swung carol. Limply curls
    The final sandwich on the platter

Till hark! a herald Messenger
    (Room 414) lifts loudly up
His quavering tenor. Salesmen stir
    Libation for his Lily cup.

'Noel,' he pipes, 'Noel, Noel.'
    Some wag beats tempo with a ruler.
And the plump blonde from Personnel
    Is sick behind the water cooler.

MARGARET ATWOOD

Cat's Eye, 1990

MY parents have bridge parties. They push the furniture in the living room to the walls and unfold two metal bridge-tables and eight bridge-chairs. In the middle of each table there are two china dishes, one with salted nuts, the other with mixed candies. These candies are called 'bridge mixture'. There are also two ashtrays on each table.

Then the doorbell begins to ring and the people come in. The house fills with the alien scent of cigarettes, which will still be there in the morning along with a few uneaten candies and salted nuts, and with bursts of laughter that get louder as time passes. I lie in my bed listening to the bursts of laughter. I feel isolated, left out. Also I don't understand why this activity, these noises and smells, is called 'bridge'. It is not like a bridge.

Sometimes Mr Banerji comes to these bridge parties. I lurk in the corner of the hallway in my flannelette pyjamas, hoping to catch a glimpse of him. I don't have a crush on him or anything like that. My wish to see him is anxiety, and fellow-feeling. I want to see how he is managing, how he is coping with his life, with having to eat turkeys, and with other things. Not very well, judging from his dark, haunted-looking eyes and slightly hysterical laughter. But if he can deal with whatever it is that's after him, and something is, then so can I. Or this is what I think.

'Masques and mummeries'

—⊰◆⊱—

GEORGE CAVENDISH
The Life and Death of Cardinal Wolsey, 1641

AND when it pleased the King's majesty for his recreation to repair unto the Cardinal's house (as he did divers times in the year), at which time there wanted no preparations or goodly furniture with viands of the finest sort that might be provided for money or friendship. Such pleasures were then devised for the King's comfort and consolation as might be invented or by man's wit imagined. The banquets were set forth with masques and mummeries in so gorgeous a sort and costly manner that it was an heaven to behold. There wanted no dames or damsels meet or apt to dance with the maskers or to garnish the place for the time, with other goodly disports. Then was there all kind of music and harmony set forth with excellent voices both of men and children.

I have seen the King suddenly come in thither in a masque with a dozen of other maskers all in garments like shepherds, made of fine cloth of gold and fine crimson satin paned, and caps of the same with visors of good proportion of visonamy; their hairs and beards either of fine gold wires or else of silver, and some being of black silk, having sixteen torches bearers besides drums, and other persons attending upon them with visors and clothed all in satin of the same colors. And at his coming and before he came into the hall, ye shall understand that he came by water to the water gate without any noise, where against his coming was laid charged many chambers. At whose landing they were all shot off, which made such a rumble in the air that it was like thunder. It made all the noblemen, ladies and gentlewomen to muse what it should mean, coming so suddenly, they sitting quietly at a solemn banquet under this sort.

First ye shall perceive that the tables were set in the chamber of presence, banquet-wise covered, my lord Cardinal sitting under the cloth of estate and there having all his service all alone. And then was there set a lady and a nobleman or a gentleman and a gentlewoman throughout all the tables in the chamber on the one side, which was made and joined as it were but one table.

ADA LEVERSON

The Limit, 1911

VAN Buren had had many pleasures, many gratifications since he had been in London; his dreams – the dreams inspired by Du Maurier's drawings when he was a little boy – had been very nearly realised. Perhaps the greatest triumph that he had had yet was the evening of the Artists' Fancy Ball.

He had succeeded in making up a party to go in costume. He was always making up parties, and he had for many years been obsessed by a longing to dress up.

Harry, in mockery of his passion for everything English, had advised him to go as an Ancient Briton, with a coat of blue paint. Scorning such ribald chaff, he had ordered a magnificent costume of chain armour. Greatly to his satisfaction he had persuaded Hereford Vaughan to go as Shakespeare, Valentia and Daphne respectively as Portia in scarlet and Rosalind in green.

A large party were to dine at Van Buren's rooms before the ball. Fancy dress has the effect of bringing out odd, unexpected little characteristics in people. For example, Harry, good-looking and a dandy, quite a romantic type, hated dressing up, and cared nothing whatever about his costume; while Romer, the sober and serious, enjoyed it immensely, and appeared to think his appearance of the utmost importance – almost a matter of life and death.

The women were far less self-conscious in costume than the men, and cared far less how they looked, probably because women are always more or less in fancy dress, and it was not so much of a novelty to them.

Valentia had pointed out that Shakespeare, to be quite correct, should wear ear-rings; so Vaughan called at her house on the way to Van Buren's, as she had promised to lend him some.

'He won't know how to put them on,' said Daphne, drawing on

her long boots. 'Probably he hasn't had his ears pierced; you must
go and screw them on for him.'

HENRY FIELDING

Tom Jones, 1749

Chap. VII. – Containing the whole humours of a masquerade.

OUR cavaliers now arrived at that temple, where Heydegger,
the great *arbiter deliciarum*, the great highpriest of pleasure,
presides; and, like other heathen priests, imposes on his votaries by
the pretended presence of the deity, when in reality no such deity is
there. Mr Nightingale, having taken a turn or two with his companion, soon left him, and walked off with a female, saying, 'Now
you are here, sir, you must beat about for your own game.' Jones
began to entertain strong hopes that his Sophia was present; and
these hopes gave him more spirits than the lights, the music, and the
company; though these are pretty strong antidotes against the spleen.
He now accosted every woman he saw, whose stature, shape, or air,
bore any resemblance to his angel; to all of whom he endeavoured
to say something smart, in order to engage an answer, by which he
might discover that voice which he thought it impossible he should
mistake. Some of these answered by a question, in a squeaking voice,
'Do you know me?' much the greater number said, 'I don't know
you, sir,' and nothing more: some called him an impertinent fellow:
some made him no answer at all: some said, 'Indeed, I don't know
your voice, and I shall have nothing to say to you;' and many gave
him as kind answers as he could wish, but not in the voice he desired
to hear. Whilst he was talking with one of these last, who was in the
habit of a shepherdess, a lady in a domino came up to him, and,
slapping him on the shoulder, whispered him at the same time in the
ear, 'If you talk any longer with that trollop, I will acquaint Miss
Western.' Jones no sooner heard that name, than, immediately
quitting his former companion, he applied to the domino, begging
and entreating her to show him the lady she had mentioned, if she
was then in the room. The mask walked hastily to the upper end of
the innermost apartment before she spoke; and then, instead of
answering him, sat down, and declared she was tired. Jones sat
down by her, and still persisted in his entreaties. At last, the lady

coldly answered, 'I imagined Mr Jones had been a more discerning lover, than to suffer any disguise to conceal his mistress from him.' 'Is she here, then, madam?' replied Jones, with some vehemence. Upon which the lady cried, 'Hush, sir, you will be observed. I promise you, upon my honour, Miss Western is not here.' Jones now, taking the mask by the hand, fell to entreating her, in the most earnest manner, to acquaint him where he might find Sophia; and, when he could obtain no direct answer, he began to upbraid her gently for having disappointed him the day before; and concluded, saying, 'Indeed, my good fairy queen, I know your majesty very well, notwithstanding the affected disguise of your voice. Indeed, Mrs Fitzpatrick, it is a little cruel to divert yourself at the expense of my torments.' The mask answered, 'Though you have so ingeniously discovered me, I must still speak in the same voice, lest I should be known by others. And do you think, good sir, that I have no greater regard for my cousin, than to assist in carrying on an affair between you two, which must end in her ruin, as well as your own? Besides, I promise you, my cousin is not mad enough to consent to her own destruction, if you are so much her enemy to tempt her to it.' 'Alas, madam,' said Jones, 'you little know my heart, when you call me an enemy of Sophia.' 'And yet to ruin anyone,' cries the other, 'you will allow is the act of an enemy: and when by the same act you must knowingly and certainly bring ruin on yourself, is it not folly or madness, as well as guilt? Now, sir, my cousin has very little more than her father will please to give her; very little for one of her fashion. You know him, and you know your own situation.' Jones vowed he had no such design on Sophia; that he would rather suffer the most violent of deaths than sacrifice her interest to his desires. He said, he knew how unworthy he was of her every way; that he had long ago resolved to quit all such aspiring thoughts but that some strange accidents had made him desirous to see her once more, when he promised he would take leave of her for ever. 'No, madam,' continued he, 'my love is not of that base kind, which seeks its own satisfaction at the expense of what is most dear to its object. I would sacrifice every thing to the possession of my Sophia, but Sophia herself.' Though the reader may have already conceived no very sublime idea of the virtue of the lady in the mask, and though possibly she may hereafter appear not to deserve one of the first characters of her sex; yet, it is certain, these generous sentiments made a strong impression upon her, and greatly added to the affection she had before conceived for our young hero. The lady now, after a silence of a few moments, said, she did not see his pretensions to Sophia so much in the light of presumption, as of imprudence. 'Young fellows', says she, 'can never have too aspiring thoughts. I love ambition in a young man, and I would have you cultivate it as much as possible. Perhaps you may succeed with those who are infinitely superior in fortune; nay, I am convinced there are women – but don't you think me a strange creature, Mr Jones, to be thus giving advice to a man, with whom I am so little acquainted, and one, with whose behaviour to me I have so little reason to be pleased?' Here Jones began to apologise, and to hope he had not offended in any thing he had said of her cousin; to which the mask answered, 'And are you so little versed in the sex, as to imagine you can well affront a lady more, than by entertaining her with your passion for another woman? If the fairy queen had conceived no better opinion of your gallantry, she would scarce have appointed you to meet her at a masquerade.'

SOPHIA MURPHY

The Duchess of Devonshire's Ball
from the Duchess of Devonshire's Introduction, 1984

THE difference was that the guests arrived in gondolas instead of carriages because the ball was given in Venice to celebrate the rebirth of the Palazzo Labia. The munificent host was Charles de Beistegui and the year was 1951. Andrew and I were lucky enough to be invited.

Several impressions have lasted in my mind. One was the entrance of Jacques Fath, a well-known Paris dressmaker at that time, wearing a headdress of ostrich feathers as tall as himself and shimmering in a gold lamé jacket and a sort of golden skirt slashed with white satin. Another was Daisy Fellowes, famed for her elegance and regularly voted the Best Dressed Woman by Americans, who went as The Americas from the Tiepolo painting on the staircase wall of the residence of the Prince Bishop at Würzburg in Germany. There was a decidedly Red Indian flavour in this *entrée* and her attendants were stained brown. Her dress was a vast affair of billowing chiffon printed in a pattern of leopard skin, the first time this was seen. Afterwards it became high fashion and everything from luggage to furnishing material appeared in leopard skin design.

The Tiepolo fresco on the walls of the Palazzo Labia portrays Antony and Cleopatra. So many women threatened to be Cleopatra that the host, seeing trouble ahead, thought it best to decide the matter himself and nominated Diana Cooper for the role.

Another similarity to the subject of this book was that a friend of mine, who described to me how much she enjoyed watching it all without having to take part, arrived at the back door and climbed to the gallery of the great reception room where she saw the assembly of the *entrées* and all that was happening, unencumbered by fancy dress. She was not in mourning, like poor Mrs Hwfa Williams. She just could not be bothered to dress up.

Charles de Beistegui went one better than the Devonshires. He provided wine and food and entertainment on the *campo* outside for the citizens of Venice, and at least one Frenchman of noble birth, who thought he should have been asked to the ball, enjoyed himself immensely among the crowd who were climbing greasy poles for chickens and hams.

GUY DE MAUPASSANT

The Mask, 1890

THERE was a fancy-dress ball at the Élysée-Montmartre that evening to celebrate Mid-Lent, and the crowd was pouring into the brightly lit passage that led to the dancehall like water into a lock. The overwhelming clamour of the orchestra was bursting through the walls and the roof like a musical storm, to spread throughout the neighbourhood, arousing in the streets and even in the depths of the nearby houses that irresistible desire to jump about, keep warm and have fun which slumbers deep in the human animal.

The regular frequenters of the place were arriving from all parts of Paris, people from all classes of society who enjoyed vulgar, noisy fun which was a little squalid and slightly depraved. There were clerks, pimps and tarts – tarts of every sort, from those in common cotton to those in the finest batiste, rich tarts, old and bejewelled, and poor tarts of sixteen eager to paint the town red, go with men and spend money. There were men of the world in evening dress prowling about in the sweating crowd, in search of young flesh, fruit with the bloom rubbed off but still tasty, their eyes skinned and their noses following the scent. And there were masked dancers who seemed chiefly inspired by the desire to have a good time.

Groups of people had already gathered around the famous quadrilles to watch their capers. The swaying hedge, the quivering mass of men and women encircling the four dancers, coiled itself round like a snake, advancing and withdrawing in response to the movements of the four performers.

VIOLET TREFUSIS

Prelude to Misadventure, 1942

THE Tour Eiffel which for so many years had been taken for granted, suddenly found itself the 'vedette du jour'; it was interviewed, tested, talked over, walked over, fought over.

People said: 'You are mad! And a fancy dress ball into the bargain! You will be pelted with rotten eggs, if not worse, by the communists of Belville.' 'It isn't a fancy dress ball,' I objected. 'My guests will merely come in the dress of the period, the period of the Inauguration; it is out of politeness to the Eiffel Tower so that it shouldn't feel démodée, once we are all up there.' People shrugged, people tapped their foreheads significantly, but they came. The dinner was to be cooked in the lift – there was nowhere else to cook it. My more unconventional friends were beside themselves with delight. We were not pelted with rotten eggs by the communists of Belville. On the contrary: the crowd that collected at the foot of the Tower clapped itself silly.

People arrived on tandems, in 'spanking dog carts', on bicycles, in bloomers. They had muffs, feather boas, buttoned boots, fans, *carnets de bal*, hats with seagulls, swallows, humming birds, aigrettes. Jewels were largely astronomical: crescent moons, comets, constellations. Gentlemen who looked as though they were protected from the world by their moustache bent over coquettish ladies who drew patterns on the ground with the point of their parasol. There were dashing cavalry officers with throttlingly high collars, 'très Gyp'; a contemporary Colette with a tiny waist and oblique cat's eyes flirted with a 1900 Boni de Castellane. . . .

I made an unrehearsed entrée with Serge Lifar: we polka-ed madly round the platform of the first floor, where my guests were assembled. In the middle of all this, a lady who must have been in her prime when the Eiffel Tower made its début, the Marquise de M. was announced. Chignon, tortoiseshell lorgnette, feather boa, 'galbe', all were perfect. Lifar rushed up to her in his effusive way: 'Oh, Madame, *do* tell us who made you that wonderful wig et la merveilleuse poitrine postiche?'

There was a deathly silence.

Madame de M. put up her lorgnette and glared at Serge as though he were a hair in the soup. 'I fear you are mistaken, Monsieur, I was not aware that this was to be a fancy dress ball.'

In spite of this and similar incidents, or perhaps because of them, the party was an unqualified success.

DAPHNE DU MAURIER

Rebecca, 1938

YES, the dress had been copied exactly from my sketch of the portrait. The puffed sleeve, the sash and the ribbon, the wide floppy hat I held in my hand. And my curls were her curls, they stood out from my face as hers did in the picture. I don't think I have ever felt so excited before, so happy and so proud. I waved my hand at the man with the fiddle, and then put my finger to my lips for silence. He smiled and bowed. He came across the gallery to the archway where I stood.

'Make the drummer announce me,' I whispered, 'make him beat the drum, you know how they do, and then call out Miss Caroline de Winter. I want to surprise them below.' He nodded his head, he understood. My heart fluttered absurdly, and my cheeks were burning. What fun it was, what mad ridiculous childish fun! I smiled at Clarice still crouching on the corridor. I picked up my skirt in my hands. Then the sound of the drum echoed in the great hall, startling me for a moment, who had waited for it, who knew that it would come. I saw them look up surprised and bewildered from the hall below.

'Miss Caroline de Winter,' shouted the drummer.

I came forward to the head of the stairs and stood there, smiling, my hat in my hand, like the girl in the picture. I waited for the clapping and laughter that would follow as I walked slowly down the stairs. Nobody clapped, nobody moved.

They all stared at me like dumb things. Beatrice uttered a little cry and put her hand to her mouth. I went on smiling, I put one hand on the banister.

'How do you do, Mr de Winter,' I said.

Maxim had not moved. He stared up at me, his glass in his hand. There was no colour in his face. It was ashen white. I saw Frank go to him as though he would speak, but Maxim shook him off. I hesitated, one foot already on the stairs. Something was wrong, they had not understood. Why was Maxim looking like that? Why did they all stand like dummies, like people in a trance?

Then Maxim moved forward to the stairs, his eyes never leaving my face.

'What the hell do you think you are doing?' he asked. His eyes blazed in anger. His face was still ashen white.

I could not move, I went on standing there, my hand on the banister.

'It's the picture,' I said, terrified at his eyes, at his voice. 'It's the picture, the one in the gallery.'

There was a long silence. We went on staring at each other. Nobody moved in the hall. I swallowed, my hand moved to my throat. 'What is it?' I said. 'What have I done?'

If only they would not stare at me like that with dull blank faces. If only somebody would say something. When Maxim spoke again I did not recognize his voice. It was still and quiet, icy cold, not a voice I knew.

'Go and change,' he said, 'it does not matter what you put on. Find an ordinary evening frock, anything will do. Go now, before anybody comes.'

I could not speak, I went on staring at him. His eyes were the only living things in the white mask of his face.

'What are you standing there for?' he said, his voice harsh and queer. 'Didn't you hear what I said?'

I turned and ran blindly through the archway to the corridors beyond. I caught a glimpse of the astonished face of the drummer who had announced me. I brushed past him, stumbling, not looking where I went. Tears blinded my eyes.

'But not all of us were experts in out-of-door etiquette'

ALAIN FOURNIER
The Lost Domain, 1913

ON reaching the bank of the Cher we undressed under the dry willows. They shielded us from prying eyes but not from the sun. Our feet on the hot sand and caked mud, we had visions of the bottle of lemonade which was cooling in a spring at the Grand Fons, a spring that bubbled up through the bank of the river. Looking into it you could see the grass waving deep underneath, but its surface was never quite free from two or three insects that looked like woodlice. But the water was so pure that fishermen never hesitated to kneel down, their hands on either bank, and drink from it.

Unfortunately, today was no exception to the rule . . . For, once dressed and seated tailor-fashion in a circle round the bottle to take our turn at one of the only two tumblers, having politely invited Monsieur Seurei to have first go, there was only enough of the frothy liquid to make each throat prickle and redouble its thirst. So, one after another, we were driven to the contemned spring, lowering our faces cautiously to the surface of the limpid water. But not all of us were experts in out-of-door etiquette. For some of us, I for one, scarcely succeeded in quenching our thirst: either because of a dislike for water as a beverage, or because the fear of swallowing a woodlouse tightened our throats, or because the transparence of the water made it hard to judge the right distance, with the result that faces plunged in and noses were filled with something so icy it seemed to burn . . . Despite these hazards and drawbacks, it seemed to us, on the hot dry bank of the Cher, that all the coolness of the world was imprisoned in this little pool, and to this day when I hear the word 'spring' my mind returns to linger over it.

RUDYARD KIPLING

Plain Tales from the Hills, 1888

WE gathered by the bank. Someone had brought out a banjo which is a most sentimental instrument and three or four of us sang. You must not laugh at this. Our amusements in out of the way Stations are very few indeed. Then we talked in groups or together, lying under the trees, with the sun-baked roses dropping their petals on our feet, until supper was ready. It was a beautiful supper, as cold and as iced as you could wish; and we stayed long over it.

I had felt that the air was growing hotter and hotter; but nobody seemed to notice it until the moon went out and a burning hot wind began lashing the orange-trees with a sound like the noise of the sea. Before we knew where we were the dust storm was on us, and everything was roaring, whirling darkness. The supper-table was blown bodily into the tank. We were afraid of staying anywhere near the old tomb for fear it might be blown down. So we felt our way to the orange-trees where the horses were picketed and waited for the storm to blow over. Then the little light that was left vanished, and you could not see your hand before your face. The air was heavy with dust and sand from the bed of the river, that filled boots and pockets, and drifted down necks, and coated eyebrows and moustaches.

It was one of the worst dust storms of the year. We were all huddled together close to the trembling horses, with the thunder chattering overhead, and the lightning spurting like water from a sluice, all ways at once. There was no danger, of course, unless the horses broke loose. I was standing with my head downwind and my hands over my mouth, hearing the trees thrashing each other. I could not see who was next me till the flashes came. Then I found that I was packed near Saumarez and the eldest Miss Copleigh, with my own horse just in front of me. I recognized the eldest Miss Copleigh, because she had a puggree round her helmet, and the youngest had not. All the electricity in the air had gone into my body, and I was quivering and tingling from head to foot – exactly as a corn shoots and tingles before rain. It was a grand storm. The wind seemed to be picking up the earth and pitching it to leeward in great heaps: and the heat beat up from the ground like the heat of the Day of Judgement.

The storm lulled slightly after the first half hour, and I heard a despairing little voice close to my ear, saying to itself, quietly and softly, as if some lost soul were flying about with the wind, 'Oh my God!' Then the younger Miss Copleigh stumbled into my arms, saying, 'Where is my horse? Get my horse. I want to go home. I want to go home. Take me home.'

DRUE HEINZ
A New England Clambake, 1983

BY far the messiest of all picnics is the famous American institution called the clambake or, before the price of lobster flew too high out of the water, the lobsterbake. In the twenties and thirties it was entirely different, and even grand. The famous Marshall Field, for instance, would anchor his great yacht off a beautiful stretch of beach in Maine and instruct his crew to go to it. This meant prepare a clambake for the next evening at sundown for his twenty guests.

Nowadays it is every man for himself. However the menu has not really changed since the Republic was formed, nor has the way settlers learned to cook the corn and shellfish in the ad hoc ovens, or pits, invented by the Indians. The New England or Yankee clambake is as much a national feast as is Thanksgiving. And most people have a last glorious binge on the beach at the end of August before they return to the city from their long summer holidays.

The first clambake I attended was in Martha's Vineyard on a lovely beach of dunes capped with long willowy beachgrass. I was told to bring a sweater, although the temperature at 5 p.m. was about 85 degrees. I was given a basket to carry, surprisingly heavy. I found out later that it was full of vodka and gin. We arrived to find a blazing fire and much consternation. It was supposed to have turned to embers by then, but the wind had risen and whipped up the blaze. And the smoke – Oh Lord – had everyone coughing, rubbing their eyes, retreating frantically from the 'bake' pits and yelling for drinks.

Soon we were consoled with large gins in paper cups, and someone kept running the line of teary-eyed spectators offering ice, ice, anyone? And along came a teenager shaking peanuts out of a large bag. Unfortunately, most of them fell to the sand as we swayed in the wind which was becoming stronger and colder. Meanwhile the younger, more durable element had managed to damp down the fire and were endeavouring to place the clams around the blistery seaweed whose water would cook them.

Hours passed, the moon came up, and the wind changed. We had to turn our backs to the fire and wrap our much-needed sweaters around us, at the same time trying to keep the sand from getting into every nook and cranny of our weather-whipped bodies.

But then came the cry, 'Clams up!' Several young men appeared with plates piled with clams, sweet potatoes, corn, a small lobster, and a large paper napkin. My nearest companion turned to grab a plateful when a gust of wind caught us and everything fell into the sand. 'Don't touch it yet, it's burning hot,' went down the line. So we all had another restorative drink.

Eventually we found a bit of everything, gratiné with sand. What to do? Obviously stagger to the sea, wash the food off quickly in the water, and eat it with our fingers. I tried, goodness knows, I tried! But I remember only getting wet to the thighs as a big wave struck, knocking the plate from my hand. Thank heavens it was dark. As I trudged back, jeans clinging dankly to my thighs, someone said, 'What wonderful clams. Didn't you think the lobster was great?' I replied, 'Yes, absolutely wonderful, never had anything so good, but it sure makes one thirsty.'

At least I had managed to hold onto my cup and received an immediate fill-up. As I neared the fire, I managed to salvage a baked potato from a friendly helper. I was torn between eating it or stashing it behind my knee as one does at an Irish point-to-point. We now crouched wetly in the moonlight. Someone started to sing, 'By the sea, by the beautiful sea,' and I looked around wildly for anyone who might be leaving in a car. At last I spied a Land-rover driving off, and begged a lift. 'We're full,' they said. 'You'll have to get in the back.' I clambered in, and what did I see but the remains of the clams, buttery corn on the cob, baby lobster, hard rolls and plates of sweet potatoes. Bumping along the potholed road back to the Vineyard I had the best, and possibly the last, clambake I would ever enjoy.

HUBERT E. H. JENNINGHAM
Life in a French Château, 1867

UNDER the shade of some trees, a party of about twenty girls were indulging in reminiscences of their childhood, by dancing one after the other to every tune they had learnt in the nursery. A few little boys were permitted to join in these frolics, and when they had danced

> A la tour d'Avignon,
> . . . .
> Tout en rond,

these little urchins became the heroes of the *fête*. They were taken possession of by the young ladies, and kissed and caressed (however ugly they might be), and told that they were 'des anges, des petits bijoux, des petits amours'. Then, as if no one was present, these grown-up girls rebegan their shouts. Their mirth appeared to know no bounds; they screamed, they laughed, they talked, and the only signs they gave of being aware that others were present, were occasional glances, promptly checked, to the right, where some two dozen men, decked out in the most elaborate and killing get-ups imaginable, had taken up a position to look at the young ladies, and appeared at the distance like so many mushrooms in a field.

KATHERINE MANSFIELD
The Garden Party, 1922

AND after all the weather was ideal. They could not have had a more perfect day for a garden party if they had ordered it. Windless, warm, the sky without a cloud. Only the blue was veiled with a haze of light gold, as it is sometimes in early summer. The gardener had been up since dawn, mowing the lawns and sweeping them, until the grass and the dark flat rosettes where the daisy plants had been seemed to shine. As for the roses, you could not help feeling they understood that roses are the only flowers that impress people at garden parties; the only flowers that everybody is certain of knowing. Hundreds, yes, literally hundreds, had come out in a single night; the green bushes bowed down as though they had been visited by archangels.

Breakfast was not yet over before the men came to put up the marquee.

'Where do you want the marquee put, mother?'

'My dear child, it's no use asking me. I'm determined to leave everything to you children this year. Forget I am your mother. Treat me as an honoured guest.'

But Meg could not possibly go and supervise the men. She had washed her hair before breakfast, and she sat drinking her coffee in a green turban, with a dark wet curl stamped on each cheek. Jose, the butterfly, always came down in a silk petticoat and a kimono jacket.

'You'll have to go, Laura; you're the artistic one.'

Away Laura flew, still holding her piece of bread-and-butter. It's so delicious to have an excuse for eating out of doors, and besides, she loved having to arrange things; she always felt she could do it so much better than anybody else.

Four men in their shirt-sleeves stood grouped together on the garden path. They carried staves covered with rolls of canvas, and they had big tool-bags slung on their backs. They looked impressive. Laura wished now that she was not holding that piece of bread-and-butter, but there was nowhere to put it, and she couldn't possibly throw it away.

MICHAEL GRANT

The Picnic Papers, 1983

JULIUS Caesar followed up the celebration of his Triumphs over his enemies by presiding – sweating profusely, we are told – over an open-air dinner in the public squares of Rome, attended by many tens if not hundreds of thousands of Romans who drank a good Italian wine (Falernian) and ate, among other things, six thousand eels 'lent' to Caesar by a former political opponent. The dictator liked doing things on a large scale, and this may have been the biggest picnic of all time (picnic? Yes, according to the *Concise Oxford Dictionary*, 'pleasure party including meal out of doors').

Queen Cleopatra did not attend Caesar's party because she was not in Rome, although she arrived shortly afterwards. But if she had been at the dinner she would surely have felt like one of her royal Greek forbears, Queen Arsinoe III of Egypt, who described the picnickers at Alexandria's Feast of Flagons as 'a squalid kind of party – a mixed crowd gorging up stale food'. Arsinoe would scarcely have been better pleased if she had attended some of the numerous similar festivals in Italy, which gave the opportunity for a good deal of fairly unrestrained eating and drinking. For example at the annual Festival of Anna Perenna, on 15 March, people camped out with their girlfriends in tents or huts of leafy boughs or reeds, and everyone drank themselves silly. At the Hilaria, the spring festival of the Great Mother, it was the custom to offer the goddess an extraordinarily pungent, garlicky salad ('its powerful whiff smites the nostrils', remarked a poet), and no doubt the revellers ate the leftovers.

D. H. LAWRENCE
Women in Love, 1920

EVERY year Mr Crich gave a more or less public water-party on the lake. There was a little pleasure-launch on Willey Water and several rowing-boats, and guests could take tea either in the marquee that was set up in the grounds of the house, or they could picnic in the shade of the great walnut tree at the boat-house by the lake. This year the staff of the Grammar School was invited, along with the chief officials of the firm. Gerald and the younger Criches did not care for this party, but it had become customary now, and it pleased the father, as being the only occasion when he could gather some people of the district together in festivity with him. For he loved to give pleasures to his dependents and to those poorer than himself. But his children preferred the company of their equals in wealth. They hated their inferiors' humility or gratitude or awkwardness.

Nevertheless they were willing to attend at this festival, as they had done almost since they were children, the more so, as they all felt a little guilty now, and unwilling to thwart their father any more, since he was so ill in health. Therefore, quite cheerfully Laura prepared to take her mother's place as hostess, and Gerald assumed responsibility for the amusements on the water.

Birkin had written to Ursula saying he expected to see her at the party, and Gudrun, although she scorned the patronage of the

Criches, would nevertheless accompany her mother and father if the weather were fine.

The day came blue and full of sunshine, with little wafts of wind. The sisters both wore dresses of white crêpe, and hats of soft grass. But Gudrun had a sash of brilliant black and pink and yellow colour wound broadly round her waist, and she had pink silk stockings, and black and pink and yellow decoration on the brim of her hat, weighing it down a little. She carried also a yellow silk coat over her arm, so that she looked remarkable, like a painting from the Salon. Her appearance was a sore trial to her father, who said angrily:

'Don't you think you might as well get yourself up for a Christmas cracker, an' ha' done with it?'

But Gudrun looked handsome and brilliant, and she wore her clothes in pure defiance. When people stared at her, and giggled after her, she made a point of saying loudly, to Ursula:

'*Regarde, regarde ces gens-là! Ne sont-ils pas de hiboux incroyables?*' And with the words of French in her mouth, she would look over her shoulder at the giggling party.

'No, really, it's impossible!' Ursula would reply distinctly. And so the two girls took it out of their universal enemy. But their father became more and more enraged.

Ursula was all snowy white, save that her hat was pink, and entirely without trimming, and her shoes were dark red, and she carried an orange-coloured coat. And in this guise they were walking all the way to Shortlands, their father and mother going in front.

They were laughing at their mother, who, dressed in a summer material of black and purple stripes, and wearing a hat of purple straw, was setting forth with much more of the shyness and trepidation of a young girl than her daughters ever felt, walking demurely beside her husband, who, as usual, looked rather crumpled in his best suit, as if he were the father of a young family and had been holding the baby whilst his wife got dressed.

KITTY VINCENT

Lipstick, 1925

'NO, my dear, I cannot say that I really know the Bishop of Runnymede; I have merely met him at garden-parties and entertainments of that description. You know I make a "bee-line", as my boy so amusingly puts it, for Bishops at garden-parties. They are quite extraordinarily *dans leur assiette* much more so than ordinary men. They know by instinct where the best strawberries are to be found, and exactly how to secure an ice. They are full of *petits soins*; I suppose that their profession teaches them so much about ministering to souls that by instinct they know what to do for the body. What do you say, my dear? You only laughed? Will you forgive me if I say that I do not think the laugh was in the best of taste. . . .'

NANCY MILFORD
Zelda Fitzgerald, 1970

T HE 'script' (short for subscription) dances were held out of doors at Oak Park, where there was a large old dance pavilion with a hardwood floor. A group of young men, usually college boys, hired a dance band and then they posted a list of girls' names on the door at Harry's. Harry's was an ice-cream parlor where the boys, who were called 'Jelly Beans', or 'Jellies', loafed and hung out with their girls. A young man then signed his name next to the name of the girl he wanted to take; it was first come first served, with the prettiest, most popular girls signed for first. The only hitch from the girls' point of view was that they had almost no say about who signed for them, and their only out was refusing to go.

There were chaperones at the dances, but Zelda completely ignored them. She danced cheek to cheek, which was considered improper, and it took very little persuasion to get her to sneak out during intermission to the cars which were parked just out of sight. She 'boodled' (which was local slang for necking in cars at a place called Boodler's Bend), she smoked, and she drank gin, if there was any, or corn liquor cut with Coke, if there wasn't.

ANTHONY TROLLOPE
Can you Forgive Her?, 1865

YARMOUTH is not a happy place for a picnic. A picnic should be held among green things. Green turf is absolutely an essential. There should be trees, broken ground, small paths, thickets and hidden recesses. There should, if possible, be rocks, old timber, moss and brambles. There should certainly be hills and dales, – on a small scale, and, above all, there should be running water. There should be no expanse. Jones should not be able to see all Greene's movements, nor should Augusta always have her eye upon her sister Jane. But the spot chosen for Mr Cheesacre's picnic at Yarmouth had none of the virtues above described. It was on the sea-shore. Nothing was visible from the site but sand and sea. There were no trees there and nothing green; – neither was there any running water. But there was a long, dry, flat strand; there was an old boat half turned over, under which it was proposed to dine; and in addition to this, benches, boards, and some amount of canvas for shelter were provided by the liberality of Mr Cheesacre. Therefore it was called Mr Cheesacre's picnic.

But it was to be a marine picnic, and therefore the essential attributes of other picnics were not required. The idea had come from some boating expeditions, in which mackerel had been caught, and during which food had been eaten, not altogether comfortably, in the boats. Then a thought had suggested itself to Captain Bellfield that they might land and eat their food, and his friend Mr Cheesacre had promised his substantial aid. A lady had surmised that Ormesby sands would be the very place for dancing in the cool of the evening. They might 'Dance on the sand,' she said, 'and yet no footing seen.' And so the thing had progressed, and the picnic been inaugurated.

'I dreamed I was at this party . . .'

JAMES THURBER
Alarms and Diversions: 'The Ladies of Orlon', 1957

ONE night, I dreamed I was at this party. A young lady had been carelessly flung onto the sofa beside me, her long legs loosely intertwined and her stuffing showing plainly at one shoulder seam. 'You're losing your sawdust,' I told her anxiously. 'Nonsex,' she said, and I suddenly realized that she and all the other women guests were dolls. Such a dream could be construed as meaning that I have reached the time of life when I seek to deny the actuality of the American Woman and to reduce her to the level of an insentient plaything. Actually, the latent meaning of this dream goes far deeper than that, and consists of a profound anxiety on my part as to what would happen to our world if the stature of Woman decreased.

A lovely woman with a taffeta xiphisternum might conceivably make this artificiality a part of her mysterious allure – I have known the kind of lady whose charm could even take the ugliness out of a thrug sutured with silk to her thisbe – but a gentleman of like kidney, let us say, could surely never regain the position he held in our competitive society before his operation. Man is used to being repaired with silver plates and pins, and it is doubtful whether his ego could long sustain a body consisting largely, or in part, of dress material. It may be, then, that a gradual textilization of the human species is one of the desperate strategies of Nature in her ceaseless effort to save our self-destructive race from the extinction of which it seems so massively enamored. Nature and I have long felt that the hope of mankind is womankind, that the physically creative sex must eventually dominate the physically destructive sex if we are to survive on this planet. The simplest things last longest, the microbe outlives the mastodon, and the female's simple gift of creativity happily lacks the ornaments and handicaps of male artifice, pretension, power and balderdash.

MIKHAEL BULGAKOV

The Master and Margarita, 1973 (posthumous)

'LET the ball commence!' shrieked the cat in a piercing voice. Margarita screamed and shut her eyes for several seconds. The ball burst upon her in an explosion of light, sound and smell. Arm in arm with Koroviev, Margarita found herself in a tropical forest. Scarlet-breasted parrots with green tails perched on lianas and hopping from branch to branch uttered deafening screeches of 'Ecstasy! Ecstasy!' The forest soon came to an end and its hot, steamy air gave way to the cool of a ballroom with columns made of a yellowish, iridescent stone. Like the forest the ballroom was completely empty except for some naked Negroes in silver turbans holding candelabra. Their faces paled with excitement when Margarita floated into the ballroom with her suite, to which Azazello had now attached himself. Here Koroviev released Margarita's arm and whispered:

'Walk straight towards the tulips!'

A low wall of white tulips rose up in front of Margarita. Beyond it she saw countless lights in globes, and rows of men in tails and starched white shirts. Margarita saw then where the sound of ball music had been coming from. A roar of brass deafened her and the soaring violins that broke through it poured over her body like blood. The orchestra, all hundred and fifty of them, were playing a polonaise.

Seeing Margarita the tail-coated conductor turned pale, smiled and suddenly raised the whole orchestra to its feet with a wave of his arm. Without a moment's break in the music the orchestra stood and engulfed Margarita in sound. The conductor turned away from the players and gave a low bow. Smiling, Margarita waved to him.

'No, no, that won't do,' whispered Koroviev. 'He won't sleep all night. Shout to him "Bravo, king of the waltz!"'

Margarita shouted as she was told, amazed that her voice, full as a bell, rang out over the noise of the orchestra. The conductor gave a start of pleasure, placed his left hand on his heart and with his right went on waving his white baton at the orchestra.

'Not enough,' whispered Koroviev. 'Look over there at the first violins and nod to them so that every one of them thinks you recognize him personally. They are all world famous. Look, there . . . on the first desk – that's Joachim! That's right! Very good . . . Now – on we go.'

'Who is the conductor?' asked Margarita as she floated away.

'Johann Strauss!' cried the cat. 'May I be hung from a liana in the tropical forest if any ball has ever had an orchestra like this! I arranged it! And not one of them was ill or refused to come!'

There were no columns in the next hall, but instead it was flanked by walls of red, pink and milky-white roses on one side and on the other by banks of Japanese double camellias. Fountains played between the walls of flowers and champagne bubbled in three ornamental basins, the first of which was a translucent violet in colour, the second ruby, the third crystal. Negroes in scarlet turbans were busy with silver scoops filling shallow goblets with champagne from the basins. In a gap in the wall of roses was a man bouncing up and down on a stage in a red swallow-tail coat, conducting an unbearably loud jazz band. As soon as he saw Margarita he bent down in front of her until his hands touched the floor, then straightened up and said in a piercing yell:

'Alleluia!'

He slapped himself once on one knee, then twice on the other, snatched a cymbal from the hands of a nearby musician and struck it against a pillar.

As she floated away Margarita caught a glimpse of the virtuoso bandleader, struggling against the polonaise that she could still hear behind her, hitting the bandsmen on the head with his cymbal while they crouched in comic terror.

At last they regained the platform where Koroviev had first met Margarita with the lamp. Now her eyes were blinded with the light streaming from innumerable bunches of crystal grapes. Margarita stopped and a little amethyst pillar appeared under her left hand.

'You can rest your hand on it if you find it becomes too tiring,' whispered Koroviev.

A black-skinned boy put a cushion embroidered with a golden poodle under Margarita's feet. Obeying the pressure of an invisible hand she bent her knee and placed her right foot on the cushion.

Margarita glanced around. Koroviev and Azazello were standing in formal attitudes. Besides Azazello were three young men, who vaguely reminded Margarita of Abadonna. A cold wind blew in her back. Looking round Margarita saw that wine was foaming out of the marble wall into a basin made of ice. She felt something warm and velvety by her left leg. It was Behemoth.

Margarita was standing at the head of a vast carpeted staircase stretching downwards in front of her. At the bottom, so far away that she seemed to be looking at it through the wrong end of a telescope, she could see a vast hall with an absolutely immense fireplace, into whose cold, black maw one could easily have driven a five-ton lorry. The hall and the staircase, bathed in painfully bright light, were empty. Then Margarita heard the sound of distant trumpets. For some minutes they stood motionless.

'Where are the guests?' Margarita asked Koroviev.

'They will be here at any moment, your majesty. There will be no lack of them. I confess I'd rather be sawing logs than receiving them here on this platform.'

'Sawing logs?' said the garrulous cat. 'I'd rather be a tram-conductor and there's no job worse than that.'

WILLIAM CARLOS WILLIAMS
The Dance, 1944

IN Brueghel's great picture, The Kermess, the dancers go round, they go round and around, the squeal and the blare and the tweedle of bagpipes, a bugle and fiddles tipping their bellies (round as the thick-sided glasses whose wash they impound) their hips and their bellies off balance to turn them. Kicking and rolling about the Fair Grounds, swinging their butts, those shanks must be sound to bear up under such rollicking measures, prance as they dance in Breughel's great picture, The Kermess.

LEWIS CARROLL
Alice in Wonderland, 1865

THERE was a table set out under a tree in front of the house, and the March Hare and the Hatter were having tea at it: a Dormouse was sitting between them, fast asleep, and the other two were resting their elbows on it, and talking over its head. 'Very uncomfortable for the Dormouse,' thought Alice; 'only, as it's asleep, I suppose it doesn't mind.'

The table was a large one, but the three were all crowded together at one corner of it. 'No room! No room!' they cried out when they saw Alice coming. 'There's *plenty* of room!' said Alice indignantly, and she sat down in a large arm-chair at one end of the table.

'Have some wine,' the March Hare said in an encouraging tone.

Alice looked all round the table, but there was nothing on it but tea. 'I don't see any wine,' she remarked.

'There isn't any,' said the March Hare.

'Then it wasn't very civil of you to offer it,' said Alice angrily.

'It wasn't very civil of you to sit down without being invited,' said the March Hare.

'I didn't know it was *your* table,' said Alice; 'it's laid for a great many more than three.'

'Your hair wants cutting,' said the Hatter. He had been looking at Alice for some time with great curiosity, and this was his first speech.

'You shouldn't make personal remarks,' Alice said with some severity; 'it's very rude.'

The Hatter opened his eyes very wide on hearing this; but all he *said* was 'Why is a raven like a writing-desk?'

'Come, we shall have some fun now!' thought Alice. 'I'm glad they've begun asking riddles – I believe I can guess that,' she added aloud.

JOHN BUNYAN
The Pilgrim's Progress, 1678

NOW when Feeble-mind and Ready-to-halt saw that it was the head of Giant Despair indeed, they were very jocund and merry. Now Christiana, if need was, could play upon the viol, and her daughter Mercy upon the lute: so since they were so merry disposed, she played them a lesson, and Ready-to-halt would dance. So he took Despondency's daughter, Much-afraid, by the hand, and to dancing they went in the road. True, he could not dance without one crutch in his hand, but I promise you he footed it well: also the girl was to be commended, for she answered the music handsomely.

As for Mr Despondency, the music was not so much to him; he was for feeding, rather than dancing, for that he was almost starved. So Christiana gave him some of her bottle of spirits for present relief, and then prepared him something to eat; and in a little time the old gentleman came to himself, and began to be finely revived.

Now I saw in my dream, when all these things were finished, Mr Great-heart took the head of Giant Despair, and set it upon a pole by the highway side, right over against the pillar that Christian erected for a caution to pilgrims that came after, to take heed of entering into his grounds.

ROBERT HERRICK

'Oberon's Feast', 1648

A LITTLE mushroom table spread,
  After short prayers they set on bread;
A moon-parched grain of purest wheat,
With some small glittering grit to eat
His choice bits with; then in a trice
They make a feast less great than nice.
But all this while his eye is serv'd,
We must not think his ear was starv'd:
But that there was in place to stir
His spleen, the chirring Grasshopper;
The merry Cricket, puling Fly,
The piping Gnat for minstrelsy.
And now, we must imagine first,
The Elves present to quench his thirst
A pure seed-pearl of infant dew,
Brought and besweetened in a blue
And pregnant violet; which done,
His kittenish eyes begin to run
Quite through the table, where he spies

The horns of papery Butterflies,
Of which he eats, and tastes a little
Of what we call the Cuckoo's spittle.
A little puffball pudding stands
By, yet not blessed by his hands,
Thar was too coarse, but then forthwith
He ventures boldly on the pith
Of sugared rush, and eats the sagg
And well bestrutted Bee's sweet bag:
Gladding his palate with some store
Of Emmets' eggs, what would he more?
But beards of Mice, a Newt's stewed thigh,
A Bloated Earwig, and a Fly;
With the red-capped worm, that's shut
Within the concave of a Nut,
Brown as his Tooth, a little Moth,
Late fastened in a piece of cloth:
With withered cherries; Mandrake's ears;
Mole's eyes; to these, the slain-Stag's tears;
The unctuous dewlaps of a Snail;
The broke-heart of a Nightingale
O'ercome in music; with a wine,
Ne'er ravished from the flattering Vine,
But gently pressed from the soft side
Of the most sweet and dainty Bride,
Brought in a dainty daisy, which
He fully quaffs up to bewitch
His blood to height; this done, commended
Grace by his Priest; *The feast is ended.*

THE BROTHERS GRIMM

Household Fairy Tales: 'Cat-Skin', 1812

BUT when the king had ordered a feast to be got ready for the
third time, it happened just the same as before.

'You must be a witch, Cat-skin,' said the Cook; 'for you always
put something into the soup, so that it pleases the king better than
mine.'

However, he let her go up as before. Then she put on the dress which sparkled like the stars, and went into the ball-room in it: and the king danced with her again, and thought she had never looked so beautiful as she did then: so whilst he was dancing with her, he put a gold ring on her finger without her seeing it, and ordered that the dance should be kept up a long time. When it was at an end, he would have held her fast by the hand; but she slipt away and sprang so quickly through the crowd that he lost sight of her: and she ran as fast as she could into her little cabin under the stairs. But this time she kept away too long, and stayed beyond the half-hour; so she had not time to take off her line dress, but threw her fur mantle over it, and in her haste did not soot herself all over, but left one finger white.

Then she ran into the kitchen, and cooked the king's soup; and as soon as the cook was gone, she put the golden brooch into the dish. When the king got to the bottom, he ordered Cat-skin to be called once more, and soon saw the white finger and the ring that he had put upon it whilst they were dancing; so he seized her hand, and kept fast hold of it, and when she wanted to loose herself and spring away, the fur cloak fell off a little on one side, and the starry dress sparkled underneath it. Then he got hold of the fur and tore it off, and her golden hair and beautiful form were seen, and she could no longer hide herself: so she washed the soot and ashes from off her face, and showed herself to be the most beautiful princess upon the face of the earth. But the king said, 'You are my beloved bride, and we will never more be parted from each other.'

RICHARD BARHAM

Ingoldsby Legends: 'The Witches Frolic', 1840

THEN up and spake that sonsie quean,
     And she spake both loud and clear:
'Oh, be it for weal, or be it for woe,
Enter friend, or enter foe,
     Rob Gilpin is welcome here! –

'Now tread we a measure! a hail! a hail!
Now tread we a measure,' quoth she –
     The heart of Robin Beat thick and throbbing –
     'Roving Rob, tread a measure with me!'

'Ay, lassie!' quoth Rob, as her hand he gripes,
'Though Satan himself were blowing the pipes!'

Now around they go, and around, and around,
With hop-skip-and-jump, and frolicsome bound,
    Such sailing and gliding, Such sinking and sliding,
    Such lofty curvetting, And grand pirouetting;
Ned, you would swear that Monsieur Gilbert
And Miss Taglioni were capering there!

And oh! such awful music! ne'er
Fell sounds so uncanny on mortal ear.
There were the tones of a dying man's groans,
Mix'd with the rattling of dead men's bones:
Had you heard the shrieks, and the squeals, and the squeaks,
You'd not have forgotten the sound for weeks.

And around, and around, and around they go,
Heel to heel, and toe to toe,
Prance and caper, curvet and wheel,
Toe to toe, and heel to heel.
''Tis merry, 'tis merry, Cummers, I trow,
To dance thus beneath the nightshade bough!' –
'Goody Price, Goody Price, now riddle me right;
Where may we sup this frolicsome night?'

'Mine host of the Dragon hath mutton and veal!
The Squire hath partridge, and widgeon, and teal,
But old Sir Thopas hath daintier cheer,
A pasty made of the good red deer,
A huge grouse pie, and a fine Florentine,
A fat roast goose, and a turkey and chine.

Part Three

REVELRY

'*Unrhymed, unrythmical, the chatter goes . . .*'

W. H. AUDEN

'At the Party', 1962

UNRHYMED, unrhythmical, the chatter goes:
Yet no one hears his own remarks as prose.

Beneath each topic tunelessly discussed
The ground-bass is reciprocal mistrust.

The names in fashion shuttling to and fro
Yield, when deciphered, messages of woe.

You cannot read me like an open book.

I'm more myself than you will ever look.

Will no one listen to my little song?

Perhaps I shan't be with you very long.

A howl for recognition, shrill with fear,
Shakes the jam-packed apartment, but each ear
Is listening to its hearing, so none hear.

W. M. MALLOCK

The New Republic, 1877

LAURENCE, though he had forewarned his guests of his *menu*
before they left the drawing-room, yet felt a little anxious when
they sat down to dinner; for he found it not altogether easy to get

the conversation started. Lady Ambrose, who was the first to speak, began somewhat off the point.

'What a charming change it is, Mr Laurence,' she said, 'to look out on the sea when one is dressing, instead of across South Audley Street!'

'Hush!' said Laurence softly, with a grave, reproving smile.

'Really,' said Lady Ambrose, 'I beg your pardon. I thought Dr Jenkinson had said grace.'

'If he has,' said Laurence, 'it is very good of him, for I am afraid he was not asked. But what I mean is, that you must only talk of what is on the cards; so be good enough to look at your *menu*, and devote your attention to the Aim of Life.'

'Really, this is much too alarming,' said Lady Ambrose. 'How is one to talk at so short a notice on a subject one has never thought about before?'

'Why, to do so,' said Laurence, 'is the very art of conversation; for in that way, one's ideas spring up fresh like young roses that have all the dew on them, instead of having been kept drying for half a lifetime between the leaves of a book. So do set a good example, and begin, or else we shall never be started at all; and my pet plan will turn out a fiasco.'

There was, indeed, as Laurence said this, something very near complete silence all round the table. It was soon broken.

'Are you High-church or Low-church?' was a question suddenly uttered in a quick eager girl's voice by Miss Prattle, a young lady of eighteen, to the astonishment of the whole company. It was addressed to Dr Jenkinson who was sitting next her.

Had a pin been run into the Doctor's leg, he could not have looked more astounded, or given a greater start. He eyed his fair questioner for some time in complete silence.

'Can you tell me the difference?'

SIDNEY SMITH

Snatches of Table-talk, date unknown

'MACAULAY improves. I have observed in him, of late, flashes of silence.'

'There was Hallam, his mouth full of cabbage and contradiction.'

'Those eminent Dissenters – Shadrach, Meshek and Abednego.'

'I heard Jeffrey speak disrepectfully of the Equator!'

'Birmingham – a place of loud noises and bad smells.'

'What ideas are more inseparable than beer and Britannia?'

'When Rogers the banker gave dinner he had all the candles placed on high the better to show off his pictures but casting his guests in a groping gloom. Smith remarked, "Above, there is a blaze of light but below, nothing but night and a gnashing of teeth".'

'She looked as if she had walked straight out of the Ark.'

'He began to fumble for his brains.'

'His talk is mere pothooks and hangers.'

'Madam, I have been looking for a person who disliked gravy all my life: let us swear eternal friendship.'

'Let onions lurk within the bowl
And, scarce suspected, animate the whole.'

'Serenely full, the epicure would say,
Fate cannot harm me – I have dined today.'

WILLIAM SHAKESPEARE

Antony and Cleopatra, 1606–7

Act I, Scene VII

On board POMPEY'S *Galley, lying near* MISENUM.

Music. Enter two or three Servants, *with a banquet.*

1. SERV. Here they'll be, man. Some o' their plants are ill-rooted already; the least wind i' the world will blow them down.

2 SERV. Lepidus is high-coloured.

1 SERV. They have made him drink alms-drink.

2 SERV. As they pinch one another by the disposition, he cries out. 'No more;' reconciles them to his entreaty, and himself to the drink.

1 SERV. But it raises the greater war between him and his discretion.

2 SERV. Why, this it is to have a name in great men's fellowship: I had as lief have a reed that will do me no service, as a partisan I could not heave.

1 SERV. To be called into a huge sphere, and not to be seen to move in 't, are the holes where eyes should be, which pitifully disaster the cheeks.

A sennet sounded. Enter CAESAR, ANTONY, LEPIDUS, POMPEY, AGRIPPA, MECAENAS, ENOBARBUS, MENAS, *with other* CAPTAINS.

Ant. [*To* CAESAR.] Thus do they, Sir: they take the flow o' the Nile
By certain scales i' the pyramid; they know,
By the height, the lowness, or the mean, if dearth,
Or foison, follow: the higher Nilus swells,
The more it promises; as it ebbs, the seedsman
Upon the slime and ooze scatters his grain,
And shortly comes to harvest.

LEP. You have strange serpents there.

ANT.   Ay, Lepidus.

LEP. Your serpent of Egypt is bred, now, of your mud by the operation of your sun: so is your crocodile.

ANT. They are so.

POM. Sit, – and some wine! – A health to Lepidus.

LEP. I am not so well as I should be, but I'll ne'er out.

ENO. Not till you have slept; I fear me, you'll be in till then.

LEP. Nay, certainly, I have heard, the Ptolemies' pyramises are very goodly things; without contradiction, I have heard that.

MEN. [*Aside to* POM.] Pompey, a word.

POM. [*Aside to* MEN.] Say in mine ear: what is't?

MEN. [*Aside to* POM.] Forsake thy seat, I do beseech thee, captain,
And hear me speak a word.

POM. [*Aside to* MEN.] Forbear me till anon. –
This wine for Lepidus.

LEP. What manner o' thing is your crocodile?

ANT. It is shaped, Sir, like itself; and it is as broad as it hath breadth; it is just so high as it is, and moves with its own organs; it lives by that which nourisheth it; and the elements once out of it, it transmigrates.

LEP. What colour is it of?

ANT. Of its own colour too.

LEP. 'Tis a strange serpent.

ANT. 'Tis so: and the tears of it are wet.

EDITH SITWELL

The English Eccentrics: 'Porson, a Tiresome Guest', 1933

YET, in earlier life, who more gallant than the Professor, who more assiduous in their attentions to the Fair? It is rumoured, indeed, that he once carried a young lady round the room in his teeth. But that was before dinner, and after dinner, the Professor, though equally manly, was less urbane. Indeed Mr Timbs tells us that, whilst at Cambridge, 'his passion for smoking, which was then going out among the younger generation, his large and indiscriminate potations, and his occasional use of the poker with a very refractory controversialist, had caused his company to be shunned by all except the few to whom his wit and scholarship were irresistible'. Apparently, the gifts in question did not always prove irresistible to the Fellows of Trinity, who when the use of the poker seemed imminent, would slink out of the Common Room, and leave the Professor sitting at the table, emitting no sign of life excepting a perpetual eruption of smoke. In the morning, the servants were accustomed to seeing him sitting where he had been left, with no appearance of having moved, even once, during his night-long vigil.

These vigils became a source of anxiety in the houses which the Professor frequented, and it became necessary, at last, for the sake of preserving the health and sanity of the hosts, that the Professor should be told that he must never stay to a later hour than eleven. He showed no resentment at this mandate, but kept the agreement, honourably, and to the letter. But, 'though he never attempted to exceed the hour limited, he would never stir before', and woe betide the host who suggested such a breach of faith. But this state of affairs did not extend to every house, or to every host, and there were houses in which the Professor behaved like a lion rampant. The unfortunate Mr Horne Tooke, for instance, was one of Professor Porson's unhappier hosts, for he was foolish enough to invite the Professor to dine with him on a night that he knew had been preceded by three nights in which the Professor had refused all entreaties on the part of his hosts that he should go home to bed. Mr Tooke thought, therefore, that Professor Porson would relent on this occasion. But the night wore on, and Mr Tooke was worn out, for the Professor became more and more animated, passing from one learned theme to another. The poker was out of sight and out of mind, but insensibility, at any costs, might have been preferred.

Dawn broke, the birds sang, the milkmen shouted, the Professor continued his monologue. At last, in mid morning, the exhausted Mr Tooke proclaimed that he had an engagement to meet a friend for breakfast in a coffee-house at Leicester Square. The Professor was delighted, and announced that he would come too. But in the end, Providence came to the rescue of Mr Tooke and, soon after the Professor and he were seated in the coffee-house, the Professor's attention was distracted for an instant, and Mr Tooke, seizing the opportunity, fled as fast as his legs would carry him, nor did he pause for breath until he had reached Richmond Buildings. Having reached this haven of refuge, he barricaded himself in, and ordered his servant not to admit the Professor even if he should attempt to batter down the door. For 'a man', Mr Tooke observed, 'who could sit up four nights successively, could sit up forty'.

RENATA ADLER

Speedboat, 1971

JUST two nights ago, I went to a party with three large dinner tables. It was mixed, the rich and famous and the reporters who had helped them on their way. There were some intellectual sharks, some arrivistes, some sheep, good souls, professors, editors, some radicals, who themselves invite poets, novelists, sophomore rioters, and visiting Englishmen to dinner, which is served by maids. This party was given to two kind, intelligent Americans I knew from college. They wanted to do good and to *know*, like people out of E. M. Forster or Henry James. The purpose was for the senator of an American liberal state and an Indian dignitary, a woman, to meet a cross section of American opinion. They met it. The first course was aspic. The dignitary thought somebody was going to attack her for Indian educational policies in Kerala. No one knew anything about India at all. She relaxed and grew bored. The senator thought he was going to meet the young and learn about them. I was sitting next to him. I said I thought he and I might be among the last three people in the room who still believed in the electoral process. He said, 'Thanks, sweetheart.'

Suddenly, after dessert, a lady at my table – a donor to controversial social causes now half persuaded to devote her money to the cause of saving art – said she thought the dinner would be wasted if the conversation did not become general, if it was all private bon mots spliced together, or just gossip. She thought we ought to talk about America today. She called first on one of those social academics, a man who had *vécu* a bit, whose bow tie was perpetually atilt, perhaps to show himself at an eccentric angle to the dinner jackets that he wore, what they implied. He rose, red-faced and angry, to his feet. He said he felt this country now was the world's most murderous and corrupt. He happened to know, he said, of two deaths at Kent State that had not been reported, and of other grave matters he was not at liberty to disclose. He felt the only hope for humanity now lay in the vitality and idealism of the third world.

The lady who led the discussion, unperturbed, asked a tireless, self-effacing worker in the cause of civil rights whether he had anything to say 'about all this'. He leaned his head against the wall, then stood up. 'Bertram,' he said. 'I am so offended by what you have just said. I don't know what to say to you.' He sat down. The lady called upon a poet, a surrealist who, with clear reluctance got to his feet and said, turning to the Indian lady, 'I think in this country we need to disburden ourselves of our, our burden of rationality.' He sat down. It did not seem exactly India's problem.

LAURENCE STERNE
A Sentimental Journey, 1768

MONS. le Count de B****, merely because he had done me one kindness in the affair of my passport, would go on and do me another, the few days he was at Paris, in making me known to a few people of rank; and they were to present me to others, and so on.

I had got master of my *secret* just in time to turn these honours to some little account; otherwise, as is commonly the case, I should have dined or supped a single time or two round, and then by *translating* French looks and attitudes into plain English, I should presently have seen, that I had got hold of the *couvert* of some more entertaining guest; and in course, should have resigned all my places one after another, merely upon the principle that I could not keep them. – As it was, things did not go much amiss.

I had the honour of being introduced to the old Marquis de B****:
in days of yore he had signalized himself by some small feats of
chivalry in the *Cour d'amour*, and had dressed himself out to the
idea of tilts and tournaments ever since – the Marquis de B****
wished to have it thought the affair was somewhere else than in his
brain. 'He could like to take a trip to England,' and asked much of
the English ladies. Stay where you are, I beseech you, Mons. le
Marquis, said I— Les Messrs. Anglois can scarce get a kind look
from them as it is. – The Marquis invited me to supper.

Mons. P**** the farmer-general, was just as inquisitive about our
taxes – They were very considerable, he heard – If we knew but how
to collect them, said I, making him a low bow.

I could never have been invited to Mons. P****'s concerts upon
any other terms.

I had been misrepresented to Madame de Q**** as an *esprit* –
Madame de Q**** was an *esprit* herself; she burnt with impatience
to see me, and hear me talk. I had not taken my seat, before I saw
she did not care a sous whether I had any wit or no – I was let in, to
be convinced she had. – I call heaven to witness I never once opened
the door of my lips.

Madame de Q**** vowed to every creature she met, 'She had
never had a more improving conversation with a man in her life.'

There are three epochas in the empire of a French woman – She is
coquette – then deist – then *devôte*: the empire during these is never
lost – she only changes her subjects: when thirty-five years and
more have unpeopled her dominions of the slaves of love, she re-
peoples it with slaves of infidelity – and then with the slaves of the
Church.

Madame de V*** was vibrating betwixt the first of these epochas:
the colour of the rose was shading fast away – she ought to have
been a deist five years before the time I had the honour to pay my
first visit.

She placed me upon the same sopha with her, for the sake of
disputing the point of religion more closely – In short, Madame de
V*** told me she believed nothing.

I told Madame de V*** it might be her principle; but I was sure
it could not be her interest to level the outworks, without which I
could not conceive how such a citadel as hers could be defended –
that there was not a more dangerous thing in the world, than for a
beauty to be a deist – that it was a debt I owed my creed, not to
conceal it from her – that I had not been five minutes sat upon the

sopha besides her, but I had begun to form designs – and what is it, but the sentiments of religion, and the persuasion they had existed in her breast, which could have checked them as they rose up?

We are not adamant, said I, taking hold of her hand – and there is need of all restraints, till age in her own time steals in and lays them on us – but, my dear lady, said I, kissing her hand – 'tis too – too soon –

I declare I had the credit all over Paris of unperverting Madame de V***. – She affirmed to Mons. D*** and the Abbé M***, that in one half hour I had said more for revealed religion, than all their Encyclopedia had said against it – I was listed directly into Madame de V***'s *Coterie* – and she put off the epocha of deism for two years.

I remember it was in this *Coterie*, in the middle of a discourse, in which I was shewing the necessity of a *first cause*, that the young Count de Faineant took me by the hand to the furthest corner of the room, to tell me my *solitaire* was pinned too straight about my neck – It should be *plus badinant*, said the Count, looking down upon his own – but a word, Mons. Yorick, *to the wise* –

– And from the wise, Mons. le Count, replied I, making him a bow – *is enough*.

The Count de Faineant embraced me with more ardour than ever I was embraced by mortal man.

For three weeks together, I was of every man's opinion I met. – *Pardil ce Mons. Yorick a autant d'esprit que nous autres. – Il raisonne bien*, said another. – *C'est un bon enfant*, said a third. – And at this price I could have eaten and drank and been merry all the days of my life at Paris; but 'twas a dishonest *reckoning* – I grew ashamed of it – it was the gain of a slave – every sentiment of honour revolted against it – the higher I got, the more I was forced upon my *beggarly system* – the better the *Coterie* – the more children of Art – I languished for those of Nature: and one night after a most vile prostitution of myself to half a dozen different people, I grew sick – went to bed – ordered La Fleur to get me horses in the morning to set out for Italy.

T. S. ELIOT
The Cocktail Party, 1950

JULIA. Is that her Aunt Laura?

EDWARD.   No; another aunt
    Whom you wouldn't know. Her mother's sister
    And rather a recluse.

JULIA.   Her favourite aunt?

EDWARD. Her aunt's favourite niece. And she's rather difficult.
    When she's ill, she insists on having Lavinia.

JULIA. I never heard of her being ill before.

EDWARD. No, she's always very strong. That's why when she's ill
   She gets into a panic.

JULIA.   And sends for Lavinia.
    I quite understand. Are there any prospects?

EDWARD. No, I think she put it all into an annuity.

JULIA. So it's very unselfish of Lavinia
    Yet very like her. But really, Edward,
    Lavinia may be away for weeks,
    Or she may come back and be called away again.
    I understand these tough old women –
    I'm one myself. I feel as if I knew
    All about that aunt in Hampshire.

EDWARD.   Hampshire?

JULIA. Didn't you say Hampshire?

EDWARD.   No, I didn't say Hampshire.

JULIA. Did you say Hampstead?

EDWARD.   No, I didn't say Hampstead.

JULIA. But she must live somewhere.

EDWARD.   She lives in Essex.

JULIA. Anywhere near Colchester? Lavinia loves oysters.

EDWARD. No. In the *depths* of Essex.

KINGSLEY AMIS
Take a Girl Like You, 1960

IN the same direction through the crowds of people, who seemed
to have doubled in numbers since she rushed upstairs to Patrick.
The new ones had perhaps had a long way to come, and that would
have been understandable, because you could hardly hope to get
together fifty people of so much the same sort, and the sort they
were, just from round about. They were all throwing themselves into
enjoying themselves, both sexes with half-closed eyes and half-open
mouths, but the women with their mouths in something like smiles,
the men with theirs in a loose O that brought the lower lip a little
forward, as in pictures of men who knew the Royal Family. The way
they held their drinks and cigarettes was different, too: the women
had their hands apart as if they had just finished a French shrug, the
men in the position of a boxer whose guard has begun to drop. But
the enjoyment thing was the same with both, reminding Jenny of TV
commercials that showed how frantic a party could get on prune
juice or chocolate biscuits, only these people would have been a bit
old for anything like that.

CARL van VECHTEN
Parties, 1930

HAMISH had been to a tea, as cocktail parties are still
occasionally called in New York, for the great English novelist,
attended by most of the local literati. The visiting celebrity talked a
great deal about himself, his plots and plans, and the others talked a
great deal about themselves, their plots and plans. Fortunately,
nobody listened to anybody else. Hamish left this house to drift, by
way of taxi, into another cocktail party given for a lady who had
left society to become an actress by an actress who had given up the
stage to become a lady. They both explained why at great length,
although everybody had heard the story many times before. But that
was quite all right because again nobody listened. With a Negro
poet and Gareth Johns, the novelist, whom he encountered at this
party, Hamish went on to an apartment in Harlem where the drinks
were better and the guests more attractive-looking, but he was still

restless and an hour or so later, he drove down through the Park
and went to a fourth party in Gramercy Park where he ran into
Noma Ridge.

Hello, Hamish, she accosted him, you must begin to believe that
I'm pursuing you.

Well, aren't you? he inquired.

Not particularly. I don't mind telling you I think you're wonderful.
I think you're swell.

There's music to that, Hamish retorted.

I know, Noma assented impatiently. Do stop talking nonsense.
It's David I want.

Oh, that's your line, is it?

It's part of my line. Not the best part, perhaps. I'd like to tell
you . . .

I'm sure you would. Everybody's been telling me all the afternoon.
Why?

You know perfectly well why, but we can't talk here. Let's run
over to Donald's.

Where it's more public.

That's what I mean. Nobody will listen to us here. It's a waste of
time talking before these people.

At the Wishbone, however, it developed that Noma must have
been speaking ironically, as she asked for a private room.

That's easy, Donald assured her. The private rooms are always
empty. My customers are exhibitionists.

Ushered into a small green chamber, they seated themselves side by
side on a couch, crossed their legs decorously, and Hamish proceeded
to attack the drink that red-headed Freddie provided for him.

JEREMY TAYLOR
Sermons, 1653

IT is certain, great knowledge, if it be without vanity, is the most
severe bridle of the tongue. For so have I heard, that all the noises
and prating of the pool, the croaking of frogs and toads, is hushed
and appeased upon the instant of bringing upon them the light of a
candle or torch. Every beam of reason, and ray of knowledge, checks
the dissolutions of the tongue.

WILLIAM GERHARDIE
My Sinful Earth, 1947

FROM time to time the butler appeared on the threshold, announcing the guests as they came up the steps; and presently he ceased announcing, and at a sign they all trooped down again to dinner. As the footman pushed up the chair behind him, Frank began to take his dispositions. In a moment of periodical unemployment when both his partners were engaged in conversations, he would prick his ears – for he was curious about his fellow men – and listen. Admiral Battersea was saying in his hoarse, sea-grunting way to the pretty, dark-eyed woman at his side: 'The Prince of Wales, I hear, kept very fit during the trip by taking a great deal of exercise.'

He found Lord de Jones at his side peculiarly congenial. Did he know the Kerrs? Didn't he! Eva? 'The darling!' said de Jones. And Mrs Kerr?

Lord de Jones's silence seemed to hold a lot.

'She craved for impossible things,' Dickin suggested.

'And she got them,' said de Jones.

'What she wanted.'

'Exactly what she wanted. They were Impossible.'

They covered many a familiar plane – Russia, Vienna, the Tyrol. 'Did you know her father?' asked de Jones. 'I went out to Russia as a young man. I was taken to their country place by him. She had just got married. Lovely. She was lovely then; really lovely. Just like Eva now. If I'd known her three days earlier she wouldn't have married Kerr.' He was pensive. 'Eva might have been my daughter.' He stopped, as if realizing the superfluity of his reflections. 'It doesn't matter now. Nothing matters now. A journey with her round the world. And then – the *coup de grâce*! It is finished . . .' The butler was removing his plate. He looked ironically at Frank. 'It is finished,' he said, a strange light in his greenish eyes.

'Would you mind it awfully?' he asked Frank.

'What?'

'If I were to end it all.'

'How do you mean?'

'At a stroke. The world and its suffering.'

'But I thought you were concerned to grow more wheat.'
'Wheat!' said de Jones, drinking lugubriously. 'Wheat!'

ANGUS WILSON

Anglo-Saxon Attitudes, 1956

HE addressed himself aggressively to Robin as they awaited the
arrival of the first guests. He was one business tycoon to
another. It was not at all what Robin cared for in Marie Hélène's
lovely gold and white Regency drawing-room, where the arts were
intended to exercise a rather genteel, flattened out, *convenable*
supremacy.

'What's your wastage, Middleton?' Yves asked, and before Robin
could inquire the meaning of this somewhat cryptic question, he
followed it up with a machine-gun fire of searching business questions intended to flatten Robin out, lay him stone dead with their
ruthless drive, their dead-hit punch, their incredible grasp of detail.
'What do your absentee figures show?' he asked. 'What's your
pension load? Have you got a record of your pay-out in widows'
benefits? Where's your man-hours production graph taking you?
What's your loss in toilet time?' These and many other questions
which had once so depressed him from an American colleague in the
air force he now worked off on Robin and, without waiting for a
reply, he cried, 'Good God! man, a guy's *got* to ask himself these
questions. You need an efficiency expert to give your place the
works.' And when Robin looked dejected, he patted him on the
elbow. 'That's all right,' he said, 'your worries are over. From today
you're going to be lucky. I'm going to save Middletons thousands.'

Marie Hélène, tightly swathed in crimson velvet, her bosom deadly
yellow as a Japanese corpse's beneath the fires of her opal necklace,
held up her hand in horror. 'No business talk, Yves, please,' she
cried. 'You will ruin my *soirée*.' And in hard flat tones, she said, 'Do
you think that Anouilh is *passé*? I find a terrible lack of *esprit* in his
last play. I'm afraid he has quite lost his elegance.' She gave it to him
as a copy-book model for the evening.

WALTER DE LA MARE

'The Feckless Dinner-Party', 1933

'WHO are we waiting for?' '*Soup* burnt?' '... Eight – '
  'Only the tiniest party. – Us!'
'Darling! Divine!' 'Ten minutes late – '
  'And my digest – ' 'I'm *rav*enous!'
'"Toomes"?' – 'Oh, he's new.' 'Looks crazed, I guess.'
  '"Married" – *Again*!' 'Well; more or less!'

'Dinner is *served*!' '"Dinner is served"!'
  'Is served?' 'Is served.' 'Ah, yes.'

'Dear Mr. Prout, will you take down
  The Lilith in leaf-green by the fire?
Blanche Ogleton? . . .' 'How coy a frown! –
  Hasn't she borrowed *Eve's* attire?'
'Morose Old Adam!' 'Charmed – I vow.'
  'Come then, and meet her now.'

'Now, Dr. Mallus – would you please? –
  Our daring poetess, Delia Seek?'
'The lady with the bony knees?'
  'And – *entre nous* – less song than beak.'
'Sharing her past with Simple Si – '
  '*Bare* facts! He'll blush!' 'Oh, fie!'

'And *you*, Sir Nathan – false but fair! –
  That fountain of wit, Aurora Pert.'
'More wit than It, poor dear! But there . . .'
  'Pitiless Pacha! *And* such a flirt!'
'"Flirt"! *Me?*' 'Who else?' 'You here . . . Who can . . .?'
  'In*corr*igible man!'

'And now, Mr. Simon – little me! –
  Last and – ' 'By no means least!' 'Oh, come!
What naughty, naughty flattery!

  Honey! – I *hear* the creature hum!'
'Sweets for the sweet, *I* always say!'
  '"Always"?. . . We're last.' '*This* way?' . . .

'No, sir; straight on, please.' 'I'd have vowed! –
  I came the other . . .' 'It's queer; I'm sure . . .'

'What frightful pictures!' 'Fiends!' 'The *crowd*!'
   'Such nudes!' 'I can't endure . . .'

'Yes, *there* they go.' 'Heavens! *Are* we right?'
   'Follow up closer!' ' "Prout"? – sand-blind!'
'This endless . . .' 'Who's turned down the light?'
   'Keep calm! They're close behind.'

'Oh! Dr. Mallus; what dismal stairs!'
   'I hate these old Victor . . .' 'Dry rot!'
'Darker and darker!' 'Fog!' 'The air's . . .'
   'Scarce breathable!' 'Hell!' '*What?*'

'The bannister's gone!' 'It's deep; keep close!'
   'We're going down and down!' 'What fun!'
'Damp! Why, my shoes . . .' 'It's slimy . . . Not *moss!*'
   'I'm freezing cold!' 'Let's run.'

'. . . Behind us. I'm giddy . . .' 'The catacombs . . .'
   'That shout!' 'Who's there?' 'I'm *alone!*' 'Stand back!'
'She said, Lead . . .' 'Oh!' 'Where's Toomes?' '*Toomes!*'
   'TOOMES!'
   'Stifling!' 'My skull will crack!'

'Sir Nathan! *Ai!*' 'I *say! Toomes!* Prout!'
   'Where? Where?' ' "Our silks and fine array" . . .'
'She's mad.' 'I'm dying!' 'Oh, Let me *out!*'
   'My God! We've lost our way!' . . .

And now how sad-serene the abandoned house,
Whereon at dawn the spring-tide sunbeams beat;
And time's slow pace alone is ominous,
And naught but shadows of noonday therein meet;
Domestic microcosm, only a Trump could rouse:
And, pondering darkly, in the silent rooms,
He who misled them all – the butler, Toomes.

ELIZABETH GASKELL

The Life of Charlotte Brontë, 1857

THE evening after I left you passed better than I expected. Thanks to my substantial lunch and cheering cup of coffee, I was able to wait the eight o'clock dinner with complete resignation, and to endure its length quite courageously, nor was I too much exhausted to converse; and of this I was glad, for otherwise I know my kind host and hostess would have been much disappointed. There were only seven gentlemen at dinner besides Mr Smith, but of these five were critics – men more dreaded in the world of letters than you can conceive. I did not know how much their presence and conversation had excited me till they were gone, and the reaction commenced. When I had retired for the night, I wished to sleep – the effort to do so was vain. I could not close my eyes. Night passed; morning came, and I rose without having known a moment's slumber. So utterly worn out was I when I got to Derby, that I was again obliged to stay there all night.

PHILIP LARKIN

'Vers de Société', 1971

MY *wife and I have asked a crowd of craps*
To come and waste their time and ours: perhaps
You'd care to join us? In a pig's arse, friend.
Day comes to an end.
The gas fire breathes, the trees are darkly swayed.
And so *Dear Warlock-Williams: I'm afraid* –

Funny how hard it is to be alone
I could spend half my evenings, if I wanted,
Holding a glass of washing sherry, canted
Over to catch the drivel of some bitch
Who's read nothing but *Which*;
Just think of all the spare time that has flown

Straight into nothingness by being filled
With forks and faces, rather than repaid
Under a lamp, hearing the noise of wind.

And looking out to see the moon thinned
To an air-sharpened blade.
A life, and yet how sternly it's instilled

All solitude is selfish. No one now
Believes the hermit with his gown and dish
Talking to God (who's gone too); the big wish
Is to have people nice to you, which means
Doing it back somehow.
Virtue is social. Are, then, these routines

Playing at goodness, like going to church?
Something that bores us, something we don't do well
(Asking that ass about his fool research)
But try to feel, because, however crudely,
It shows us what should be?
Too subtle, that. Too decent, too. Oh hell.

Only the young can be alone freely.
The time is shorter now for company,
And sitting by a lamp more often brings
Not peace, but other things.
Beyond the light stand failure and remorse
Whispering *Dear Warlock-Williams: Why, of course –*

RONALD FIRBANK

Inclinations, 1916

THE 'intimate' dinner arranged by Mrs Collins in honour of her elder daughter promised to be a large one. Covers for twenty guests, at a table to hold eighteen, insured nevertheless a touch of welcome snugness. In the crepuscular double drawing-room, commanding the eternal moors, county society, as it assembled, exchanged cheery greetings. It was indeed to all intents the Doncaster Meeting lot.

Discanting away from homely topics, Sir Harry Ortop had just seen a fox, it seemed, crossing Cockaway Common, while Miss Rosalba Roggers had passed a traction-engine in the Rectory Lane. 'Horrid thing; but the Scarboro' road is really a disgrace,' she pronounced, turning her attention to an angular beauty clad in sugary pink and a crown of birds' feathers.

Holding forth in a quizzical, hoarse-sweet voice, she was arraigning her husband with indescribable archness: 'He always gets into his carriage first, and then half shuts the door on you!'

Momentous in his butlerhood, Queen, supported by an extra footman, announced each new advent with an air of serene detachment.

Mr Napier Fairmile, Miss Nespole—

Entering on the heels of the former inamorato of the Countess sailed a mite of a woman enveloped fancifully in a fairy-hued cashmere shawl. The Cyclopean chatelaine of Cupingforth Castle, and one of the wealthiest women in the Riding, she was held, by local opinion, to be eccentric for preferring to live all alone, which may possibly have had its dangers for a person of her condition and sex; nevertheless, on occasion, to convince an intrusive stranger she had a male in the house, she would discharge a cartridge out of window, and knot her hair across her chin in front in a thick cascade to imitate *a beard*.

Lady Watercarriage, The Hon. Viola West-Wind, Captain Margaret-Baker—

Quite revitalised, performing her duties, Mrs Collins circulated smilingly here and there. Throwing a veil of glamour upon each guest, she had introduced Miss Dawkins twice as 'The Great Traveller'.

'I ain't going back to Australia not yet awhile. That is so!' Miss Dawkins declared, recognising across the Rector's shoulder in the damp-stained mezzotints upon the walls some views of popular thoroughfares her foot had trodden – Trafalgar Square, the Place de la Concorde, the Piazza Colonna, the Puerta del Sol. 'If I don't just spit at them!' she commented, idly opening and closing her fan.

The Farquhar of Farquhar, Mrs Lampsacus of Gisborough Park—

Already a full quarter of an hour late, they were yet not the last.

Masticating, chewing the air, Mr Collins appeared to have become involved against his will in the esoteric confidences of a pair of expansive matrons: 'In York I saw some very pretty . . . I enquired the price . . . Would you believe . . . *Need* I say I bought them!'

RADCLYFFE HALL
The Unlit Lamp, 1924

AS she sat down by Mrs Ogden, her bright brown eyes looked inquisitively round the room, resting for an instant on the admiral's portrait, and then on the relics upon the occasional table. Mrs Ogden watched her, secretly triumphant.

'Dear Lady Loo. How good of you to come to our little gathering. *My* Day I call it – very foolish of me – but after all— Oh, yes, how very kind of you— But then, why rob your hothouses for poor little me? You forgot to bring them? Oh, never mind, it's the thought that counts, is it not? Your speaking of peaches makes me feel quite homesick for Chesham – we had such acres of glass at Chesham! – Yes, that is Joan – come here, Joan dear! Naughty child, she will insist on keeping her hair short. You think it suits her? Really? Clever? Well – run away, Joan darling – yes, frankly, very clever, so Miss Rodney thinks. Attractive? You think so? Now fancy, my husband always thinks Milly is the pretty one. Shall I ask Joan to recite or shall Milly play first? What do you think? Joan first, oh, all right – Joan, dear!'

The dreaded moment had arrived; Joan, shy and awkward, floundered through her recitation.

MARCEL PROUST
Swann in Love, 1922

'WHAT are all those good people laughing at over there? There's no sign of brooding melancholy down in your corner,' shouted Mme Verdurin. 'You don't suppose I find it very amusing to be stuck up here by myself on the stool of repentance,' she went on peevishly, like a spoiled child.

Mme Verdurin was sitting upon a high Swedish chair of waxed pinewood, which a violinist from that country had given her, and which she kept in her drawing-room, although in appearance it suggested a school 'form,' and 'swore,' as the saying is, at the really good antique furniture which she had besides; but she made a point of keeping on view the presents which her 'faithful' were in the habit of making her from time to time, so that the donors might have the pleasure of seeing them there when they came to the house. She tried to persuade them to confine their tributes to flowers and sweets, which had at least the merit of mortality; but she was never successful, and the house was gradually filled with a collection of foot-warmers, cushions, clocks, screens, barometers and vases, a constant repetition and a boundless incongruity of useless but indestructable objects.

From this lofty perch she would take her spirited part in the conversation of the 'faithful,' and would revel in all their fun; but, since the accident to her jaw, she had abandoned the effort involved in real hilarity, and had substituted a kind of symbolical dumb-show which signified, without endangering or even fatiguing her in any way, that she was 'laughing until she cried'. At the least witticism aimed by any of the circle against a 'bore', or against a former member of the circle who was now relegated to the limbo of 'bores' – and to the utter despair of M. Verdurin, who had always made out that he was just as easily amused as his wife, but who, since his laughter was the 'real thing', was out of breath in a moment, and so was overtaken and vanquished by her device of a feigned but continuous hilarity – she would utter a shrill cry, shut tight her little bird-like eyes, which were beginning to be clouded over by a cataract, and quickly, as though she had only just time to avoid some indecent sight or to parry a mortal blow, burying her face in her hands, which completely engulfed it, and prevented her from seeing anything at all, she would appear to be struggling to suppress, to eradicate a laugh which, were she to give way to it, must inevitably leave her inanimate. So, stupefied with the gaiety of the 'faithful', drunken with comradeship, scandal and asseveration, Mme Verdurin, perched on her high seat like a cage-bird whose biscuit has been steeped in mulled wine, would sit aloft and sob with fellow-feeling.

Meanwhile M. Verdurin, after first asking Swann's permission to light his pipe ('No ceremony here, you understand; we're all pals!'), went and begged the young musician to sit down at the piano.

MALCOLM BRADBURY

The History Man, 1975

'I'M in a hang-up,' says Felicity. 'I'm tired of being lesbian. I'd like to be with a man.' 'You were very anti-male last time we talked,' says Howard. 'Oh, last time we talked,' says Felicity, 'that was *last term.* I was coming to terms with my sexuality then. But now I've found that my sexuality isn't the one I've come to terms with, if you can see what I mean.' 'Oh, I can,' says Howard. 'Well, that shouldn't be a problem.' 'Oh, it is, Dr Kirk, Howard,' says Felicity Phee. 'You see, the girl I'm with, Maureen, says it's reactionary. She says I'm collapsing into a syndrome of subservience. She says I have a slave mentality.' 'She does,' says Howard. 'Yes,' says Felicity, 'and, I mean, I couldn't do something reactionary, could I?' 'Oh, no, Felicity,' says Howard. 'So what would you do?' says Felicity. 'I mean, if you were me, and belonged to an oppressed sex.' 'I'd do what I wanted to,' says Howard. 'Maureen throws shoes at me. She says I'm an Uncle Tom. I had to talk to you. I said to myself, I have to talk to *him.*' 'Look, Felicity,' says Howard, 'there's only one rule. Follow the line of your own desires. Don't accept other people's versions, unless you believe them true. Isn't that right?' 'Oh Howard,' says Felicity, kissing him on the cheek, 'you're marvellous. You give such good advice.' Howard says: 'That's because it so closely resembles what people want to hear.' 'No, it's because you're wise,' says Felicity. 'Oh, boy, do I need a flat male chest for a change.'

He goes through into the kitchen. It is filled with people; a male human leg protrudes from under the table. A baby lies asleep in a carrycot on top of the refrigerator. 'Is it your view that there is a constant entity definable as virtue?' asks the Pakistani thought leader of the advanced priest, in front of the globular wallpaper. The record player roars; the booming decibels, the yelps of a youthful pop group on heat, bounce round the house. Howard takes some of the bottles of wine, dark red in the glass, and uncorks them. A stout, maternal girl comes into the kitchen and picks up a baby's bottle, which has been warming in a saucepan on the cooker. She tries the contents by squirting them delicately onto her brown arm. 'Oh, shit,' she says. 'Who's Hegel?' says a voice; Howard looks up, and it is the bra-less girl who had come to his office that morning. 'Someone who . . .' says Howard. 'It's Howard,' says Myra Beamish, standing beside him, her wig tipped slightly to one side, laughing enormously. She has her arm around Dr Macintosh, who still holds his bottle. 'Oh, Howard, you give great parties,' she says. 'Is it going well?' asks Howard. 'Oh, great,' says Myra, 'they're playing "Who am I?" in the living-room. And "What are the students going to do next?" in the dining-room. And "I gave birth at three and at five I was up and typing my thesis" in the hall.' 'There's also a thing called "Was it good for you, too, baby?" in the guest bedroom,' says Macintosh. 'It sounds like the description of a reasonable kind of party,' says Howard. 'How does someone as beastly as you manage to make life so nice for us?' asks Myra. 'It's zap,' says Howard. 'It's zing,' says Myra. 'It's zoom,' says Macintosh.

Howard picks up the new bottle, and returns to the living-room. He bears the libation about, hoping for transfiguration to follow. 'Is his vasectomy reversible or not?' asks someone.

MURIEL SPARK

The Bachelors, 1960

ISOBEL Billows's house was in a newly smartened street at World's End which lies at that other end of Chelsea. The walls and ceiling of her drawing-room were papered in a dull red and black design. She was giving a cocktail party. Isobel had been three years divorced from her husband and always said to her new friends 'I was the innocent party,' which they did not doubt, and the very statement of which proved, to some of her friends, that she was so in a sense.

Marlene Cooper's ear-rings swung with animation as she spoke seriously about spiritualism to Francis Eccles who had now got a job on the British Council. Tim, like a bright young manservant of good appearance, sinuously slid among the guests with a silver dish of shrimps; these shrimps were curled up as if in sleep on the top of small biscuits. Isobel Billows herself, large, soft-featured, middle aged, and handsome, had given up trying to introduce everyone and was surveying the standing crowd from a corner while Ewart Thornton talked to her, he having had three Martinis, in the course of which he had told Isobel that he had mounds of homework, that a grammar-school master had no status these days, that spiritualism was the meeting-ground between science and religion, and that he

always bought his shirts and flannel trousers from Marks &
Spencer's. It was at the point of his fourth Martini that Ewart's
deepest pride emerged, to enchant Isobel and make her feel she was
really in the swing by having him at her party. She listened to him
wonderingly as he told her of the real miner's cottage of his birth in
Carmarthenshire where his father still lived, and the real crofter's
cottage in Perthshire where his grandparents had lived till late.
'Latham Street Council School; Traherne Grammar School; Sheffield
Red Brick – only the brick isn't red,' boasted Ewart. 'Three shillings
and sixpence a week pocket money all the while I was a student.
From the age of ten to the age of thirteen I was employed by a
fishmonger to deliver fish after school hours and on Saturday
mornings. My earnings were four shillings a week which, with the
similar earnings of my brothers, went into the family funds. I was
given a pair of stout boots every year at Easter. Most of my clothes
were home made. We had outdoor sanitation which we shared with
two other families—'

'Were you ever in trouble with the police?' Isobel said, looking
round in the hope that someone was listening.

HUGO VICKERS

Loelia Lindsay, 1979

'THERE was a noisy lunch party at Pam Berry's,' recorded Noël
Coward in 1957. 'Loelia, Annie [Fleming], Virginia Cowles, the
ubiquitous Malcolm Muggeridge, whom I can't stand, and Patrick
Kinross. It was quite funny and everyone shrieked at once. If the
dialogue had been transcribed the critics undoubtedly would have
stated confidently that such characters did not exist.'

With this in mind and this album in prospect I decided to tape-
record a luncheon at Loelia Lindsay's house. I arrived bearing an
enormous machine which I described at the time as 'another ear at
the table'. The guests were Lady Diana Cooper, her grand-daughter,
Artemis, and Loelia's niece, Carolyn Ponsonby. While the machine
was rather conspicuous and considerably inhibited the three younger
members of the party, Diana and Loelia tended to forget its presence.

The conversation began with a discussion concerning the death of
an old friend. They had lived too long and seen too many die to face
this in other than a matter of fact manner.

DIANA: Now . . . Is it true that———is dead?

LOELIA: Yes, he's dead. I nearly rang you up but I thought why tell you bad news, not that it is all that bad news, let's face it.

DIANA: It's jolly good news.

LOELIA: Well, she doesn't take quite that line.

DIANA: Well, I take that line.

LOELIA: I take that line too. But I don't think it's the right thing to say. You say: 'I do understand you are feeling rather sad.' That is the line.

DIANA: How did he die?

LOELIA: He died in really rather a strange way. . . .

The manner of his departing was then described in considerable detail, the death itself registering on tape as a click of the fingers, followed by silence.

DIANA: Well, this morning the news was broken to me as 'not to be relied upon'.

LOELIA: What? That he's dead? You can rely on me, I promise. Ab-so-lutely!

DIANA: I'm afraid I said, 'How wonderful!'

During the lunch itself, the 'extra ear' coped admirably with the slower conversation, punctuated with the sound of knives and forks on plates. What was especially fascinating was that the machine caught nuances which escaped me at the time. Listening to it alone later, I realized how skilfully Loelia brought us all into the conversation in turn, and how, once we were drawn in, we then stayed in, and general conversation was established. I learned for the first time that there is an art in entertaining beyond good food and carefully chosen guests. Diana had been talking of her wartime visit to Shwe Dagon in Rangoon, and saying with pride that she had had to remove not only her shoes but also her stockings.

NGAIO MARSH

Final Curtain, 1947

THE poor small banquet was, if nothing else, a tribute to the zeal of Sir Henry's admirers in the Dominions and the United States of America. Troy had not seen its like for years. He himself, she noticed, ate a mess of something that had been put through a sieve. Conversation was general, innocuous, and sounded a little as if it had been carefully memorized beforehand. It was difficult not to look at Miss Orrincourt's diamonds. They were a sort of visual *faux pas* which no amount of blameless small-talk could shout down. Troy observed that the Ancreds themselves constantly darted furtive glances at them. Sir Henry continued bland, urbane, and, to Troy, excessively gracious. She found his compliments, which were adroit, rather hard to counter. He spoke of her work and asked if she had done a self-portrait. 'Only in my student days when I couldn't afford a model,' said Troy. 'But that's very naughty of you,' he said. 'It is now that you should give us the perfect painting of the perfect subject.'

'Crikey!' thought Troy.

They drank Rudesheimer. When Barker hovered beside him, Sir Henry, announcing that it was a special occasion, said he would take half a glass. Millamant and Pauline looked anxiously at him.

'Papa, darling,' said Pauline. '*Do* you think—?' And Millamant murmured: 'Yes, Papa. *Do* you think—?'

'Do I think what?' he replied, glaring at them.

'Wine,' they murmured disjointedly. 'Dr Withers . . . not really advisable . . . however.'

'Fill it up, Barker,' Sir Henry commanded loudly, 'fill it up.'

Troy heard Pauline and Millamant sigh windily.

Dinner proceeded with circumspection but uneasily. Paul and Fenella were silent. Cedric, on Troy's right hand, conversed in feverish spasms with anybody who would listen to him. Sir Henry's flow of compliments continued unabated through three courses, and to Troy's dismay, Miss Orrincourt began to show signs of marked hostility.

'And unextinguished laughter shakes the skies.'

ALEXANDER POPE

'Hephaestus', 1716

HE said, and to her hands the goblet heaved
Which, with a smile, the white-armed Queen received.
Then to the rest he filled; and in his turn
Each to his lips applied the nectared urn.
Vulcan with awkward grace his office plies
And unextinguished laughter shakes the skies.
   Thus the blest gods the genial day prolong,
In feasts ambrosial, and celestial song.
Apollo tuned the lyre; the Muses round
With voice alternate aid the silver sound.
Meantime the radiant Sun, to mortal sight
Descending swift, rolled down the rapid light.
Then to their starry domes the gods depart,
The shining monuments of Vulcan's art:
Jove on his couch reclined his awful head
And Juno slumbered on the golden bed.

ANON

Sir Gawain and the Green Knight, Fourteenth Century

BUT Arthur would not eat until all were served.
He was charming and cheerful, child-like and gay,
And loving active life, little did he favour

Lying down for long or lolling on a seat,
So robust his young blood and his beating brain.
Still, he was stirred now by something else:
His noble announcement that he never would eat
On such a fair feast-day till informed in full
Of some unusual adventure, as yet untold,
Of some momentous marvel that he might believe,
About ancestors, or arms, or other high theme;
Or till a stranger should seek out a strong knight of his,
To join with him in jousting, in jeopardy to lay
Life against life, each allowing the other
The favour of Fortune, the fairer lot.
Such was the King's custom when he kept court,
At every fine feast among his free retinue
       In hall.
    So he throve amid the throng,
    A ruler royal and tail,
    Still standing staunch and strong,
    And young like the year withal.

Erect stood the strong King, stately of mien,
Trifling time with talk before the topmost table.
Good Gawain was placed at Guinevere's side,
And Agravain of the Hard Hand sat on the other side,
Both the King's sister's sons, staunchest of knights.
Above, Bishop Baldwin began the board,
And Ywain, Urien's son ate next to him.
These were disposed on the dais and with dignity served,
And many mighty men next, marshalled at side tables.
Then the first course came in with such cracking of trumpets,
(Whence bright bedecked blazons in banners hung)
Such din of drumming and a deal of fine piping,
Such wild warbles whelming and echoing
That hearts were uplifted high at the strains.
Then delicacies and dainties were delivered to the guests,
Fresh food in foison, such freight of full dishes
That space was scarce at the social tables
For the several soups set before them in silver
       On the cloth.
    Each feaster made free with the fare,
    Took lightly and nothing loth:

Twelve plates were for every pair.
Good beer and bright wine both.

NOËL COWARD

'I Went to a Marvellous Party', 1929

QUITE for no reason I'm here for the season,
And high as a kite.
Living in error
With Maude at Cap Ferrat
Which couldn't be right.

Everyone's here and frightfully gay,
Nobody cares what people say,
Tho' the Riviera seems really much queerer
Than Rome at its height
Yesterday night

chorus
I went to a marvellous party
I must say the fun was intense,
We all had to do what the people we knew
Would be doing a hundred years hence.
Dear Cecil arrived wearing armour
Some shells and a black feather boa.
Poor Millicent wore a surrealist comb
Made of bits of mosaic from St Peter's in Rome,
But the weight was so great that she had to go home.

THE MARCHIONESS OF
LONDONDERRY (ED.)

The Russian Journals of Catherine and Martha Wilmot, 1934

ON this day the long looked for ball which had been postponed
from December 6th Old Style took place. Only a part of the
Palace was thrown open and that was lighted by ten thousand
candles.
The *Salle Blanche* is a gallery one hundred and thirty-three feet by

forty-nine with columns supporting a gallery which was filled with spectators. The room is of dazzling whiteness and without a line of gilding and with four immense stoves which had externally the appearance of banners and standards. The pillars were wreathed with candles, the whole a perfect blaze of light, and three thousand here produced literally the effect of daylight in which they themselves seemed to burn dim and blue.

When the company was assembled the doors opened and the Imperial family walked in and rarely does one find united so much grace and beauty. The Empress was dressed in white with *colonnes* of large single diamonds round her gown from her waist to her feet. She had a *couronne du moyen age* at the back of her head and a small low one on her forehead, the shape of the whole perfectly classic, not a jewel or colour but these enormous diamonds which she called *mes cailloux*, and which, except on her, must have been taken for the pickings of a great glass lustre. Altogether I never saw such a combination of simplicity and splendour.

Prince Charles of Prussia, the Empress's brother, had arrived and in compliment to the Emperor wore the light blue ribbon, the great cordon of *St André*, the first order in Russia, the Emperor and the *Héritier* having on the orange ribbon, the Black Eagle of Prussia. Great attention is paid to these details and much importance attached to them. The Grand Duchesses Marie and Olga looked lovely, their beautiful skins, fair hair, graceful figures, simple *toilettes* and amiable high bred manner delighted everyone.

The polonaises began and continued some time. They are very agreeable for those who do not dance. When the Emperor took me I endeavoured to thank him for his *cadeaux* and his kindness in thinking of me at all. '*Mais, Madame, c'était une injure d'en doûter.*' He said my letter was *charmante*, and the Empress who said the same, added, '*C'était trop bon pour lui*'. The ball began at nine. After the polonaises were quadrilles and at twelve o'clock we passed through a *Salle des Maréchaux* and a long gallery with between three and four hundred pictures of Dawe's to the supper room, an enormous *salle* with scagliola columns and blue glass lustres and lighted by four thousand candles. This was really fairyland – the endless vista, the quantities of massy plate, the abundance of lovely flowers, and, to crown all, the whole having the appearance of an *orangerie*, the supper tables being so constituted as to let the stems of the immense orange trees through so that we literally sat under their shade and perfume. The scene was perfect enchantment and eight hundred and fifty sat down to supper without the slightest confusion or squeeze. The Empress, according to the strict old etiquette of Russian hospitality, went round all the tables and spoke to every person until she fainted away. She soon recovered and after we returned to *la Salle Blanche* she retired with the rest of the Imperial family and thus ended this magnificent fête.

ROBERT SURTEES

Jorrocks's Jaunts and Jollities, 1838

THE dining-room was the breadth of the passage narrower than the front drawing-room, and, as Mr Jorrocks truly said, was *ray*ther small, but the table being excessively broad, made the room appear less than it was. It was lighted up with spermaceti candles, in silver holders, one at each corner of the table, and there was a lamp in the wall between the red-curtained windows, immediately below a brass nail, on which Mr Jorrocks's great hunting-whip and a bunch of boot-garters were hung. Two more candles in the hands of bronzed Dianas on the marble mantelpiece lighted up a coloured copy of Barraud's picture of John Warde, on Blue Ruin; while Mr Ralph Lambton, on his horse Undertaker, with his hounds and men, occupied a frame on the opposite wall. The old-fashioned cellaret sideboard, against the wall at the end, supported a large bright burning brass lamp, with raised foxes round the rim, whose effulgent rays shed a brilliant halo over eight black hats and two white ones, whereof the four middle ones were decorated with evergreens and foxes' brushes. The dinner table was crowded, not covered. There was scarcely a square inch of cloth to be seen on any part. In the centre stood a magnificent finely-spun barley sugar windmill, two feet and a half high, with a spacious sugar foundation, with a cart and horses and two or three millers at the door, and a she-miller working a ball dress flounce at a lower window.

The whole dinner, first, second, third, fourth course, – everything, in fact, except dessert – was on the table, as we sometimes see it at ordinaries and public dinners. Before both Mr and Mrs Jorrocks were two great tureens of mock turtle soup, each capable of holding a gallon, and both full up to the brim. Then there were two sorts of fish; turbot and lobster sauce, and a great salmon. A round of boiled beef and an immense piece of roast occupied the rear of these, ready to march on the disappearance of the fish and soup – and behind the walls, formed by the beef of old England, came two dishes of grouse, each dish holding three brace. The side dishes consisted of a calf's head hashed, a leg of mutton, chickens, ducks, and mountains of vegetables; and round the windmill were plum puddings, tarts, jellies, pies, and puffs.

Behind Mrs Jorrocks's chair stood Batsay with a fine brass-headed comb in her hair, and stiff ringlets down her ruddy cheeks. She was dressed in a green silk gown, with a coral necklace, and one of Mr Jorrocks's lavender and white coloured silk pocket-handkerchiefs made into an apron. Binjimin stood with the door in his hand, as the saying is, with a towel twisted round his thumb, as though he had cut it.

'Now, gentlemen,' said Mr Jorrocks, casting his eye up the table, as soon as they had all got squeezed and wedged round it, and the dishes were uncovered, *'you see your dinner*, eat whatever you like except the windmill – hope you'll be able to satisfy nature with what's on – would have had more, but Mrs J. is so werry fine, she won't stand two joints of the same sort on the table.'

'We dance and the world swirls around us'

◦◦◦

BOHUMIL HRABAL

Too Loud a Solitude, 1976

IT is evening, I'm at a dance, and in comes Marie (or Manča, as I call her), the girl I've been waiting for, ribbons trailing, ribbons braided in her hair, and the band plays and I dance only with her, we dance and the world swirls around us like a merry-go-round, and when out of the corner of my eye I look for an opening that Manča and I can polka into, I see Manča's ribbons swinging around me, borne straight out on the wind of the dance, and whenever I feel the need to slow down, the ribbons start to droop, but then I pick up again and whirl her around, and the ribbons pick up and graze my hands, the fingers that hold her hand, which holds on tightly to a white embroidered handkerchief, and for the first time I tell her I love her and she whispers back that she's loved me since school, and then all at once she presses against me, clasps me, and we're closer than we've ever been before, and she asks me to be her partner for Women's Choice, and I shout 'Yes!' but no sooner does Women's Choice begin than Manča turns pale and tells me she'll only be a second.

When she came back, her hands were cold, but we started up again and I kept her twirling so everyone could see what a good dancer I was and how good we were together, what a couple we made, and as the polka reached its dizzy peak and Manča's ribbons started fluttering through the air with her straw-coloured braid, I noticed the other couples had stopped dancing and were moving away from us in disgust, until finally they made a large ring around us, but not to admire us, no, to escape us, because centrifugal force was spraying them with something horrible, though exactly what it was neither Manča nor I could guess, until Manča's mother ran up, horror-stricken, grabbed her by the arm, and they ran out of the dance hall, out of the Lower Tavern, never to return, which meant that I didn't see her again for years.

What had happened was that Manča was so excited by her Women's Choice, so thrilled by my I love you, that she had to pop out to the tavern latrine, where, unbeknownst to her, her ribbons had dipped into the pyramid of faeces rising up to meet the board she sat on, and when she ran out into the brightly lit room and starting dancing, she splashed and splattered the dancers, every dancer within range, with the centrifugal force of her ribbons, and from that day on they called her Shithead Manča.

FRANCES BURNEY

Evelina, 1778
Queen-Ann-Street, April 5, Tuesday morning

I have a vast deal to say, and shall give all this morning to my pen. As to my plan of writing every evening the adventures of the day, I find it impracticable; for the diversions here are so very late, that if I begin my letters after them, I could not go to bed at all.

We past a most extraordinary evening. A *private* ball this was called, so I expected to have seen about four or five couple; but, Lord! my dear Sir, I believe I saw half the world! Two very large rooms were full of company; in one, were cards for the elderly ladies, and in the other, were the dancers. My mamma Mirvan, for she always calls me her child, said she would sit with Maria and me till we were provided with partners, and then join the card-players.

The gentlemen, as they passed and repassed, looked as if they thought we were quite at their disposal, and only waiting for the honour of their commands; and they sauntered about, in a careless indolent manner, as if with a view to keep us in suspense. I don't speak of this in regard to Miss Mirvan and myself only, but to the ladies in general; and I thought it so provoking, that I determined, in my own mind, that, far from humouring such airs, I would rather not dance at all, than with any one who should seem to think me ready to accept the first partner who would condescend to take me.

Not long after, a young man, who had for some time looked at us with a kind of negligent impertinence, advanced, on tiptoe, towards me; he had a set smile on his face, and his dress was so foppish, that I really believe he even wished to be stared at; and yet he was very ugly.

Bowing almost to the ground, with a sort of swing, and waving his hand with the greatest conceit, after a short and silly pause, he said, 'Madam – may I presume?'—and stopt, offering to take my hand. I drew it back, but could scarce forbear laughing. 'Allow me, Madam,' (continued he, affectedly breaking off every half moment) 'the honour and happiness – if I am not so unhappy as to address you too late – to have the happiness and honour—'

Again he would have taken my hand, but, bowing my head, I begged to be excused, and turned to Miss Mirvan to conceal my laughter. He then desired to know if I had already engaged myself to some more fortunate man? I said No, and that I believed I should not dance at all. He would keep himself, he told me, disengaged, in hopes I should relent; and then, uttering some ridiculous speeches of sorrow and disappointment, though his face still wore the same invariable smile, he retreated.

It so happened, as we have since recollected, that during this little dialogue, Mrs Mirvan was conversing with the lady of the house. And very soon after another gentleman, who seemed about six-and-twenty years old, gayly, but not foppishly, dressed, and indeed extremely handsome, with an air of mixed politeness and gallantry, desired to know if I was engaged, or would honour him with my hand. So he was pleased to say, though I am sure I know not what honour he could receive from me; but these sort of expressions, I find, are used as words of course, without any distinction of persons, or study of propriety.

Well, I bowed, and I am sure I coloured; for indeed I was frightened at the thoughts of dancing before so many people; all strangers, and, which was worse, *with* a stranger; however, that was unavoidable, for though I looked round the room several times, I could not see one person that I knew. And so, he took my hand, and led me to join in the dance.

DOROTHY PARKER

'The Waltz', from *After Such Pleasures*, 1934

W HY, *thank you so much. I'd adore to.*
        I don't want to dance with him. I don't want to dance with anybody. And even if I did, it wouldn't be him. He'd be well down among the last ten. I've seen the way he dances; it looks like something you do on St Walpurgis Night. Just think, not a quarter of an hour ago, here I was sitting, feeling so sorry for the poor girl he was dancing with. And now *I'm* going to be the poor girl. Well, well. Isn't it a small world?

And a peach of a world, too. A true little corker. Its events are so fascinatingly unpredictable, are not they? Here I was, minding my own business, not doing a stitch of harm to any living soul. And then he comes into my life, all smiles and city manners, to sue me for the favor of one memorable mazurka. Why, he scarcely knows my name, let alone what it stands for. It stands for Despair, Bewilderment, Futility, Degradation, and Premeditated Murder, but little does he wot. I don't wot his name, either; I haven't any idea what it is. Jukes, would be my guess from the look in his eyes. How do you do, Mr Jukes? And how is that dear little brother of yours, with the two heads?

Ah, now why did he have to come around me, with his low requests? Why can't he let me lead my own life? I ask so little – just to be left alone in my quiet corner of the table, to do my evening brooding over all my sorrows. And he must come, with his bows and his scrapes and his may-I-have-this-ones. And I had to go and tell him that I'd adore to dance with him. I cannot understand why I wasn't struck right down dead. Yes, and being struck dead would look like a day in the country, compared to struggling out a dance with this boy. But what could I do? Everyone else at the table had got up to dance, except him and me. There I was, trapped. Trapped like a trap in a trap.

What can you say, when a man asks you to dance with him? I most certainly will *not* dance with you, I'll see you in hell first. Why, thank you, I'd like to awfully, but I'm having labor pains. Oh, yes, *do* let's dance together – it's so nice to meet a man who isn't a scaredy-cat about catching my beri-beri. No. There was nothing for me to do, but say I'd adore to. Well, we might as well get it over with. All right, Cannon-ball, let's run out on the field. You won the toss; you can lead.

THE SPECTATOR
Thursday, 17 May 1711

S IR,

   'I am a Man in Years, and by an honest Industry in the World have acquired enough to give my Children a liberal Education, though I was an utter Stranger to it my self. My eldest Daughter, a Girl of Sixteen, has for some time been under the Tuition of Monsieur *Rigadoon*, a Dancing-Master in the City; and I was prevailed upon by her and her Mother to go last Night to one of his Balls. I must own to you, Sir, that having never been at any such Place before, I was very much pleased and surprized with that part of his Entertainment which he called *French Dancing*. There were several Young Men and Women, whose Limbs seemed to have no other Motion, but purely what the Musick gave them. After this Part was over, they began a Diversion which they call *Country Dancing*, and wherein there were also some things not disagreeable, and divers *Emblematical Figures*, Composed, as I guess, by Wise Men, for the Instruction of Youth.

   'Among the rest I observed one, which, I think, they call *Hunt the Squirrel*, in which while the Woman flies the Man pursues her; but as soon as she turns, he runs away, and she is obliged to follow.

   'The Moral of this Dance does, I think, very aptly recommend Modesty and Discretion to the Female Sex.

   'But as the best Institutions are liable to Corruptions, so, Sir, I must acquaint you that very great Abuses are crept into this Entertainment. I was amazed to see my Girl handed by, and handing young Fellows with so much Familiarity; and I could not have thought it had been in the Child. They very often made use of a most impudent and lascivious Step called *Setting*, which I know not how to describe to you, but by telling you that 'tis the very reverse of *Back to Back*. At last an impudent young Dog bid the Fidlers play a Dance called *Mol. Pately*, and after having made two or three Capers, ran to his Partner, locked his Arms in hers, and whisked her round cleverly above Ground in such manner, that I, who sat upon one of the lowest Benches, saw further above her Shoe than I can think fit to acquaint you with. I could no longer endure these Enormities, wherefore just as my Girl was going to be made a Whirligig, I ran in, seized on the Child, and carried her home.

'Sir, I am not yet old enough to be a Fool. I suppose this Diversion might be at first invented to keep up a good Understanding between young Men and Women, and so far I am not against it; but I shall never allow of these things. I know not what you will say to this Case at present, but am sure that had you been with me you would have seen matter of great Speculation.

　I am
　　Yours, &c.'

TOBIAS SMOLLETT
The Adventures of Roderick Random, 1748

BEFORE the country-dances began I received a message by a person I did not know from Bragwell, who was present, importing that nobody who knew him presumed to dance with Melinda while he was there in person, and that I would do well to relinquish her without noise, because he had a mind to lead up a country-dance with her. This extraordinary intimation, which was delivered in the lady's hearing, did not at all discompose me, who by this time was pretty well acquainted with the character of my rival. I therefore, without the least symptom of concern, bade the gentleman tell Mr Bragwell, that, since I was so happy as to obtain the lady's consent, I should not be solicitous about his; and desired the bearer himself to bring me no such impertinent messages for the future. Melinda affected a sort of confusion, and pretended to wonder that Mr Bragwell should give himself such liberties with regard to her, who had no manner of connexion with the fellow. I laid hold of this opportunity to display my valor, and offered to call him to an account for his insolence, a proposal which she absolutely refused, under pretence of consulting my safety; though I could perceive, by the sparkling of her eyes, that she would not have thought herself affronted in being the subject of a duel. I was by no means pleased with this discovery of her thoughts, which not only argued the most unjustifiable vanity, but likewise the most barbarous indifference: however, I was allured by her fortune, and resolved to gratify her pride, in making her the occasion of a public quarrel between me and Bragwell, who I was pretty certain would never drive matters to a dangerous extremity.

While we danced together, I observed this formidable rival at one end of the room, encircled with a cluster of beaux, to whom he talked with great vehemence, casting many big looks at me from time to time. I guessed the subject of his discourse; and as soon as I had handed my partner to her seat, strutted up to the place where he stood, and, cocking my hat in his face, demanded aloud if he had any thing to say to me. He answered, with a sullen tone, 'Nothing, at present, sir;' and turned about on his heel. 'Well,' said I, 'you know where I am to be found at any time.' His companions stared at one another, and I returned to the lady, whose features brightened at my approach, and immediately a whisper ran through the whole room; after which so many eyes were turned on me that I was ready to sink with confusion. When the ball broke up, I led her to her coach; and, like a true French gallant, would have got up behind it, in order to protect her from violence on the road; but she absolutely refused my offer, and expressed her concern that there was not an empty seat for me within the vehicle.

HENRY JAMES
Washington Square, 1881

THESE observations, in themselves of no great profundity, Mr Townsend seemed to offer for what they were worth, and as a contribution to an acquaintance. He looked straight into Catherine's eyes. She answered nothing; she only listened, and looked at him; and he, as if he expected no particular reply, went on to say many other things in the same comfortable and natural manner. Catherine, though she felt tongue-tied, was conscious of no embarrassment; it seemed proper that he should talk, and that she should simply look at him. What made it natural was that he was so handsome, or, rather, as she phrased it to herself, so beautiful. The music had been silent for a while, but it suddenly began again; and then he asked her, with a deeper, intenser smile, if she would do him the honour of dancing with him. Even to this inquiry she gave no audible assent; she simply let him put his arm round her waist – as she did so, it occurred to her more vividly than it had ever done before that this was a singular place for a gentleman's arm to be – and in a moment he was guiding her round the room in the harmonious rotation of the polka. When they paused, she felt that she was red; and then, for some moments, she stopped looking at him. She fanned herself, and looked at the flowers that were painted on her fan. He asked her if she would begin again, and she hesitated to answer, still looking at the flowers.

'Does it make you dizzy?' he asked, in a tone of great kindness.

Then Catherine looked up at him; he was certainly beautiful, and not at all red. 'Yes,' she said; she hardly knew why, for dancing had never made her dizzy.

THOMAS HARDY
Under the Greenwood Tree, 1872

THE ear-rings of the ladies now flung themselves wildly about, turning violent summersaults, banging this way and that, and then swinging quietly against the ears sustaining them. Mrs Crumpler – a heavy woman, who, for some reason which nobody ever thought worth inquiry, danced in a clean apron – moved so smoothly through the figure that her feet were never seen; conveying to imaginative minds the idea that she rolled on castors.

Minute after minute glided by, and the party reached the period when ladies' back-hair begins to look forgotten and dissipated; when a perceptible dampness makes itself apparent upon the faces even of delicate girls – a ghastly dew having for some time rained from the features of their masculine partners; when skirts begin to be torn out of their gathers; when elderly people, who have stood up to please their juniors, begin to feel sundry small tremblings in the region of the knees, and to wish the interminable dance was at Jericho; when (at country parties of the thorough sort) waistcoats begin to be unbuttoned, and when the fiddlers' chairs have been wriggled, by the frantic bowing of their occupiers, to a distance of about two feet from where they originally stood.

LEO TOLSTOY

Anna Karenina, 1872

THE black velvet ribbon of her locket clasped her neck with
unusual softness. That ribbon was charming, and when Kitty
had looked at her neck in the glass at home, she felt that that ribbon
was eloquent. There might be some possible doubt about anything
else, but that ribbon *was* charming. Kitty smiled, here at the ball,
when she caught sight of it again in the mirror. Her bare shoulders
and arms gave her a sensation as of cold marble, a feeling she liked
very much. Her eyes shone and she could not keep her rosy lips from
smiling at the consciousness of her own loveliness. Before she had
reached the light-coloured crowd of women in tulle, ribbons and
lace, who were waiting for partners (Kitty never long formed one of
the crowd), she was already asked for the waltz and asked by the
best dancer, the leader of the dancing hierarchy, the famous *dirigeur*
and Master of the Ceremonies, a handsome, stately married man.
George Korsunsky. He had just left the Countess Bonin, with whom
he had danced the first round of the waltz, and looking round his
domain – that is to say, a few couples who had begun to dance – he
noticed Kitty just coming in. He approached her at that peculiar free
and easy amble natural only to Masters of Ceremonies, bowed, and,
without even asking her consent, put his arm round her slim waist.
She looked about for some one to hold her fan and the mistress of
the house took it from her with a smile.

'How fine that you have come in good time,' he said with his arm
round her waist. 'It's wrong of people to come so late.'

Bending her left arm she put her hand on his shoulder, and her
little feet in their pink shoes began moving quickly, lightly and
rhythmically in time with the music, over the smooth parquet floor.

'It is a rest to waltz with you,' he said as he took the first slow
steps of the dance. 'What lightness and precision! It's delightful!' he
remarked, saying to her what he said to almost all the dancing
partners whom he really liked.

DOMINICK DUNNE

People Like Us, 1988

T HE ballroom lights dimmed, and the party-goers gasped at the beauty as the regular lighting was replaced by pink-and-turquoise fluorescent light, giving the illusion of total fantasy. Then, with a pull of a golden rope, the clouds above burst open, and butterflies, thousands of butterflies, descended from the ceiling of the ballroom, fluttering here, fluttering there.

'Oh, heaven!'

'Divine!'

'Spectacular!'

'It's the most beautiful thing I've ever seen,' cried Ruby Renthal. Ruby reached out and took hold of Elias's hand, and he, in turn, clasped his hand over hers. They looked at each other and knew that they had made it, as they always knew they would, but beyond their wildest dreams.

'Too marvelous for words,' said the Countess of Castoria.

'Oh, look,' said the First Lady, clapping her hands in delight.

Ezzie Fenwick, who knew beauty when he saw beauty, had tears in his eyes. 'Divoon,' he said.

People raced for the dance floor. Everyone wanted to dance. Abandon was the order of the night, as couples gave themselves over to the music and beauty of the Renthals' ball. The dance floor was full when the first scream came, from Rochelle Prud'homme, followed by screams from Matilda Clarke and Violet Bastedo, as the ten thousand butterflies, yellow and orange, flown up from Chile only that day, began dropping to their deaths, having been fried by the pink-and-turquoise fluorescent lights. Secret Service men rushed in past the dancers, who were now wiping dead butterflies from their hair and backs and shoulders, to rescue the First Lady before total pandemonium broke out.

'The *odor*!' cried Ezzie, waving his hand in front of his nose like a fan, as the dying butterflies kept descending.

'Turn out those fucking fluorescent lights!' screamed Elias.

'Don't say *fucking*, Elias,' whispered an agitated Ruby into her husband's ear.

Mickie, nervous sweat pouring off his brow, pulled the switch that turned off the pink-and-turquoise fluorescent lights, and the ballroom was plunged into total darkness. Fernanda Somerset screamed. On the crowded stairway, an enormously fat Albanian princess fainted and, falling, knocked over several people.

'Turn on the ballroom lights!' screamed Elias.

JULIAN FANE

Gabriel Young, 1973

THE tune finished. The band began to play a Paul Jones. Gabriel and Henrietta were separated; he was linked with the chain of men circling to the left, she with the inner chain of women circling in the other direction. When the music and the circulation stopped, Gabriel partnered the stranger opposite in the ensuing dance. The band played a second Paul Jones, and a third and a fourth, and the pace of the music quickened. Laughing female faces flashed past Gabriel as he was dragged clockwise in a gallop, and fringes and locks and tresses of hair of different colours, and swirling skirts and petticoats, and twinkling feet beneath. At one moment he danced with Lorna Worthington, whose hand was dry and horny after Henrietta's, like a monkey's paw, then he was dancing with Lady Holmes, holding or being held by her. 'What a marvellous party,' he shouted in her ear, which was on a level with his lips. In reply, in her upper-class accent, she shrieked something about Henrietta having taken such a shine to him in Paris. He would have been surprised if he had had an opportunity to consider her statement, for Henrietta's greeting had been none too warm, and she had sparred with him at dinner, and her smile during their dance turned down discouragingly, although perhaps she had wriggled her fingers in a provocative fashion. But the music changed and changed again, and he was dancing with another partner, he was revolving in another dizzy circle, catching glimpses of the mirrors, the flowers, the band, and girls, pretty girls everywhere, their cheeks rosy from their exertions, their supple rounded figures.

He grew hotter, he felt freer, and entered into the gay spirit of the proceedings, so that after the last Paul Jones he was emboldened to ask his previous temporary partners for dances. He gripped and guided them with more authority, he glided and spun and whirled and executed agile steps, grateful for their sweet feminine understanding and acceptance of his intentions, passionately susceptible. The constraints of the evening, of recent weeks and indeed months, were relieved by activity. The kaleidoscope of his cogitations was shaken into innumerable new patterns by pleasure. But he couldn't spare a second to study them. The assurance he had given his hostess, that it was a marvellous party, was the plain truth.

COVENTRY PATMORE

'The County Ball', 1909

I

WELL, Heaven be thank'd my first-love fail'd,
    As, Heaven be thank'd, our first-loves do!
Thought I, when Fanny past me sail'd,
    Loved once, for what I never knew,
Unless for colouring in her talk,
    When cheeks and merry mouth would show
Three roses on a single stalk,
    The middle wanting room to blow,
And forward ways, that charm'd the boy
    Whose love-sick mind, misreading fate,
Scarce hoped that any Queen of Joy
    Could ever stoop to be his mate.

2

But there danced she, who from the leaven
    Of ill preserv'd my heart and wit
All unawares, for she was heaven,
    Others at best but fit for it.
One of those lovely things she was
    In whose least action there can be
Nothing so transient but it has
    An air of immortality.
I mark'd her step, with peace elate,
    Her brow more beautiful than morn,
Her sometime look of girlish state
    Which sweetly waived its right to scorn;
The giddy crowd, she grave the while,
    Although, as 'twere beyond her will,
Around her mouth the baby smile,

That she was born with, linger'd still.
Her ball-dress seem'd a breathing mist,
    From the fair form exhaled and shed,
Raised in the dance with arm and wrist
    All warmth and light, unbraceleted.
Her motion, feeling 'twas beloved,
    The pensive soul of tune express'd,
And, oh, what perfume, as she moved,
    Came from the flowers in her breast!
How sweet a tongue the music had!
    'Beautiful Girl', it seem'd to say,
'Though all the world were vile and sad,
    'Dance on; let innocence be gay.'
Ah, none but I discern'd her looks,
    When in the throng she pass'd me by,
For love is like a ghost, and brooks
    Only the chosen seer's eye;
And who but she could e'er divine
    The halo and the happy trance,
When her right arm reposed on mine,
    In all the pauses of the dance!

3

Whilst so her beauty fed my sight,
    And whilst I lived in what she said,
Accordant airs, like all delight
    Most sweet when noted least, were play'd;
And was it like the Pharisee
    If I in secret bow'd my face
With joyful thanks that I should be,
    Not as many were, but with grace,
And fortune of well-nurtured youth,
    And days no sordid pains defile,
And thoughts accustom'd to the truth,
    Made capable of her fair smile?

4

Charles Barton follow'd down the stair,
    To talk with me about the Ball,
And carp at all the people there.
    The Churchills chiefly stirr'd his gall:
'Such were the Kriemhilds and Isondes

'You storm'd about at Trinity!
'Nothing at heart but handsome Blondes!
    'Folk say that you and Fanny Fry – '
'They err! Good-night! Here lies my course,
    'Through Wilton.' Silence blest my ears,
And, weak at heart with vague remorse,
    A passing poignancy of tears
Attack'd mine eyes. By pale and park
    I rode, and ever seem'd to see,
In the transparent starry dark,
    That splendid brow of chastity,
That soft and yet subduing light,
    At which, as at the sudden moon,
I held my breath, and thought 'how bright!'
    That guileless beauty in its noon,
Compelling tribute of desires
    Ardent as day when Sirius reigns,
Pure as the permeating fires
    That smoulder in the opal's veins.

ROSAMOND LEHMANN

Invitation to the Waltz, 1932

THE band burst into a fox-trot. Several couples moved out into
the room and began to dance. They must belong to the house-
party. Not noticeably lovely or well dressed. More or less alike they
looked – fairish, prettyish, of medium height, plump to thinnish, all
in the same kind of pale-coloured frock, their hair parted at the side
and waved in the same boring kind of wave. All but one. She came
in alone by the further door, and they caught sight of her for a
moment standing beside Rollo, nearly as tall as he, a narrow, high-
shouldered figure sheathed in white satin, fragile neck lifting the
small and shapely head in a long curve; black hair parted in the
middle, taken back close behind the ears and coiled low on her neck
in a heavy silky knot. Her face turned slowly, looking round the
room. They thought they saw a face of improbable beauty, pale,
modelled in planes never before thought of. A new face. She turned
away again, disappearing with Rollo through the doorway.
    They backed against the wall and stood side by side, watching the

revolving couples with bright strained expressions of interest. They could not part until some one came to part them; but they felt they hated one another. Reggie stood a little apart from them, looking at the dancers with the same air of bland appraisal. The band went on playing and he went on looking. At last he threw out a casual arm, encircling the waist of the one nearer to him, and said, gazing over her head:

'Want to dance?'

It was Olivia. Relieved, distressed, blushing, careful to avoid her sister's eye, she placed herself within his loose uncompromising grasp. He launched out with her into a sober pacing. And it was Kate who was left alone.

MARIA EDGEWORTH
Moral Tales, 1801

WHEN they entered the ball-room, Archibald Mackenzie asked Flora to dance, whilst Forester was considering where he should put his hat. 'Are you going to dance without me? I thought I had asked you to dance with me. I intended it all the time we were coming in the coach.'

Flora thanked him for his kind intentions; whilst Archibald, with a look of triumph, hurried his partner away, and the dance began. Forester saw this transaction in the most serious light, and it afforded him subject for meditation till at least half a dozen country-dances had been finished. In vain the 'Berwick Jockey', the 'Highland Laddie', and the 'Flowers of Edinburgh' were played: 'they suited not the gloomy habit' of his soul. He fixed himself behind a pillar, proof against music, mirth and sympathy; he looked upon the dancers with a cynical eye. At length he found an amusement that gratified his present splenetic humour: he applied both his hands to his ears, effectually to stop out the sound of the music, that he might enjoy the ridiculous spectacle of a number of people capering about without any apparent motive. Forester's attitude caught the attention of some of the company; indeed, it was strikingly awkward. His elbows stuck out from his ears, and his head was sunk beneath his shoulders. Archibald Mackenzie was delighted beyond measure at his figure, and pointed him out to his acquaintance with all possible expedition. The laugh and the whisper circulated with rapidity.

Henry, who was dancing, did not perceive what was going on, till his partner said to him, 'Pray, who is that strange mortal?'

'My friend,' cried Henry. 'Will you excuse me for one instant?' and he ran up to Forester, and roused him from his singular attitude. 'He is,' continued Henry, as he returned to his partner, 'an excellent young man; and he has superior abilities: we must not quarrel with him for trifles.'

With what different eyes different people behold the same objects! Whilst Forester had been stopping his ears, Dr Campbell, who had more of the nature of the laughing than of the weeping philosopher, had found much benevolent pleasure in contemplating the festive scene. Not that any folly or ridicule escaped his keen penetration; but he saw everything with an indulgent eye; and if he laughed, laughed in such a manner, that even those who were the objects of his pleasantry could scarcely have forborne to sympathise in his mirth. Folly, he thought, could be felt as properly, and quite as effectually corrected, by the tickling of a feather, as by the lash of the satirist.

ALEXANDRE DUMAS
The Lady of the Camellias, 1848

WHEN full of my sorrowful emotions, I arrived at the ball, it was already very animated. They were dancing, shouting even, and in one of the quadrilles I perceived Marguerite dancing with the Comte de N., who seemed proud of showing her off, as if he said to everybody: 'This woman is mine.'

I leaned against the mantelpiece just opposite Marguerite and watched her dancing. Her face changed the moment she caught sight of me. I saluted her casually with a glance of the eyes and a wave of the hand.

When I reflected that after the ball she would go home, not with me but with that rich fool, when I thought of what would follow their return, the blood rose to my face, and I felt the need of doing something to trouble their relations.

After the dance I went up to the mistress of the house, who displayed for the benefit of her guests a dazzling bosom and magnificent shoulders. She was beautiful, and, from the point of view of figure, more beautiful than Marguerite. I realized this fact still more clearly from certain glances which Marguerite bestowed upon her while I was talking with her. The man who was the lover of such a woman might well be as proud of M. de N., and she was beautiful enough to inspire a passion not less great than that which Marguerite had inspired in me. At that moment she had no lover. It would not be difficult to become so; it depended only on showing enough money to attract her attention.

I made up my mind. That woman should be my mistress. I began by dancing with her. Half an hour afterward, Marguerite, pale as death, put on her wrap and left the ball.

ST FRANCIS DE SALES
An Introduction to a Devout Life, 1613

DANCES and Balls in their own Nature are things indifferent, but as they are ordinarily us'd, they incline much to Evil, and are consequently full of Danger. They are us'd by Night, in Darkness and Obscurity, and it is very easy to slide obscure and vicious Accidents into a Subject so capable of Evil. They watch long at their Pastimes, and afterwards lose the Mornings, and by consequence the Opportunity of serving God. In a word, it is always Folly to change Day into Night, Light into Darkness, and good Works into Wantonness. Everyone strives who shall carry thither most Vanity; and Vanity is so great a Disposition to deprav'd Affections and dangerous and reprehensible Loves, that all those Mischiefs are easily ingender'd in Dances.

I say of Dances *Philothea,* as Physicians say of *Mushrooms*; the best of them are nothing worth, yet if you will needs eat *Mushrooms,* be sure they will be well drest: If on some Occasion, which you cannot well excuse, you must go to a Ball, see that your dance be well order'd: But how must it be well order'd? With Modesty, Gravity and honest Intention.

Eat but seldom and little of *Mushrooms* (say the Physicians) for be they never so well drest, the Quantity makes them poysonous. Dance but little and very seldom, *Philothea,* for otherwise thou puttest thy self in danger to become affectionate to it.

Mushrooms, according to *Pliny,* being spongy and porous, easily draw Infection to them, so that being near Serpents and Toads, they receive Venom from them: Masques, Dances and other Night meeting, ordinarily attract the Vices and Sins of the Time into one Place, as Quarrels, Envy, Scoffings and wanton Loves. And as these Exercises open the Pores of the Body, so they also open the Pores of the Heart, by means whereof, if any Serpent taking the Advantage, breathe into the Ear some wanton Word or lascivious Discourse, or if some *Basilisk* glance an unchaste Look or immodest Eye, the Heart thus open'd is easily seiz'd on and Poyson'd. O *Philothea*, these impertinent Recreations are ordinarily dangerous: they distract the Spirit of Devotion, weaken the forces, make Charity cold, and stir up in the Soul a thousand evil Affections; and therefore they are to be us'd with great Discretion.

But above all, they say, that after *Mushrooms* we must drink Wine; And I say, that after Dancing it is necessary to use good and holy Meditations, to hinder those dangerous Impressions, which the vain Pleasure, taken in Dancing, may have left in our Mind. But what Meditations?

That, whilst you were at the Masque, many Souls were burning in Hell-fire for Sins committed in Dancing, or by Occasion of it. Many Religious and Devout Persons were at that very time in the Presence of God, singing his Praises and Contemplating his Beauty: Oh how much more happily was their time spent than yours! Whilst you were Dancing, many Souls departed out of this World in great Anguish, many thousand Men and Women suffer'd great Pains in their Beds, in Hospitals, in the streets, by the Gout, Stone and burning Fevers. Alas! they had no rest, and will you have no compassion of them? And do not you think, that one Day you shall Groan as they did? Our B. Saviour, our Lady, the Angels and Saints beheld your Dancing. Ah how they did pity you, feeling your Heart busy'd in these Trifles, and so attentive to this Trash! Alas! whilst you were there, the time is pass'd away, and Death is come nearer; see how he mocks you and calls you to his Dance, in which the Groans of your Friends shall be the Musick, and where you shall make but one Step from Life in Death. This Dance is the true Pastime of mortal Men, since by it we pass in a Moment from Time to Eternity of Joys or Pains. I have set you down these few Considerations; God will suggest better to you, if you fear him.

HARRIS WESTON & BERT LEE

'Knees up Mother Brown', 1939

V1

I'VE just been to a 'ding-dong' down dear old Brixton way,
Old Mother Brown the Pearly Queen's a hundred years today.
Oh! what a celebration! was proper lah-di-dah!
Until they roll'd the carpet up,
And shouted 'Nah then, Ma!'

CHORUS

Knees up Mother Brown! Knees up Mother Brown!
Come along dearie let it go! Ee-i-ee-i-ee-i-oh!
It's yer blooming birthday
Let's wake up all the town!
So, knees up, knees up! Don't get the breeze up,
Knees up Mother Brown!

V2

Joe brought his concertina, and Nobby brought the beer.
And all the little nippers swung upon the chandelier!
A black-out warden passin' yell'd, Ma, pull down that blind,
Just look at what you're showin'', and we shouted 'Never mind'.

V3

And fat old Uncle 'Enry 'e quite enjoyed the fun
The buttons on his Sunday pants kept bustin' one by one!
But still 'e kept on dancin' – another one went 'pop'
He said 'I'm goin' ter keep on till me 'round-me-'ouses drop.'

V4

Then old Maria Perkins, she danced wiv all her might.
Each time she kicked 'er legs up we all shouted with delight,
'Lift up yer skirts Maria – my word, yer doin' fine!
And we can see yer washing 'anging on the Siegfried Line.'

V5

We 'ad no pig's ear' glasses – but still we didn't mind,
We drank it out of 'vauses' and whatever we could find.
We toasted good ol' Nelson there 'anging by the door,
And as we blew the froth at him he shouted with a roar:

V6

Bill drove up on 'is barrer – just like a proper swell.
And Mother Brown said 'Come inside and bring yer moke as well.'
It nibbled Grandad's whiskers, then started kicking out,
And as ma Brown went through the window we began to shout

V7

And then old Granny Western – she'd 'ad a good blow out
She 'ad two pints o' winkles wiv some cocktails and some stout
'I might 'ave indigestion,' she murmured wiv a grunt
'But lummy up to now it's all quiet on the Western front.'

V8

A crowd stood round the winder – they'd 'ad a lovely time
The kids sat on the railin's thought it was a pantomime
Pa went round wiv 'is titfer – collected one and three
We shouted 'Come on Mother, show 'em your agilitee.'

'Nor have we one or two kinds of drunkards only . . .'

THOMAS NASHE

'Pierce Pennilesse his Supplication to the Divell', 1592

NOR have we one or two kinds of drunkards only, but eight kinds. The first is ape drunk, and he leaps, and sings, and holloes, and danceth for the heavens. The second is lion drunk, and he flings the pots about the house, calls his hostess whore, breaks the glass windows with his dagger, and is apt to quarrel with any man that speaks to him. The third is swine drunk, heavy, lumpish, and sleepy, and cries for a little more drink and a few more clothes. The fourth is sheep drunk, wise in his own conceit when he cannot bring forth a right word. The fifth is maudlin drunk when a fellow will weep for kindness in the midst of his ale, and kiss you, saying, 'By God, captain, I love thee; go thy ways, thou dost not think so often of me as I do of thee; I would (if it pleased God) I could not love thee so well as I do.' And then he puts his finger in his eye and cries. The sixth is martin drunk, when a man is drunk and drinks himself sober ere he stir. The seventh is goat drunk, when, in his drunkenness, he hath no mind but on lechery. The eighth is fox drunk, when he is crafty drunk, as many of the Dutchmen be, that will never bargain but when they are drunk. All these species, and more, I have seen practised in one company at one sitting, when I have been permitted to remain sober amongst them, only to note their several humours. He that plies any one of them hard, it will make him to write admirable verses, and to have a deep casting head, though he were never so very a dunce before.

CHARLES DICKENS

David Copperfield, 1849

I BEGAN, by being singularly cheerful and light-hearted; all sorts of half-forgotten things to talk about, came rushing into my mind, and made me hold forth in a most unwonted manner. I laughed heartily at my own jokes, and everybody else's; called Steerforth to order for not passing the wine; made several engagements to go to Oxford; announced that I meant to have a dinner-party exactly like that, once a week, until further notice; and madly took so much snuff out of Grainger's box, that I was obliged to go into the pantry, and have a private fit of sneezing ten minutes long.

I went on, by passing the wine faster and faster yet, and continually starting up with a corkscrew to open more wine, long before any was needed. I proposed Steerforth's health. I said he was my dearest friend, the protector of my boyhood, and the companion of my prime. I said I was delighted to propose his health. I said I owed him more obligations than I could ever repay, and held him in a higher admiration than I could ever express. I finished by saying, 'I'll give you Steerforth! God bless him! Hurrah!' We gave him three times three, and another, and a good one to finish with. I broke my glass in going round the table to shake hands with him, and I said (in two words) 'Steerforth, you're the guiding-star of my existence.'

I went on, by finding suddenly that somebody was in the middle of a song. Markham was the singer, and he sang 'When the heart of a man is depressed with care.' He said, when he had sung it, he would give us 'Woman!' I took objection to that, and I couldn't allow it. I said it was not a respectful way of proposing the toast, and I would never permit that toast to be drunk in my house otherwise than as 'The Ladies!' I was very high with him, mainly I think because I saw Steerforth and Grainger laughing at me – or at him – or at both of us. He said a man was not to be dictated to. I said a man *was*. He said a man was not to be insulted, then. I said he was right there – never under my roof, where the Lares were sacred, and the laws of hospitality paramount. He said it was no derogation from a man's dignity to confess that I was a devilish good fellow. I instantly proposed his health.

Somebody was smoking. We were all smoking. *I* was smoking, and trying to suppress a rising tendency to shudder. Steerforth had made a speech about me, in the course of which I had been affected almost to tears. I returned thanks, and hoped the present company would dine with me to-morrow, and the day after – each day at five o'clock, that we might enjoy the pleasures of conversation and society through a long evening. I felt called upon to propose an individual. I would give them my aunt. Miss Betsey Trotwood, the best of her sex!

Somebody was leaning out of my bedroom window, refreshing his forehead against the cool stone of the parapet, and feeling the air upon his face. It was myself. I was addressing myself as 'Copperfield,' and saying, 'Why did you try to smoke? You might have known you couldn't do it.' Now, somebody was unsteadily contemplating his features in the looking-glass. That was I too. I was very pale in the looking-glass; my eyes had a vacant appearance; and my hair – only my hair, nothing else – looked drunk.

PETRONIUS

'Trimalchio's Banquet', AD 65

WE observed also some new things; for in the Gallery stood two Eunuchs, one of whom held a Silver Chamber-pot, the other counted the Balls, not those they kept tossing, but such as fell to the Ground. While we admir'd the Humour, one Menelaus came up to us, and told us we were come where we must set up for the Night, and that we had seen the beginning of our Entertainment. As he was yet talking, Trimalchio snapp'd his Fingers, at which sign the Eunuch held the Chamber-pot to him as he was playing; then calling for Water, he dipped the tips of his Fingers in it, and dry'd them on the Boys Head. 'Twould be too long to recount every thing: We went into the Hot-house, and having sweated a little, into the Cold Bath; and while Trimalchio was anointed from Head to Foot with a liquid Perfume, and rubb'd clean again, not with Linnen but with finest Flannen, his three Chyrurgeons ply'd the Muscadine, but brawling over their Cups; Trimalchio said it was his turn to drink; then wrapt in a Scarlet Mantle, he was laid on a Litter born by Six Servants, with Four Lacqueys in rich Liveries running before him, and by his side a Sedan, in which was carried his Darling, a stale bleer-eyed Catamite, more Ill-favoured than his Master Trimalchio; who as they went on, kept close to his Ear with a Flagellet, as if he had whispered him, and made him Musick all the way. Wondering, we followed, and, with Agamemnon, came to the Gate, on which hung a Tablet with this Inscription:

WHAT EVER SERVANT GOES FORTH WITHOUT HIS MASTER'S COMMAND, HE SHALL RECEIVE AN HUNDRED STRIPES.

In the Porch stood the Porter in a Green Livery, girt about with a Cherry-coloured Girdle, garbling of Pease in a Silver Charger; and over head hung a Golden Cage with a Magpye in it, which gave us an All Hail as we entred: But while I was gaping at these things, I had like to have broken my Neck backward, for on the left hand, not far from the Porter's Lodge, there was a great Dog in a Chain painted on the Wall, and over him written in Capital Letters, BEWARE THE DOG. My Companions could not forbear laughing; but I recollecting my Spirits, pursued my design of going to the end of the Wall; it was the draught of a Market-place where Slaves were bought and sold with Bills over them: There was also Trimalchio with a white Staff in his Hand, and Minerva with a Train after her entring Rome: Then having learnt how to cast Accompt, he was made Auditor; all exquisitely painted with their proper Titles; and at the end of the Gallery Mercury lifting him by the Chin, and placing him on a Judgment-Seat, Fortune stood by him with a Cornucopia, and the Three fatal Sisters winding a Golden Thread.

MARTIN CRUZ SMITH
Gorky Park, 1981

BY midnight, everyone had returned and everyone was drunk. There was a buffet of cold pork and sausages, fish, blini, cheeses and breads, pickled mushrooms, even pressed caviar. Someone was shouting poetry. At the other end of the room couples hopped to a Hungarian version of the Bee Gees. Misha was stricken with guilt and couldn't keep his eyes off Zoya sitting close to Schmidt.

'I thought we were going to spend this weekend together,' Arkady said the one time he got Zoya alone in the kitchen. 'How did Schmidt get into it?'

'I invited him.' She carried out a bottle of wine.

'To Zoya Renko' – Schmidt raised his glass at her return – 'selected yesterday by her District Committee to speak on new challenges in education before the entire City Committe, making us all very proud – especially, I'm sure, her husband.'

Arkady came out of the kitchen to find everyone looking at him except Schmidt, who was winking at Zoya. Natasha saved Arkady from more confusion by handing him a drink. A sentimental Georgian crooner slipped down on the turntable, and Schmidt and Zoya rose to dance.

They'd danced before, Arkady could tell. Balding but trim, Schmidt was very smooth on his feet, with a muscular wedge-shaped jaw accustomed to leading. He had the thick neck of a gymnast and the black-rimmed glasses of a Party thinker. His hand almost covered Zoya's back as she leaned into him.

'To Comrade Schmidt.' Misha hoisted a bottle as the song ended. 'To Comrade Schmidt we drink a toast not because he's gained a sinecure at a District Committee doing crossword puzzles and selling office supplies on the side, because I can remember once taking home a paper clip myself.'

Misha spilled some vodka and nodded happily at everyone, only getting started. 'We drink to him not because he attends Party conferences at beach resorts on the Black Sea, because last year I was allowed to fly to Murmansk. We drink not because the District Committee buys him cases of fine wine, because we all get to stand in line for a warm beer from time to time. We drink not because he wants our wives, because the rest of us can always masturbate if need be. Nor because he can drive over pedestrians in his Chaika limousine, because we have the advantage of the world's greatest subway system. Not even because his sexual habits include necrophilia, sadism and homosexuality because – please, comrades – we are no longer living in the Dark Ages. No,' Misha concluded, 'we drink to Comrade Dr Schmidt for none of these reasons. The reason we drink to him is because he is such a good Communist.'

Schmidt showed a smile as hard as a car grille.

Dancing, talking, sitting became increasingly drunken. Arkady was in the kitchen making coffee for five minutes before he realized that the film maker was lying with the dancer's wife in a corner. He backed out and left his cup. In the living room Misha sleepily danced with his head on Natasha's shoulder. Arkady climbed the steps to his bedroom, and was about to open the door when Schmidt came out and shut it.

'I drink to you,' Schmidt whispered, 'because your wife is a great screw.'

TRUMAN CAPOTE
Breakfast at Tiffany's, 1958

SOMEONE coughed, several swallowed. A Naval officer, who had been holding Mag Wildwood's drink, put it down.

'But then,' said Holly, 'I hear so many of these Southern girls have the same trouble.' She shuddered delicately, and went to the kitchen for more ice.

Mag Wildwood couldn't understand it, the abrupt absence of warmth on her return; the conversations she began behaved like green logs, they fumed but would not fire. More unforgivably, people were leaving without taking her telephone number. The Air Force colonel decamped while her back was turned, and this was the straw too much: he'd asked her to dinner. Suddenly she was blind. And since gin to artifice bears the same relation as tears to mascara, her attractions at once dissembled. She took it out on everyone. She called her hostess a Hollywood degenerate. She invited a man in his fifties to fight. She told Berman, Hitler was right. She exhilarated Rusty Trawler by stiff-arming him into a corner. 'You know what's going to happen to you?' she said, with no hint of a stutter. 'I'm going to march you over to the zoo and feed you to the yak.' He looked altogether willing, but she disappointed him by sliding to the floor, where she sat humming.

'You're a bore. Get up from there,' Holly said, stretching on a pair of gloves. The remnants of the party were waiting at the door, and when the bore didn't budge Holly cast me an apologetic glance. 'Be an angel, would you, Fred? Put her in a taxi. She lives at the Winslow.'

'Don't. Live Barbizon. Regent 4-5700. Ask for Mag Wildwood.'

'You *are* an angel, Fred.'

They were gone. The prospect of steering an Amazon into a taxi obliterated whatever resentment I felt. But she solved the problem herself. Rising on her own steam, she stared down at me with a lurching loftiness. She said, 'Let's go Stork. Catch lucky balloon,' and fell full-length like an axed oak. My first thought was to run for a doctor. But examination proved her pulse fine and her breathing regular. She was simply asleep. After finding a pillow for her head, I left her to enjoy it.

———≫∘∘∘≪———

JILLY COOPER
Octavia, 1977

HE wasn't the only one. Once those hunting types had had a few drinks, they all closed in on me, vying for my attention. Over and over again I let my glass be filled up. Never had my wit been more malicious or more sparkling. I kept them all in fits of braying laughter.

Like an experienced comedian, although I was keeping my audience happy, I was very conscious of what was going on in the wings – Jeremy, looking like a thundercloud because I was flirting so outrageously with other men, Gareth behaving like the Hamiltons' future son-in-law, whether he was coping with drinks or smiling into Lorna's eyes. Every so often, however, his eyes flickered in my direction, and his face hardened.

About ten o'clock, Bridget Hamilton wandered in, very red in the face, and carrying two saucepans, and plonked them down on a long polished table beside a pile of plates and forks.

'There's risotto here,' she said vaguely, 'if anyone's hungry.'

People surged forward to eat. I stayed put, the men around me stayed put as well. The din we were making increased until Gareth pushed his way through the crowd.

'You ought to eat something, Octavia,' he said.

I shook my head and smiled up at him insolently.

'Aren't you hungry?' drawled the MFH who was lounging beside me.

I turned to him, smiling sweetly, 'Only for you.'

A nearby group of women stopped filling their faces with risotto and talking about nappies, and looked at me in horror. The MFH's wife was among them. She had a face like a well-bred cod.

'The young gels of today are not the same as they were twenty years ago,' she said loudly.

'Of course they're not,' I shouted across at her. 'Twenty years ago I was only six. You must expect some change in my appearance and behaviour.'

She turned puce with anger at the roar of laughter that greeted this. Gareth didn't laugh. He took hold of my arm.

'I think you'd better come and eat,' he said in even tones.

'I've told you once,' I snapped, 'I don't want to eat. I want to dance. Why doesn't someone put on the record player?'

The MFH looked down at the circles of silver sequins.

'What happens to those when you dance?'

I giggled. 'Now you see me, now you don't. They've been known to shift off centre.'

There was another roar of laughter.

'Well, what are we waiting for?' said the MFH. 'Let's put a record on and dance.'

'All right,' I said, looking up at him under my lashes, 'But I must go to the loo first.'

Upstairs in the bathroom, I hardly recognized myself. I looked like some Maenad, my hair tousled, my eyes glittering, my cheeks flushed. God, the dress was so beautiful.

'And you're so beautiful too,' I added and, leaning forward, lightly kissed my reflection in the mirror.

Even in my alcoholic stare, I was slightly abashed when I turned round and saw Gareth standing watching me from the doorway.

'Don't you know it's rude to stare?' I said.

He didn't move.

'I'd like to come past – if you don't mind,' I went on.

'Oh no, you don't,' he said, grabbing my wrist.

'Oh yes I do,' I screamed, trying to tug myself away.

'Will you stop behaving like a whore!' he swore at me and, pulling me into the nearest bedroom, threw me on the bed and locked the door.

'Now I suppose you're going to treat me like a whore,' I spat at him. 'What will your precious Lorna say if she catches us here together?'

Suddenly I was frightened. There was murder in his eyes.

JOHN WILMOT, EARL OF ROCHESTER

Satires and Lampoons, 1670s

WHAT *Timon* does old Age begin t'approach
    That thus thou droop'st under a Nights debauch?
Hast thou lost deep to needy *Rogues* on Tick
Who ne're cou'd pay, and must be paid next *Week*.
Tim Neither alas, but a dull dining *Sot*,
Seiz'd me ith' *Mall*, who just my name had got;
He runs upon me, cries dear *Rogue* I'm thine,
With me some *Wits*, of thy acquaintance dine.

I tell him I'm engag'd, but as a *Whore*,
With modesty enslaves her *Spark*, the more,
The longer I deny'd, the more he prest,
At last I e'ne consent to be his *Guest*.
He takes me in his *Coach*, and as we go,
Pulls out a *Linel*, of a Sheet, or two;
Insipid, as, the praise of pious Queens,
Or *Shadwells*, unassisted former *Scenes*;
Which he admir'd, and prais'd at ev'ry *Line*.
At last it was so sharp, it must be mine.
I vow'd I was no more a *Wit*, than he,
Unpractic'd, and unblest in *Poetry*:
A *Song* to *Phillis*, I perhaps might make,
But never Rhym'd, but for my *Pintles* sake:
I envy'd no *Mans* fortune, nor his fame,
Nor ever thought of a revenge so tame.
He knew my *Stile*, he sword, and 'twas in vain,
Thus to deny the Issue of my *Brain*.
Choak'd with his flatt'ry, I no answer make,
But silent leave him to his dear mistake
Which he, by this, has spread o're the whole Town,
And me, with an officious Lye, undone.
Of a well meaning *Fool*, I'm most afraid,
Who sillily repeats, what was well said.
But this was not the worst, when he came home,
He askt are *Sidley, Buchurst, Savill*, come?
No, but there were above *Halfwit* and *Huffe*
Kickum, and *Dingboy*. Oh 'tis well enough.
They're all brave *Fellows* cryes mine *Host*, let's Dine,
I long to have my *Belly* full of *Wine*,
They'll write, and fight I dare assure you,
They're Men, *Tam Marte quam Mercurio*.
I saw my error, but 'twas now too late,
No means, nor hopes, appear of a retreat.
Well we salute, and each *Man* takes his Seat.
Boy (says my *Sot*) is my *Wife* ready yet?
A *Wife* good *Gods*! A *Fop* and *Bullys* too!
For one poor *Meale*, what must I undergo?
In comes my *Lady* strait, she had been *Fair*,
Fit to give love, and to prevent despair.
But *Age, Beauties* incurable Disease,

Had left her more desire, than pow'r to please.
As *Cocks* will strike, although their *Spurrs* be gone,
She with her old bleer *Eyes* to smite begun:
Though nothing else, she (in despight of time)
Preserv'd the affectation of her prime;
However you begun, she brought in love,
And hardly from that subject would remove.
We chancd to speak of the *French Kings* success;
My *Lady* wonder'd much how *Heav'n* cou'd bless,
A *Man*, that lov'd Two *Women* at one time;
But more how he to them excus'd his Crime.
She askt *Huffe*, if *Loves* flame he never felt?
He answer'd bluntly – do you think I'm gelt?
She at his plainness smil'd, then turn'd to me,
Love in young *Minds*, preceeds ev'n *Poetry*.
You to that passion can no *Stranger* be,
But *Wits*, are giv'n to inconstancy.
She had run on I think till now, but *Meat*
Came up, and suddenly she took her seat.
I thought the *Dinner* wou'd make some amends,
When my good *Host* cryes out – y'are all my *Friends*,
Our own plain *Fare*, and the best *Terse* the *Bull*
Affords, I'll give you and your *Bellies* full:
As for *French Kickshaws*, *Cellery*, and *Champoon*,
Ragous and *Fricasses*, introth we'ave none.
Here's a good *Dinner* towards thought I, when strait
Up comes a piece of *Beef*, full *Horsmans* weight;
Hard as the *Arse* of *Mosely*, under which,
The *Coachman* sweats, as ridden by a *Witch*.
A Dish of *Carrets*, each of 'em as long,
As *Tool*, that to fair *Countess*, did belong;
Which her small *Pillow*, cou'd not so well hide,
But *Visiters*, his flaming Head espy'd.
Pig, *Goose*, and *Capon*, follow'd in the *Rear*,
With all that *Country Bumpkins*, call good Cheer:
Serv'd up with Sauces all of *Eighty Eight*,
When our tough *Youth*, wrestled, and threw the Weight.
And now the *Bottle*, briskly flies about,
Instead of *Ice*, wrapt up in a wet *Clowt*.
A Brimmer follows the Third bit we eat,
Small *Bear*, becomes our drink, and Wine, our Meat.

The *Table* was so large, that in less space,
A Man might safe, Six old *Italians* place:
Each Man had as much room, as *Porter*, *Blunt*,
Or *Harris*, had, in *Cullens*, *Bushel Cunt*.
And now the *Wine* began to work, mine *Host*
Had been a *Collonel* we must hear him boast
Not of *Towns* won, but an *Estate* he lost
For the *Kings* Service, which indeed he spent
Whoring, and Drinking, but with good intent.
He talkt much of a Plot, and *Money* lent
In *Cromwells* time. My *Lady* she
Complain'd our love was course, our *Poetry*,
Unfit for modest Eares: small *Whores*, and *Play'rs*
Were of our Hair-brain'd *Youth*, the only cares;
Who were too wild for any virtuous *League*,
Too rotten to consummate the Intrigue,
Falkland, she prais'd, and *Sucklings*, easie Pen,
And seem'd to taste their former parts again.
Mine *Host*, drinks to the best in *Christendome*,
And decently my *Lady*, quits the Room.
Left to our selves, of several things we prate,
Some regulate the *Stage*, and some the *State*.
Halfwit, cries up my Lord of *Orrery*,
Ah how well *Mustapha*, and *Zanger* dye!
His sense so little forc'd, that by one *Line*,
You may the other easily divine.
　　And which is worse, if any worse can be,
　　He never said one word of it to me.
There's fine *Poetry*! you'd swear 'twere *Prose*,
So little on the Sense, the Rhymes impose.
Damn me (says *Dingboy*) in my mind *Gods-swounds*
Etheridge, writes *Airy Songs*, and soft *Lampoons*,
The best of any *Man*; as for your *Nowns*,
Grammar, and Rules of Art, he knows 'em not,
Yet writ Two talking *Plays*, without one *Plot*.
　　Huffe, was for *Settle*, and *Morocco*, prais'd,
Said rumbling words, like Drums, his courage rais'd.
　　Whose broad-built-bulks, the boyst'rous Billows, bear,
　　Zaphee and Sally, Mugadore, Oran,
　　The fam'd Arzile, Alcazer, Tituan.
Was ever braver Language writ by *Man*?

Kickum for *Crown* declar'd, said in *Romance*,
He had out done the very *Wits*, of *France*.
Witness *Pandion*, and his *Charles the Eight*;
Where a young *Monarch*, careless of his Fate,
Though Forreign Troops, and *Rebels*, shock his State,
Complains another sight afflicts him more.
(*Videl.*) *The Queens Galleys rowing from the Shore,*
Fitting their Oars and Tackling to be gon
Whilst sporting Waves smil'd on the rising Sun.
Waves smiling on the *Sun*! I'm sure that's new,
And 'twas well thought on, give the *Devil* his due.
Mine *Host*, who had said nothing in an hour,
Rose up, and prais'd the *Indian Emperor*.
As if our Old World, *modestly withdrew,*
And here in private had brought forth a New.
There are Two *Lines*! who but he durst presume
To make the old *World*, a new withdrawing Room,
Whereof another *World* she's brought to *Bed*!
What a brave *Midwife* is a *Laureats* head!
But pox of all these *Scriblers*, what do'e think.
Will *Souches* this year any *Champoone* drink?
Will *Turene* fight him? without doubt says *Huffe*,
When they Two meet, their meeting will be rough.
Damn me (says *Dingboy*) the *French*, *Cowards* are,
They pay, but the *English, Scots,* and *Swiss* make *War*.
In gawdy *Troops*, at a review they shine,
But dare not with the *Germans, Battel* joyn;
What now appears like courage, is not so,
'Tis short pride, which from success does grow;
On their first blow, they'll shrink into those fears,
They shew'd at *Cressy, Agincourt, Poytiers*;
Their loss was infamous, *Honor* so stain'd,
Is by a *Nation* not to be regain'd.
What they were then I know not, now th'are brave,
He that denies it – lyes and is a *Slave*
(Says *Huffe* and frown'd) says *Dingboy*, that do I,
And at that word, at t'others *Head* let fly
A greasie *Plate*, when suddenly they all,
Together by the Eares in Parties fall.
Halfwit, with *Dingboy* joynes, *Kickum* with *Huffe*
Their Swords were safe, and so we let 'em cuff

Till they mine *Host*, and I, had all enough.
Their rage once over, they begin to treat,
And Six fresh *Bottles*, must the peace compleat.
I ran down Stairs, with a Vow never more
To drink Bear Glass, and hear the *Hectors* roar.

THOMAS JORDAN

'The Epicure', date unknown

L ET us drink and be merry, dance, joke, and rejoice,
    With claret and sherry, theorbo and voice!
The changeable world to our joy is unjust,
    All treasure's uncertain,
    Then down with your dust!
In frolics dispose your pounds, shillings, and pence,
For we shall be nothing a hundred years hence.

We'll sport and be free with Moll, Betty, and Dolly,
Have oysters and lobsters to cure melancholy:
Fish-dinners will make a man spring like a flea.
    Dame Venus, love's lady,
    Was born of the sea;
With her and with Bacchus we'll tickle the sense,
For we shall be past it a hundred years hence.

Your most beautiful bride who with garlands is crown'd
And kills with each glance as she treads on the ground,
Whose lightness and brightness doth shine in such splendour
    That none but the stars
    Are thought fit to attend her,
Though now she be pleasant and sweet to the sense,
Will be damnable mouldy a hundred years hence.

Then why should we turmoil in cares and in fears,
Turn all our tranquill'ty to sighs and to tears?
Let's eat, drink, and play till the worms do corrupt us,
    'Tis certain, *Post mortem*
    Nulla voluptas.
For health, wealth and beauty, wit, learning and sense,
Must all come to nothing a hundred years hence.

CHARLES LAMB

'Confessions of a Drunkard' from *The Last Essays of Elia*, 1813

I BELIEVE that there are constitutions, robust heads and iron insides, whom scarce any excesses can hurt; whom brandy (I have seen them drink it like wine), at all events whom wine, taken in ever so plentiful measure, can do no worse injury to than just to muddle their faculties, perhaps never very pellucid. On them this discourse is wasted. They would but laugh at a weak brother, who, trying his strength with them, and coming off foiled from the contest, would fain persuade them that such agonistic exercises are dangerous. It is to a very different description of persons I speak. It is to the weak, the nervous; to those who feel the want of some artificial aid to raise their spirits in society to what is no more than the ordinary pitch of all around them without it. This is the secret of our drinking. Such must fly the convivial board in the first instance, if they do not mean to sell themselves for term of life.

Twelve years ago I had completed my six and twentieth year. I had lived from the period of leaving school to that time pretty much in solitude. My companions were chiefly books, or at most one or two living ones of my own book-loving and sober stamp. I rose early, went to bed betimes, and the faculties which God had given me, I have reason to think, did not rust in me unused.

About that time I fell in with some companions of a different order. They were men of boisterous spirits, sitters up a-nights, disputants, drunken; yet seemed to have something noble about them. We dealt about the wit, or what passes for it after midnight, jovially. Of the quality called fancy I certainly possessed a larger share than my companions. Encouraged by their applause, I set up for a profest joker! I, who of all men am least fitted for such an occupation, having, in addition to the greatest difficulty which I experience at all times of finding words to express my meaning, a natural nervous impediment in my speech!

Reader, if you are gifted with nerves like mine, aspire to any character but that of a wit. When you find a tickling relish upon your tongue disposing you to that sort of conversation, especially if you find a preternatural flow of ideas setting in upon you at the sight of a bottle and fresh glasses, avoid giving way to it as you would fly your greatest destruction. If you cannot crush the power of fancy, or that within you which you mistake for such, divert it, give it some other play. Write an essay, pen a character or description, – but not as I do now, with tears trickling down your cheeks.

To be an object of compassion to friends, of derision to foes; to be suspected by strangers, stared at by fools; to be esteemed dull when you cannot be witty, to be applauded for witty when you know that you have been dull; to be called upon for the extemporaneous exercise of that faculty which no premeditation can give; to be spurred on to efforts which end in contempt; to be set on to provoke mirth which procures the procurer hatred; to give pleasure and be paid with squinting malice; to swallow draughts of life-destroying wine which are to be distilled into airy breath to tickle vain auditors; to mortgage miserable morrows for nights of madness; to waste whole seas of time upon those who pay it back in little inconsiderable drops of grudging applause – are the wages of buffoonery and death.

SUSANNA JOHNSTON

Five Rehearsals, 1984

'SO, what got into you?' asked Janet as the three women closed in together in the sitting-room. The men stayed behind, drinking more.

'I'm in love with Johann. That's all.' Van wiped away tears from her eyes and chain smoked. Mrs Shelton, kind and fastidious, leant forward. 'Don't dear. You're a bit drunk. You'll be OK. You mustn't be in love with him. He doesn't know how to behave.'

'Greta. How dare you? He's one of our oldest friends. Mervyn knew him when he first came to England in the early days, before he married Myra. Mervyn hadn't lived here long himself. I agree, though, Johann doesn't and never will know how to behave. The way he sat there picking his nose.'

They were joined by the small band of men, now terribly intoxicated. Wallace came over to where Van sat, weeping and lonely. He squeezed and kissed her with exaggerated passion. In her drunken state she rejoiced. To be kissed like that in front of Johann. Greta, dainty, did her best to distract the others but had no luck with Mervyn. His eyes bulged as he queued for his fun. Soon it came. He wrenched her from Wallace's arms, a rag doll, lifted her skirt and felt about inside her knickers. Johann was inert but Janet's tiny black eyes were upon them.

'Now,' she said, pushing all guests towards the door, 'I want you to leave. I want to go to bed with my husband. When you have excited him sufficiently' – this to Van – 'he will come to bed with me. Get out the lot of you. And Johann, another time bring Carola.'

JOHANN WOLFGANG von GOETHE

Faust, 1808

ALTMAYER. Here's to liberty: bring in the wine!
MEPHISTOPHELES
  I'd drink a glass to liberty, my friend,
  If only local vintage weren't so bad.
SIEBEL. You'd best not air that notion here, egad!
MEPHISTOPHELES.
  Agreed; I fear the landlord to offend,
  Or I would offer every worthy guest
  From our own cellar something of the best.
SIEBEL. In that case, good, I'll say 'twas my request.
FROSCH. But give no nips; such samples, Sir, I hate:
  A real good glass-full we appreciate.
  For if it's my judicious word you ask,
  You have to fill my gullet for the task.
ALTMAYER (*sotto voce*).
  They come from Rheinland, I presume.
MEPHISTOPHELES. Give me a gimlet.
BRANDER.   What's that for?
  You surely haven't casks outside the door?
ALTMAYER.
  The landlord's tools are there, across the room.
MEPHISTOPHELES (*takes the gimlet*).
  (*To Frosch*) Now say, what's yours? A sparkling wine perhaps?
FROSCH. How's this? – Have you varieties, good Sir?
MEPHISTOPHELES. I'll give you all whatever you prefer.
ALTMAYER (*to Frosch*).
  Aha, you soon begin to lick your chaps.
FROSCH. Well, if I have to choose, I'll call for Rhein:

First in our Fatherland's good gift of wine.

MEPHISTOPHELES (*boring a hole in the table-edge, where Frosch is sitting*).

Fetch me some wax to make the spigots, quick!

ALTMAYER. It's nothing but a conjuring trick.

MEPHISTOPHELES (*to Brander*). And yours?

BRANDER.   Champagne, dear Sir, is mine,

And let it be a foaming, sparkling wine.

(*Mephistopheles bores; meanwhile one of them has made the wax spigots, and plugged them in.*)

BRANDER. One can't be always banning foreign stuff,

We have to look abroad for much that's fine:

A German hates a Frenchman sure enough,

But has a true affection for his wine.

SIEBEL (*as Mephistopheles comes towards his place at the table*).

Sour vintages I always shall pass by:

I much prefer the sweet wines to the dry.

MEPHISTOPHELES.

Just say the word, and you shall have Tokay.

ALTMAYER. Sirs, look me in the face and let's be frank:

Is this a foolery or a silly prank?

MEPHISTOPHELES.

Tut, tut. In such distinguished company

Unseemly joking would be out of place.

Therefore speak up, Sir, what's the wine to be,

And I'll endeavour then to please Your Grace.

ALTMAYER. I'm not particular, if that's the case.

(*The holes are now bored and the stoppers fixed.*)

MEPHISTOPHELES (*with curious gestures*).

Sweet grapes are on a wine-stock borne,

The he-goat has a branch of horn.

Wine comes from juice, the grape from wood,

The table yields us wine as good.

Deep Nature has her wonders still,

So draw the bungs and drink your fill.

ALL (*drawing the spigots and seeing the wines of their choice flowing into their glasses*).

O grand! In fountains! To it, with a will!

MEPHISTOPHELES.

My compliments! And don't let any spill.

(*They drink again and again.*)

SEVERAL (*singing*). Hell's Hottentots we are for wine,
  And lap the liquor as it flows;
  And happy as a hundred swine
  We drink, and don't care if it snows.
MEPHISTOPHELES.
  Now they're let loose, in democratic bliss.
FAUST. Come, let us go, I've had enough of this.
MEPHISTOPHELES. Why rush away?
  For if you stay
  A revelation shall you see
  Of charming bestiality.
    (*Siebel drinks recklessly and spills the wine on the floor, where
    it bursts into flame.*)
ALL. Help! Fire! Give help! A hellish flame!
MEPHISTOPHELES.
  Peace, friendly Element, be quiet and tame.
  (*To the drinkers.*) A spot of purging fire, in wisdom's name.
SIEBEL. We'll make you sorry for it, all the same:
  Who d'you take us for, man? What's your game?
FROSCH. I'll stop his jokes, no matter what he says.
ALTMAYER. And see him quietly off the premises.
SIEBEL. Come, come! How dare you, Sir, begin
  Your hocus-pocus in our inn?
MEPHISTOPHELES. Silence, old beer-can!
SIEBEL.   Broomstick, this to me!
  Will you add insult, Sir, to injury?
BRANDER. He's asking for it! Watch the fighting start!
ALTMAYER (*draws a plug from the table and receives a spurt of
  fire*). Fire, fire!
SIEBEL. Stab me this outlaw, practising black art!
  He's anybody's game! Strike for the heart!
    (*They draw their knives and advance upon Mephistopheles.*)
MEPHISTOPHELES (*with solemn gestures*).
  Mirage mount on sight and word,
  Vision, sense and place be blurred,
  And minds be distantly transferred.
    (*They stand and look at each other amazed.*)
ALTMAYER.
  Where may I be? And what this lovely land?
FROSCH. And vineyards!
SIEBEL. Ay, and clustering grapes to hand.

BRANDER. And here beneath the roof of green
  The richly loaded stems are seen.
    (*He takes Siebel by the nose; the rest treat each other the same,*
    and all raise their knives.)
MEPHISTOPHELES (*solemnly, as before*).
  Illusion take your scales from off their eyes:
  The Devil's humour let them recognize!
    (*He vanishes with Faust. The drinkers let go of each other.*)

CYRIL CONNOLLY

The Rock Pool, 1936

SOME party! Those two women from Antibes passed out and
had to be put in Duff's bedroom. And then Tahiti! She said she'd
broken her knee doing the *grand écart*, and Duff and Varna had to
carry her down to the village. Imagine carrying her half a kilometre!
They had to get a doctor and she screamed so when he touched her
he couldn't find out if anything was the matter. Then Sonia had a
row with the colonial. She told me about it when she came to say
good morning to me.

ABRAHAM COWLEY

'Drinking', 1668

THE thirsty earth soaks up the rain,
  And drinks and gapes for drink again;
The plants suck in the earth, and are
With constant drinking fresh and fair;
The sea itself (which one would think
Should have but little need of drink)
Drinks ten thousand rivers up,
So filled that they o'erflow the cup.
The busy Sun (and one would guess
By 's drunken fiery face no less)
Drinks up the sea, and when he's done,
The Moon and Stars drink up the Sun:
They drink and dance by their own light,

They drink and revel all the night:
Nothing in Nature's sober found,
But an eternal health goes round.
Fill up the bowl, then, fill it high,
Fill all the glasses there – for why
Should every creature drink but I?
Why, man of morals, tell me why?

IVAN TURGENEV

The Torrents of Spring, 1897

AT one of the tables near were sitting several officers of the Garrison of the Maine. From their glances and whispering together it was easy to perceive that they were struck by Gemma's beauty; one of them, who had probably stayed in Frankfort, stared at her persistently, as at a figure familiar to him; he obviously knew who she was. He suddenly got up, and glass in hand – all the officers had been drinking hard, and the cloth before them was crowded with bottles – approached the table at which Gemma was sitting. He was a very young flaxen-haired man, with a rather pleasing and even attractive face, but his features were distorted with the wine he had drunk, his cheeks were twitching, his blood-shot eyes wandered, and wore an insolent expression. His companions at first tried to hold him back, but afterwards let him go, interested apparently to see what he would do, and how it would end.

Slightly unsteady on his legs, the officer stopped before Gemma, and in an unnaturally screaming voice, in which, in spite of himself, an inward struggle could be discerned, he articulated, 'I drink to the health of the prettiest confectioner in all Frankfort, in all the world (he emptied his glass), and in return I take this flower, picked by her divine little fingers!' He took from the table a rose that lay beside Gemma's plate. At first she was astonished, alarmed, and turned fearfully white ... then alarm was replaced by indignation; she suddenly crimsoned all over, to her very hair – and her eyes, fastened directly on the offender, at the same time darkened and flamed, they were filled with black gloom, and burned with the fire of irrepressible fury. The officer must have been confused by this look; he muttered something unintelligible, bowed, and walked back to his friends. They greeted him with a laugh, and faint applause.

TOBIAS SMOLLETT

Humphrey Clinker, 1771

THE continual swimming of those phantoms before my eyes gave me a swimming of the head, which was also affected by the foul air, circulating through such a number of rotten human bellows. I therefore retreated towards the door, and stood in the passage to the next room, talking to my friend Quin: when an end being put to the minuets, the benches were removed to make way for the country-dances; and the multitude rising at once, the whole atmosphere was put in commotion. Then, all of a sudden, came rushing on me an Egyptian gale, so impregnated with pestilential vapors, that my nerves were overpowered, and I dropped senseless on the floor.

You may easily conceive what a clamor and confusion this accident must have produced in such an assembly. I soon recovered, however, and found myself in an easy chair, supported by my own people. Sister Tabby, in her great tenderness, had put me to the torture, squeezing my head under her arm, and stuffing my nose with spirit of hartshorn, till the whole inside was excoriated. I no sooner got home than I sent for doctor Cl— who assured me I needed not be alarmed, for my swooning was entirely occasioned by an accidental impression of fetid effluvia on nerves of uncommon sensibility. I know not how other people's nerves are constructed; but one would imagine they must be made of very coarse materials, to stand the shock of such a horrid assault. It was, indeed, *a compound of villanous smells*, in which the most violent stinks and the most powerful perfumes contended for the mastery. Imagine to yourself a high exalted essence of mingled odours, arising from putrid gums, imposthumated lungs, sour flatulencies, rank armpits, sweating feet, running sores and issues, plasters, ointments, and embrocations, Hungary-water, spirit of lavender, assafoetida drops, musk, hartshorn, and sal volatile; besides a thousand frowsy steams, which I could not analyse. Such, O Dick! is the fragrant ether we breathe in the polite assemblies of Bath: such is the atmosphere I have exchanged for the pure, elastic, animating air of the Welsh mountains. *O rus, quando te aspiciam?* – I wonder what the devil possessed me—

Part Four

ENDINGS

ALEXANDER SERGEYEVITCH PUSHKIN

The Moor of Peter the Great, 1828

'ARE you raving, greybeard?' interrupted the fool, Yekimovna. 'Or are you blind? That's the imperial sledge – the Tsar's come.'

Gavrila Afanassyevitch hurriedly stood up from the table; everybody rushed over to the windows, and indeed they saw the Tsar, leaning on his orderly's shoulder, mounting the steps. There was a general confusion. The host rushed forward to meet Peter: the servants dashed hither and thither, as if demented: the guests took fright, and some even began to think of how to leave for home as soon as possible. Peter's thundering voice was suddenly heard in the hall: all fell silent, and the Tsar entered, accompanied by his host, overcome with joy.

'Good day, ladies and gentlemen,' said Peter cheerfully.

Everyone bowed low. The Tsar's sharp eyes sought out the host's young daughter in the crowd: he summoned her to him. Natalya Gavrilovna advanced boldly enough, even though she was blushing not only to her ears, but also down to her shoulders.

'You become more beautiful every day,' the Tsar said to her, and as was his habit, he kissed her on the forehead: then, turning to the guests, he said:

'I have disturbed you? You were dining? Sit down again, I beg of you, and give me some aniseed-vodka, Gavrila Afanassyevitch.'

The host rushed over to his stately steward, snatched the tray from his hands, and himself filled a golden goblet and handed it to the Tsar with a bow. Peter drank the vodka, ate a biscuit and for the second time invited the guests to continue with their dinner. All resumed their former places with the exception of the dwarf and the housekeeper, who did not dare to remain at a table honoured by the presence of the Tsar. Peter sat down next to his host and asked for some soup. The imperial orderly handed him a wooden spoon mounted with ivory and a knife and fork with green bone handles, for Peter never used any cutlery other than his own. The dinner, which a moment before had been noisy with laughter and conversation, was continued in silence and constraint. The host, through respect and delight, ate nothing; the guests also stood on ceremony and listened with reverence as the Tsar conversed in German with the captive Swede about the campaign of 1701. The fool, Yekimovna, spoken to on one or two occasions by the Tsar, replied with a sort of shy *hauteur*, which, be it noted, was by no means a sign of natural stupidity on her part. The dinner finally came to an end. The Tsar stood up, and after him all the guests.

'Gavrila Afanassyevitch,' he said to his host, 'I'd like a word with you in private.'

And taking him by the arm, he led him into the drawing-room, and shut the door behind him. The guests remained in the dining-room, whispering to each other about this unexpected visit and, for fear of being indiscreet, quickly dispersed one after another for home, without thanking their host for his hospitality. His father-in-law, daughter and sister conducted them quietly to the door and remained alone in the dining-room, waiting for the Tsar to come out.

BARONESS ORCZY

The Scarlet Pimpernel, 1905

FOR one moment there was dead silence from the little boudoir. Beyond from the brilliant ballroom, the sweet notes of the gavotte, the frou-frou of rich dresses, the talk and laughter of a large and merry crowd, came a strange, weird accompaniment to the drama which was being enacted here.

Sir Andrew had not uttered another word. Then it was that that extra sense became potent in Marguerite Blakeney. She could not see, for her eyes were closed: she could not hear, for the noise from the ballroom drowned the soft rustle of the momentous scrap of paper: nevertheless she knew, as if she had both seen and heard, that

Sir Andrew was even now holding the paper to the flame of one of the candles.

At the exact moment that it began to catch fire, she opened her eyes, raised her hand, and with two dainty fingers, had taken the burning scrap of paper from the young man's hand. Then she blew out the flame, and held the paper to her nostril with perfect unconcern.

'How thoughtful of you, Sir Andrew,' she said gaily, 'surely 'twas your grandmother who taught you that the smell of burnt paper was a sovereign remedy against giddiness.'

She sighed with satisfaction, holding the paper tightly between her jewelled fingers; that talisman which perhaps would save her brother Armand's life. Sir Andrew was staring at her, too dazed for the moment to realize what had actually happened; he had been taken so completely by surprise, that he seemed quite unable to grasp the fact that the slip of paper, which she held in her dainty hand, was one perhaps on which the life of his comrade might depend.

Marguerite burst into a long, merry peal of laughter.

'Why do you stare at me like that?' she said playfully. 'I assure you I feel much better: your remedy has proved most effectual. This room is most delightfully cool,' she added, with the same perfect composure, 'and the sound of the gavotte from the ballroom is fascinating and soothing.'

She was prattling on in the most unconcerned and pleasant way, whilst Sir Andrew, in an agony of mind, was racking his brains as to the quickest method he could employ to get that bit of paper out of that beautiful woman's hand. Instinctively, vague and tumultuous thoughts rushed through his mind: he suddenly remembered her nationality, and, worst of all, recollected that horrible tale about the Marquis de St Cyr, which in England no one had credited, for the sake of Sir Percy, as well as for her own.

'What? Still dreaming and staring?' she said, with a merry laugh. 'You are most ungallant, Sir Andrew: and now I come to think of it, you seemed more startled than pleased when you saw me just now. I do believe after all, that it was not concern for my health, nor yet a remedy taught you by your grandmother, that caused you to burn this tiny scrap of paper . . . I vow it must have been your lady love's last cruel epistle you were trying to destroy. Now confess,' she added, playfully holding up the scrap of paper, 'does this contain her final *congé*, or a last appeal to kiss and make friends?'

'Whichever it is, Lady Blakeney,' said Sir Andrew, who was

gradually recovering his self-possession, 'this little note is undoubtedly mine, and . . .'

Not caring whether his action was one that would be styled illbred
towards a lady, the young man had made a bold dash for the note:
but Marguerite's thoughts flew quicker than his own: her actions,
under pressure of this intense excitement, were swifter and more
sure. She was tall and strong, she took a quick step backwards and
knocked over the small Sheraton table which was already top-heavy,
and which fell with a crash, together with the massive candelabra
upon it.

She gave a quick cry of alarm.

'The candles, Sir Andrew. Quick!'

WILLIAM SHAKESPEARE

Macbeth, 1605–6

Act III, Scene IV

LEN.   May it please your highness sit?
[*The Ghost of* BANQUO *appears, and sits in* MACBETH'S *place.*]
MACB. Here had we now our country's honour roof'd,
      Were the grac'd person of our Banquo present;
      Who may I rather challenge for unkindness,
      Than pity for mischance!
ROSSE.   His absence, Sir,
      Lays blame upon his promise. Please it your highness
      To grace us with your royal company?
MACB. The table's full.
LEN.   Here is a place reserv'd, Sir.
MACB. Where?
LEN. Here, my good lord. What is't that moves your highness?
MACB. Which of you have done this?
LORDS.   What, my good lord?
MACB. Thou canst not say I did it: never shake
      Thy gory locks at me.
ROSSE. Gentlemen, rise; his highness is not well.
LADY M. Sit, worthy friends: my lord is often thus,
      And hath been from his youth: pray you, keep seat;
      The fit is momentary; upon a thought

He will again be well: if much you note him,
You shall offend him, and extend his passion:
Feed, and regard him not. Are you a man?
MACB. Ay, and a bold one, that dare look on that
  Which might appal the devil.
LADY M.   O proper stuff!
This is the very painting of your fear:
This is the air-drawn dagger, which, you said,
Led you to Duncan. O, these flaws and starts
(Impostors to true fear) would well become
A woman's story at a winter's fire,
Authoriz'd by her grandam. Shame itself!
Why do you make such faces? When all's done,
You look but on a stool.
MACB. Pr'ythee, see there! behold! look! lo! how say you?
Why, what care I? If thou canst nod, speak too.
If charnel-houses, and our graves, must send
Those that we bury back, our monuments
Shall be the maws of kites.   [*Ghost disappears*]

ROBERT COOVER

Gerald's Party, date unknown

'I T – it's only a party—!' I protested.
  'Only! do you think I'm *blind*? You've got drug addicts here!
You've got perverts, anarchists, pimps and peeping toms! Adulterers!
You've got dipsomaniacs! You've got whores, thugs, thieves, athe-
ists, sodomists and out-and-out lunatics! There isn't *anything* they
wouldn't do!' He seemed almost to have grown. He was rigid,
powerful – yet his hand was trembling as he picked up a piece of
paper. 'In this world, nothing, – *nothing*, I tell you is ever wholly
concealed. I know what's in their sick stinking hearts.'
  'Look at this! It's a drawing of the murder scene. Only it was
drawn *before the murder*. We can *prove* this. Somebody was
planning this homicide all along! You see? Somebody here, *in this
house*. Down to the *last vile detail* – except that they apparently
meant to strike her womb instead of the breast – at least that must
be the true *meaning* of the crime – you can see here the blood, the
hideous weapon between her legs.'

HUGO VICKERS

Gladys, Duchess of Marlborough, 1979

EVELYN Waugh recorded that at the dinner there were two
ambassadors and 'about forty hard-faced middle-aged peers and
peeresses'. Gladys looked 'very battered with fine diamonds', while
Sunny wore his Garter riband and a silk turban over a bandaged
eye. As Waugh left, Gladys turned to him and declared: 'Ah, you are
like Marlborough. He has such a mundane mind. He will go to any
party for which he is sent a printed invitation.'

That insult was a mild one compared to others to which Gladys
subjected Marlborough. There had been an occasion on which he
had struck Gladys on the way to a luncheon party, causing her to
arrive with a black eye. There were rows about servants, Marlborough claiming that Gladys upset them and they left, and an atmosphere soon reigned in which neither party could do anything right.
In her misery, Gladys responded by kicking out. One night Sunny
was talking about politics. From the other end of the table Gladys
suddenly shouted at him 'Shut up! You know nothing about politics.
I've slept with every prime minister in Europe and most kings. You
are not qualified to speak.' Sunny dug nervously into his dinner. On
another occasion she instigated a conversation about communism,
ingeniously involving the footmen in the conversation and creating
general discomfort. And at one dinner she produced a revolver and
placed it beside her. A rather startled guest at her side inquired:
'Duchess, what are you going to do with that?' to which she replied:
'Oh! I don't know. I might just shoot Marlborough!'

LORD BYRON

Childe Harold's Pilgrimage, 1812

from *Canto III*

XXI
There was a sound of revelry by night,
And Belgium's capital had gather'd then
Her Beauty and her Chivalry, and bright
The lamps shone o'er fair women and brave men:

A thousand hearts beat happily: and when
Music arose with its voluptuous swell,
Soft eyes look'd love to eyes which spake again,
And all went merry as a marriage bell:
But hush! hark! a deep sound strikes like a rising knell!

XXII

Did ye not hear it? – No: 'twas but the wind,
Or the car rattling o'er the stony street:
On with the dance! let joy be unconfined:
No sleep till morn, when Youth and Pleasure meet
To chase the glowing Hours with flying feet.
But hark! – that heavy sound breaks in once more,
As if the clouds its echo would repeat;
And nearer, clearer, deadlier than before!
Arm! arm! it is – it is – the cannon's opening roar!

XXIII

Within a window'd niche of that high hall
Sate Brunswick's fated chieftain; he did hear
That sound, the first amidst the festival,
And caught its tone with Death's prophetic ear;
And when they smiled because he deem'd it near.
His heart more truly knew that peal too well
Which stretch'd his father on a bloody bier,
And roused the vengeance blood alone could quell:
He rushed into the field, and, foremost fighting, fell.

XXIV

Ah! then and there was hurrying to and fro,
And gathering tears, and tremblings of distress,
And cheeks all pale, which but an hour ago
Blush'd at the praise of their own loveliness:
And there were sudden partings, such as press
The life from out young hearts, and choking sighs
Which ne'er might be repeated: who would guess
If ever more should meet those mutual eyes,
Since upon night so sweet such awful morn could rise!

XXV

And there was mounting in hot haste: the steed,
The mustering squadron, and the clattering car,
Went pouring forward with impetuous speed,

And swiftly forming in the ranks of war;
And the deep thunder peal on peal afar;
And near, the beat of the alarming drum
Roused up the soldier ere the morning star:
While throng'd the citizens with terror dumb,
Or whispering, with white lips – 'The foe!
    They come! they come!'

XXVI

And wild and high the 'Camerons' gathering' rose,
The war-note of Lochiel, which Albyn's hills
Have heard, and heard, too, have her Saxon foes:
How in the noon of night that pibroch thrills
Savage and shrill! But with the breath which fills
Their mountain-pipe, so fill the mountaineers
With the fierce native daring which instils
The stirring memory of a thousand years,
And Evan's, Donald's fame rings in each clansman's ears!

GEORGE BERNARD SHAW

Pygmalion, 1912

CLEARLY Eliza will not pass as a duchess yet and Higgins's bet remains unwon. But the six months are not yet exhausted: and just in time Eliza does actually pass as a princess. For a glimpse of how she did it imagine an Embassy in London one summer evening after dark. The hall door has an awning and a carpet across the sidewalk to the kerb, because a grand reception is in progress. A small crowd is lined up to see the guests arrive.

A Rolls-Royce car drives up. Pickering in evening dress, with medals and orders, alights, and hands out Eliza, in opera cloak, evening dress, diamonds, fan, dowers and all accessories. Higgins follows. The car drives off: and the three go up the steps and into the house, the door opening for them as they approach.

Inside the house they find themselves in a spacious hall from which the grand staircase rises. On the left are the arrangements for the gentlemen's cloaks. The male guests are depositing their hats and wraps there.

On the right is a door leading to the ladies' cloakroom. Ladies are

going in cloaked and coming out in splendour. Pickering whispers to
Eliza and points out the ladies' room. She goes into it. Higgins and
Pickering take off their overcoats and take tickets for them from the
attendant.

One of the guests, occupied in the same way, has his back turned.
Having taken his ticket, he turns round and reveals himself as an
important looking young man with an astonishingly hairy face. He
has an enormous moustache, flowing out into luxuriant whiskers.
Waves of hair cluster on his brow. His hair is cropped closely at the
back, and glows with oil. Otherwise he is very smart. He wears
several worthless orders. He is evidently a foreigner, guessable as a
whiskered Pandour from Hungary; but in spite of the ferocity of his
moustache he is amiable and genially voluble.

HOSTESS. Ah, here is Professor Higgins: he will tell us. Tell us all
about the wonderful young lady, Professor.

HIGGINS [*almost morosely*] What wonderful young lady?

HOSTESS. You know very well. They tell me there has been nothing
like her in London since people stood on their chairs to look at
Mrs Langtry.

Nepommuck joins the group, full of news.

HOSTESS. Ah, here you are at last, Nepommuck. Have you found
out all about the Doolittle lady?

NEPOMMUCK. I have found out all about her. She is a fraud.

HOSTESS. A fraud! Oh no.

NEPOMMUCK. YES. yes. She cannot deceive me. Her name cannot
be Doolittle.

HIGGINS. Why?

NEPOMMUCK. Because Doolittle is an English name. And she is not
English.

HOSTESS. Oh, nonsense! She speaks English perfectly.

NEPOMMUCK. Too perfectly. Can you shew me any English woman
who speaks English as it should be spoken? Only foreigners who
have been taught to speak it speak it well.

HOSTESS. Certainly she terrified me by the way she said How d'ye
do. I had a schoolmistress who talked like that: and I was mortally
afraid of her. But if she is not English what is she?

NEPOMMUCK. Hungarian.

ALL THE REST. Hungarian!

NEPOMMUCK. Hungarian. And of royal blood. I am Hungarian.
My blood is royal.

HIGGINS. Did you speak to her in Hungarian?

NEPOMMUCK. I did. She was very clever. She said 'Please speak to me in English: I do not understand French.' French! She pretends not to know the difference between Hungarian and French. Impossible: she knows both.

HIGGINS. And the blood royal? How did you find that out?

NEPOMMUCK. Instinct, maestro, instinct. Only the Magyar races can produce that air of the divine right, those resolute eyes. She is a princess.

HOST. What do you say, Professor?

HIGGINS I say an ordinary London girl out of the gutter and taught to speak by an expert. I place her in Drury Lane.

NEPOMMUCK. Ha ha ha! Oh, maestro, maestro, you are mad on the subject of cockney dialects. The London gutter is the whole world for you.

HIGGINS [to the Hostess] What does your Excellency say?

HOSTESS. Oh, of course I agree with Nepommuck. She must be a princess at least.

HOST. Not necessarily legitimate, of course. Morganatic perhaps. But that is undoubtedly her class.

HIGGINS. I stick to my opinion.

HOSTESS. Oh, you are incorrigible.

   The group breaks up, leaving Higgins isolated. Pickering joins him.

PICKERING. Where is Eliza? We must keep an eye on her.
   Eliza joins them.

LIZA. I don't think I can bear much more. The people all stare so at me. An old lady has just told me that I speak exactly like Queen Victoria. I am sorry if I have lost your bet. I have done my best: but nothing can make me the same as these people.

PICKERING. You have not lost it, my dear. You have won it ten times over.

HIGGINS. Let us get out of this. I have had enough of chattering to these fools.

PICKERING. Eliza is tired: and I am hungry. Let us clear out and have supper somewhere.

PATRICK LEIGH-FERMOR
The Violins of St Jacques, 1953

THE floor was bare. But, before the dancers could disperse to the lantern-lit terraces – the heat seemed to be growing more oppressive every minute – they were arrested by a shrill cry from the head of the stairs: 'Please wait a moment, everybody!'

It was Anne-Jules, standing on the landing with Pierrot at his side. They were dressed from head to foot in palm-leaves, and wore tall gold necromancer's hats painted with a pattern of stars and planets and snakes. They advanced to the head of the stairs, turned back to back with a precision that must have been often rehearsed and slid down opposite banisters which deposited them simultaneously on the empty dance-floor. Advancing to the middle, Pierrot placed a footstool under the central chandelier, and on top of this Anne-Jules placed his mysterious basket. Then, bowing towards his father's table, he said, 'Vos Excellences. Monsieur le comte, madame la comtesse, messieurs, mesdames, mesdemoiselles, nous allons vous wévéler le woi du Carnaval.' Bending to the square basket, he opened a trap door in the side and intoned the following words:

> Beauté supwême et toute puissante,
> et majesté du carnaval,
> Dans les tenèbwes languissantes,
> Sors du palais, diwige le bal!

Both boys then began a low, soft coaxing whistle and, in a stage whisper, said in unison, 'Sors, Sardanapale!' The long drawn whistling continued, and the guests craned forward with a flutter of curiosity. 'Sors, Sardanapale!', Anne-Jules and Pierrot repeated, and a dark object appeared from the little wicker door. It moved from side to side for a few seconds, curled downwards to the floor, and then, followed by two flowing yards of scaly and noiseless sinuosity as thick as a wrist, began to move across the parquet. There was a general gasp and one or two half-suppressed screams. Following it, Anne-Jules changed his whistle to a succession of staccato notes and the snake raised its head high in the air. Its head was followed by an erect pillar of trunk which stretched every second longer until its entire length, rising from and balancing on a small terminal circle of tail, seemed to be standing perpendicular. The terrible triangular and horny head, lowered at right angles to its trunk, swayed from side to side with a drunken-seeming motion. A forked tongue darted swiftly in and out of hissing jaws.

A shock of terror at the sight of the *fer de lance*, poised in the classical posture preparatory to striking, ran through the room like a wave of electricity. The bite of the trigonocephalus brings certain death within the hour. In a sudden scurry the dancers crowded back from the possible ambit of its leap. The Count was the first to break the silence.

'Anne-Jules,' he shouted, 'do you know how to make that brute get back into the basket?'

Anne-Jules looked at his father round-eyed with feigned surprise. 'Yes, papa.'

'Then do so directly.'

Still softly whistling, he approached the poised serpent from behind, caught hold of the back of the hissing head, then, lifting it in the air, gathered up the heavy slack with his other hand and walked to where Pierrot was holding the basket open. Everyone held their breath. The Countess, white as chalk, was feverishly fingering her châtelaine. Anne-Jules dropped the tail through the trap-door and coiled the long body after it until only the head remained outside. With a murmur of 'tentre, Sardanapale,' he dropped it inside and Pierrot closed the lid.

There was a universal escape of breath and a slightly hysterical rush of talk. The Count strode to the basket, picked it up and handed it to Gentilien, whose pupils were revolving in apprehensive circles of white.

'Take this brute away and destroy it. And you,' he said severely, turning to Anne-Jules, 'go straight up to bed and stay there!'

The two little wizards, their conical hats hanging dejectedly now, made for the stairs and, climbing sadly to the landing, vanished.

'I apologise for my son's ridiculous behaviour,' the Count said, with a circular gesture to his guests, and then waved to the band. Raggedly at first they struck up a polka. He seized Berthe round the waist and off they galloped, the musicians recovering the beat once more from their master's determined pacings. Other couples joined them and soon, in a hubbub of chatter, the Ball revived.

THE BIBLE
Daniel, Chapter 5

BELSHAZZAR the king made a great feast to a thousand of his lords, and drank wine before the thousand.

Belshazzar, whiles he tasted the wine, commanded to bring the golden and silver vessels which his father Nebuchadnezzar had taken out of the temple which *was* in Jerusalem: that the king, and his princes, his wives, and his concubines, might drink therein.

Then they brought the golden vessels that were taken out of the temple of the house of God which *was* at Jerusalem: and the king, and his princes, his wives, and his concubines, drank in them.

They drank wine, and praised the gods of gold, and of silver, of brass, of iron, of wood, and of stone.

In the same hour came forth fingers of a man's hand, and wrote over against the candlestick upon the plaister of the wall of the king's palace: and the king saw the part of the hand that wrote.

Then the king's countenance was changed, and his thoughts troubled him, so that the joints of his loins were loosed, and his knees smote one against another.

The king cried aloud to bring in the astrologers, the Chaldeans, and the sooth-sayers. *And* the king spake, and said to the wise *men* of Babylon, Whosoever shall read this writing, and shew me the interpretation thereof, shall be clothed with scarlet, and *have* a chain of gold about his neck, and shall be the third ruler in the kingdom.

Then came in all the king's wise *men*: but they could not read the writing, nor make known to the king the interpretation thereof.

Then was king Belshazzar greatly troubled, and his countenance was changed in him and his lords were astonished.

MARGARET ATWOOD
Life Before Man, 1980

NATE is talking with a girl in a white dress. He's never seen her before, though she claims to have met him at one of Martha's parties, two years ago, she says. She's telling Nate about her job. She makes plastic models of Holstein cows which are sold to breeders and dealers. The cows have to be made exactly to scale, perfect in every detail. She's hoping to go into painted portraits of individual cows, for which she could get more money. She asks Nate what his sign is.

Nate knows he should leave the party. He's done his duty. But the girl seizes his hand and bends over his palm, squinting at his life line. He can see a short distance down the front of her dress. He watches this pinched landscape idly. He isn't very good at casual encounters.

Martha is there, right beside his ear. She wants to have a word with him, she says. She takes his other hand and he allows himself to be led from the living room, down the hall into the bedroom. Coats are piled on the bed.

'You're disgusting,' Martha says. 'You make me want to puke.'

Nate blinks at her, bending his head towards her as if this will help him to understand. Martha punches him in the face, then begins kicking him in the shins. She's hampered by the long skirt of her dress, so she slugs him, aiming for the belly, hitting him in the rib cage. Nate catches her arms and holds her against him. Now she's crying. He could throw her onto the bed, roll her up in coats to hold her still, then try to find out what he's done.

'What did I do?' he says.

'Making up to her at my party, right in front of me. You always try to humiliate me,' Martha says, her voice coming in spurts. 'You know what? You succeed.'

'I wasn't,' Nate says, 'We were talking about plastic cows.'

MADAME DE SÉVIGNÉ
Letters, 26 April 1671

Paris, Sunday, 26th April, 1671

'THIS letter will not go till Wednesday; but indeed it is not a letter but an account Moreuil has given me for you of what happened at Chantilly. I wrote to you on Friday, telling you Vatel had stabbed himself – here is the story in detail. The King arrived on Thursday evening, when all went well – the hunting, the lanterns, the moonlight, the walks in the garden, the supper in a place decorated with jonquils. But there was no roast served at some of the tables, because of the great number of unexpected guests. This upset Vatel very much. He went about saying, "I have lost my honour – I can't endure this." And he told Gourville that he had been so much worried by the preparations that he had not slept for the last twelve nights. Gourville did all he could to comfort him; but he could not get the failure of the roast (though there was plenty at the King's table) out of his head.

'Gourville spoke to the Prince, who went to Vatel's room and said to him, "Vatel, everything is going well. Nothing could have been better than the King's supper." He replied, "Your Highness's kindness completes my distress. I know there was no roast for two tables." "Not at all," said the Prince, "don't distress yourself, for everything is going well."

'Midnight comes – the fireworks are a failure. They can hardly be seen, the sky is so cloudy. They had cost 16,000 francs. At four o'clock in the morning Vatel gets up and wanders about. The whole household is asleep. He comes across one of the purveyors who has just arrived. He finds that he has brought only two loads of fish. "Is this all?" he asks. "Yes, Monsieur," says the man, not knowing that orders had been given to others. Vatel waits for some time: but as no more carts arrive, he thinks there is no more fish to be had. He goes to Gourville and says, "Sir, I shall not be able to bear this disgrace. I shall not survive the loss of my honour and reputation." Gourville makes light of the matter; whereupon Vatel mounts to his chamber, puts his sword against the door and runs himself through. Twice he merely wounds himself, but at the third stroke he falls down dead.

'Loads of fish arrive from all quarters. Vatel is not to be found. People go to his chamber: they knock; they force the door; they find him lying in his blood. The Prince is greatly distressed. His son weeps, for all the arrangements for his journey to Burgundy depended on Vatel.'

MARY WESLEY

A Dubious Legacy, 1992

THE dinner table was a shambles. Maisie was screaming, Trask swearing and Pilar yelling, 'Aie! Aie!' at the top of her voice. Some of the candles had been snuffed, some had fallen and spitted their grease as Margaret danced on the table among the debris of the meal. As she danced she crushed the lilies of the valley underfoot. She had ripped the Dior dress, tearing the bodice, so that she was

naked to the waist. Flame from a candle had scorched up her skirt:
the smell of singeing mingled with the lilies. But worse than the smell
of burning Dior was the stink of scorched feathers as she whirled the
cockatoo round her head, then dipped it low to catch in the candles.
Maisie was screaming on a high, hysterical, undulating note and
Peter was being sick into the tulips.

Trask, Ebro, James and Matthew made futile grabs at Margaret
but, evading them, she stamped and danced, whirling the cockatoo.

Then Antonia leapt upon the table. Margaret crowed, 'I dare you
to come closer.' As Antonia hesitated she tore off the bird's head
and flung it in Antonia's face, shouting, 'Hah! Come on! Come on!'
and began ripping the bird's wings.

Henry, bursting past Ebro, hurled himself on to the table and,
catching Margaret round the knees, brought her down among the
glass and china. As she went down she tore at his face with her
bloody hands. The table collapsed under their weight and Antonia,
terrified, cried, 'Help! I am falling!' And Margaret, struggling with
Henry, bit him in the neck.

Matthew said, 'Oh *dear*!' and helped Antonia to her feet. Maisie
and Pilar stopped screaming, Barbara ran into James's arms, buried
her face against his dinner jacket and sobbed, but nobody spoke
until Henry said, 'Give us a hand, somebody,' and extricated himself
and his wife from the broken table, setting her carefully on her feet
as Hector and Calypso arrived at a run to see what was happening.

They heard Henry say, 'You must not get cold, Margaret.' He was
quiet and solicitous after the shrill pandemonium. They saw him
take off his jacket and wrap it round her nakedness. 'Are you all
right?' he asked. 'Are you hurt? No? That's good.' The bite on his
neck was bleeding but he was gentle with Margaret, setting her
upright, holding her steady.

WILLIAM SHAKESPEARE

Romeo and Juliet, 1596

Act I, Scene V

Enter [CAPULET, LADY CAPULET, JULIET, TYBALT,
NURSE *and*] *all the* Guests *and* Gentlewomen *to the Masquers.*

CAP. Welcome, gentlemen, ladies that have their toes

Unplagu'd with corns will walk a bout with you.
Ah my mistresses, which of you all
Will now deny to dance? She that makes dainty,
She I'll swear hath corns. Am I come near ye now?
Welcome, gentlemen. I have seen the day
That I have worn a visor and could tell
A whispering tale in a fair lady's ear,
Such as would please. 'Tis gone, 'tis gone, 'tis gone,
You are welcome, gentlemen: come, musicians, play.
A hall, a hall, give room! And foot it girls!
                    Music plays and they dance.
More light, you knaves, and turn the tables up.
And quench the fire, the room is grown too hot.
Ah sirrah, this unlook'd-for sport comes well.
Nay sit, nay sit, good cousin Capulet,
For you and I are past our dancing days.
How long is't now since last yourself and I
Were in a masque?
COUSIN CAP.   By'r Lady, thirty years.
CAP. What, man, 'tis not so much, 'tis not so much.
    'Tis since the nuptial of Lucentio,
    Come Pentecost as quickly as it will,
    Some five and twenty years: and then we masqu'd.
COUSIN CAP. 'Tis more, 'tis more, his son is elder, sir:
    His son is thirty.
CAP.   Will you tell me that?
    His son was but a ward two years ago.
ROMEO. What lady's that which doth enrich the hand
    Of yonder knight?
SER.   I know not, sir.
ROMEO. O, she doth teach the torches to burn bright.
    It seems she hangs upon the cheek of night
    As a rich jewel in an Ethiop's ear;
    Beauty too rich for use, for earth too dear.
    So shows a snowy dove trooping with crows
    As yonder lady o'er her fellows shows.
    The measure done, I'll watch her place of stand,
    And touching hers, make blessed my rude hand.
    Did my heart love till now? Forswear it, sight.
    For I ne'er saw true beauty till this night.
TYB. This by his voice should be a Montague.

Fetch me my rapier, boy. [*Exit Boy.*] What, dares the slave
Come hither, cover'd with an antic face,
To fleer and scorn at our solemnity?
Now by the stock and honour of my kin,
To strike him dead I hold it not a sin.

CAP. Why how now, kinsman, wherefore storm you so?

TYB. Uncle, this is a Montague, our foe:
A villain that is hither come in spite
To scorn at our solemnity this night.

CAP. Young Romeo is it?

TYB.   'Tis he, that villain Romeo.

CAP. Content thee, gentle coz, let him alone,
A bears him like a portly gentleman;
And, to say truth, Verona brags of him
To be a virtuous and well-govern'd youth.
I would not for the wealth of all this town
Here in my house do him disparagement.
Therefore be patient, take no note of him.
It is my will, the which if thou respect,
Show a fair presence and put off these frowns,
An ill-beseeming semblance for a feast.

TYB. It fits when such a villain is a guest:
I'll not endure him.

CAP.   He shall be endur'd.
What, goodman boy! I say he shall! Go to,
Am I the master here or you? Go to.
You'll not endure him! God shall mend my soul,
You'll make a mutiny among my guests,
You will set cock-a-hoop, you'll be the man!

TYB. Why, uncle, 'tis a shame.

CAP.   Go to, go to.
You are a saucy boy. Is't so indeed?
This trick may chance to scathe you. I know what.
You must contrary me. Marry, 'tis time.
Well said, my hearts! You are a princox, go
Be quiet, or – More light! More light! – For shame,
I'll make you quiet. What, cheerly, my hearts!

TYB. Patience perforce with wilful choler meeting
Makes my flesh tremble in their different greeting.
I will withdraw; but this intrusion shall
Now seeming sweet, convert to bitt'rest gall.   *Exit.*

SAINT-SIMON

at Versailles, date unknown

MME de Charlus was greedy and a great gambler. She used to spend whole nights wildly doubling against increasing odds, for at that time they played lansquenet for high stakes, at the house of Mme la Princesse de Conti, the sister of Monsieur le Prince. One Friday night, Mme de Charlus was supping there with a large company. She was ill-dressed as usual, but for once, most fashionably, wearing one of those headdresses called commodes, that were not fastened in any way to the ladies' heads. They were vastly high constructions and were removed or put on just as men take off and put on their wigs and nightcaps.

Mme de Charlus was sitting next to Le Tellier, the Archbishop of Rheims. As she was removing the top of a boiled egg, she leaned forward to take the salt and accidentally stuck her head into the flame of a neighbouring candle. The Archbishop, seeing her on fire, hurled himself at the headdress and flung it to the ground, whereupon Mme de Charlus, in amazement and fury at finding herself thus dis-wigged for no apparent reason, threw her egg into the Archbishop's face, and it ran down all over him. He did nothing but laugh, and the entire company was in fits at seeing the ancient grey, dirty head of Mme de Charlus, and the omelet she had made on the Archbishop. Especially comic was her rage and abuse, for she imagined that she had been insulted and would hear no excuse, and then suddenly perceived that she had been left bald before all the world. By this time, the headdress had been burnt and Mme la Princesse de Conti had sent for another, but before it could be placed upon her head there was plenty of time to contemplate her charms, and for her to continue with her furious protests.

Gambling was again forbidden, under threat of severe penalties.

HORACE

'A Fiasco of a dinner-party', *from Satires VIII*, 35 BC

HORACE. How did you like your dinner with the rich Nasidienus? Yesterday, when I tried to get you as my own guest, I was told you had been dining there since midday.

FUNDANIUS. So much so that never in my life did I have a better
time.

HOR. Tell me, if you don't mind, what was the first dish to appease
an angry appetite?

FUN. First there was a wild boar. It was caught when a gentle south
wind was blowing, as the father of the feast kept telling us.
Around it were pungent turnips, lettuces, radishes – such things as
whet a jaded appetite – skirret, fish-pickle, and Coan lees. When
these were removed, a high-girt slave with purple napkin wiped
well the maple-wood table, while a second swept up the scraps
and anything that could offend the guests. Then, like an Attic
maid bearing Ceres' sacred emblems, there came forward dusky
Hydaspes with Caecuban wine, and Alcon with Chian, unmixed
with brine. Then said our host: 'If Alban is more to your taste,
Maecenas, or Falernian, we have both.'

HOR. O the misery of wealth! But who, Fundanius, were those at
dinner, with whom you had so fine a time? I am eager to know.

FUN. Myself at the top, then next to me Viscus of Thurii, and below,
if I remember, Varius. Then Vibidius and Servilius Balatro, the
'shades' that Maecenas had brought with him. Above our host
was Nomentanus; below him, Porcius, who made us laugh by
swallowing whole cheese-cakes at a mouthful. Nomentanus was
there to see that if anything perchance escaped our notice, he
might point it out with his forefinger; for the rest of the folk – we,
I mean – eat fowl, oysters, and fish, which had a flavour far
different from any we knew, as, for instance, was made clear at
once, after he had handed me the livers of a plaice and a turbot, a
dish I had never tasted before. After this he informed me that the
honey-apples were red because picked in the light of a waning
moon. What difference that makes you would learn better from
himself.

Then said Vibidius to Balatro: 'Unless we drink him bankrupt,
we shall die unavenged,' and he calls for larger cups. Then did
paleness overspread the face of the host, who dreaded nothing so
much as hard drinkers, either because they chaff one too freely or
because fiery wines dull the delicate palate. Vibidius and Balatro
tilt whole decanters of wine into Allifan goblets. All followed suit,
save the guests on the lowest couch, who did no harm to the
flagons.

Then is brought in a lamprey, outstretched on a platter, with
shrimps swimming all round it. Upon this the master: 'This,' said

he, 'was caught before spawning; if taken later, its flesh would
have been poorer. The ingredients of the sauce are these: oil from
Venafrum of the first pressing, roe from the juices of the Spanish
mackerel, wine five years old, but produced this side of the sea,
poured in while it is on the boil – after boiling, Chian suits better
than anything else – white pepper, and vinegar made from the
fermenting of Lesbian vintage. I was the first to point out that one
should boil in the sauce green rockets and bitter elecampane;
Curtillus would use sea-urchins, unwashed, inasmuch as the yield
of the sea-shellfish itself is better than a briny pickle.'

Meantime the canopy spread above came down in mighty ruin
upon the platter, trailing more black dust than the North-wind
raises on Campanian plains. We feared a worse disaster, but
finding there was no danger recover ourselves. Rufus drooped his
head and wept as if his son had fallen by an untimely fate. What
would have been the end, had not Nomentanus, the philosopher,
thus rallied his friend: 'Ah, Fortune, what god is more cruel
toward us than thou! How thou dost ever delight to make sport
of the life of man!' Varius could scarce smother a laugh with his
napkin. Balatro, who sneers at everything, said: 'These are the
terms of life, and therefore the meed of fame will never equal your
labour. To think that, in order that I may have lavish entertainment, you are to be racked and tortured with every anxiety, lest
the bread be burned, lest sauce be served ill-seasoned, that all your
slaves may be properly attired and neat for waiting! Then, too,
these risks besides – the canopy falling, as it did just now, or a
numskull stumbling and breaking a dish. But one who entertains
is like a general: mishaps oft reveal his genius, smooth going hides
it.' To this replies Nasidienus, 'Heaven grant you every blessing
you crave, so kind a man are you, so civil a guest!' and calls for
his slippers. Then on each couch you might note the buzz of
whispers in secret ears exchanged.

HOR. No play would I have rather seen; but pray tell me, what did
you find to laugh at next?

FUN. While Vibidius is asking the servants whether the flagon also
was broken, since cups were not brought him when called for, and
while we were laughing at pretended jests, Balatro egging us on,
back you come, Nasidienus, with altered brow, as if bent on
mending misfortune by art. Then follow servants, bearing on a
huge charger the limbs of a crane sprinkled with much salt and
meal, and the liver of a white goose fattened on rich figs, and

hares' limbs torn off, as being more dainty than if eaten with the loins. Then we saw blackbirds served with the breast burnt, and pigeons without the rumps – real dainties, did not our host unfold their laws and properties. But on we ran, taking our revenge on him by tasting nothing at all, as though the things were blasted with Canidia's breath, more deadly than African serpents.

MAX PEMBERTON

The Ripening Rubies, date unknown

'THE plain fact is,' said Lady Faber, 'we are entertaining thieves. It positively makes me shudder to look at my own guests, and to think that some of them are criminals.'

We stood together in the conservatory of her house in Portman Square, looking down upon a brilliant ballroom, upon a glow of colour, and the radiance of unnumbered gems. She had taken me aside after the fourth waltz to tell me that her famous belt of rubies had been shorn of one of its finest pendants; and she showed me beyond possibility of dispute that the loss was no accident, but another of those amazing thefts which startled London so frequently during the season of 1893. Nor was hers the only case. Though I had been in her house but an hour, complaints from other sources had reached me. The Countess of Dunholm had lost a crescent brooch of brilliants; Mrs Kenningham-Hardy had missed a spray of pearls and turquoise; Lady Hallingham made mention of an emerald locket which was gone, as she thought, from her necklace; though, as she confessed with a truly feminine doubt, she was not positive that her maid had given it to her. And these misfortunes, being capped by the abstraction of Lady Faber's pendant, compelled me to believe that of all the startling stories of thefts which the season had known the story of this dance would be the most remarkable.

These things and many more came to my mind as I held the mutilated belt in my hand and examined the fracture, while my hostess stood, with an angry flush upon her face, waiting for my verdict. A moment's inspection of the bauble revealed to me at once its exceeding value, and the means whereby a pendant of it had been snatched.

'If you will look closely,' said I, 'you will see that the gold chain here has been cut with a pair of scissors. As we don't know the name of the person who used them, we may describe them as pickpocket's scissors.'

'Which means that I am entertaining a pickpocket,' said she, flushing again at the thought.

'Or a person in possession of a pickpocket's implements,' I suggested.

'How dreadful,' she cried, 'not for myself, though the rubies are very valuable, but for the others. This is the third dance during the week at which people's jewels have been stolen. When will it end?'

NATHANIEL HAWTHORNE
Tanglewood Tales, 1852–3

EACH of the strangers was invited to sit down; and there they were, two and twenty storm-beaten mariners, in worn and tattered garb, sitting on two and twenty cushioned and canopied thrones, so rich and gorgeous that the proudest monarch had nothing more splendid in his stateliest hall.

Then you might have seen the guests nodding, winking with one eye, and leaning from one throne to another, to communicate their satisfaction in hoarse whispers.

'Our good hostess has made kings of us all,' said one. 'Ha! do you smell the feast? I'll engage it will be fit to set before two and twenty kings.'

'I hope', said another, 'it will be, mainly good substantial joints, sirloins, spareribs, and hinder quarters, without too many kick-shaws. If I thought the good lady would not take it amiss, I should call for a fat slice of fried bacon to begin with.'

Ah, the gluttons and gormandisers! You see how it was with them. In the loftiest seats of dignity, on royal thrones, they could think of nothing but their greedy appetite, which was the portion of their nature that they shared with wolves and swine; so that they resembled those vilest of animals far more than they did kings – if, indeed, kings were what they ought to be.

But the beautiful woman now clapped her hands; and immediately there entered a train of two and twenty serving-men, bringing dishes of the richest food, all hot from the kitchen fire, and sending up such a steam that it hung like a cloud below the crystal dome of the saloon. An equal number of attendants brought great flagons of wine, of various kinds, some of which sparkled as it was poured out, and went bubbling down the throat; while, of other sorts, the purple liquor was so clear that you could see the wrought figures at the bottom of the goblet. While the servants supplied the two and twenty guests with food and drink, the hostess and her four maidens went from one throne to another, exhorting them to eat their fill, and to quaff wine abundantly, and thus to recompense themselves, at this one banquet, for the many days when they had gone without a dinner. But, whenever the mariners were not looking at them (which was pretty often, as they looked chiefly into the basins and platters), the beautiful woman and her damsels turned aside and laughed. Even the servants, as they knelt down to present the dishes, might be seen to grin and sneer while the guests were helping themselves to the offered dainties.

And once in a while the strangers seemed to taste something that they did not like.

'Here is an odd kind of a spice in this dish,' said one. 'I can't say it quite suits my palate. Down it goes, however.'

'Send a good draught of wine down your throat,' said his comrade on the next throne. 'That is the stuff to make this sort of cookery relish well. Though I must needs say the wine has a queer taste too. But the more I drink of it the better I like the flavour.'

Whatever little fault they might find with the dishes, they sat at dinner a prodigiously long while; and it would really have made you ashamed to see how they swilled down the liquor and gobbled up the food. They sat on golden thrones, to be sure, but they behaved like pigs in a sty; and, if they had had their wits about them, they might have guessed that this was the opinion of their beautiful hostess and her maidens. It brings a blush into my face to reckon up, in my own mind, what mountains of meat and pudding, and what gallons of wine, these two and twenty guzzlers and gormandisers ate and drank. They forgot all about their homes, and their wives and children, and all about Ulysses, and everything else, except this banquet, at which they wanted to keep feasting for ever. But at length they began to give over, from mere incapacity to hold any more.

'That last bit of fat is too much for me,' said one.

'And I have not room for another morsel,' said his next neighbour, heaving a sigh. 'What a pity! My appetite is as sharp as ever.'

In short, they all left off eating, and leaned back on their thrones with such a stupid and helpless aspect as made them ridiculous to behold. When their hostess saw this, she laughed aloud; so did her four damsels; so did the two and twenty serving-men that bore the dishes, and their two and twenty fellows that poured out the wine. And the louder they all laughed, the more stupid and helpless did the two and twenty gormandisers look. Then the beautiful woman took her stand in the middle of the saloon, and stretching out a slender rod (it had been all the while in her hand, although they never noticed it till this moment), she turned it from one guest to another, until each had felt it pointed at himself. Beautiful as her face was, and though there was a smile on it, it looked just as wicked and mischievous as the ugliest serpent that ever was seen; and fat-witted as the voyagers had made themselves, they began to suspect that they had fallen into the power of an evil-minded enchantress.

'Wretches,' cried she, 'you have abused a lady's hospitality; and in this princely saloon your behaviour has been suited to a hog-pen. You are already swine in everything but the human form, which you disgrace, and which I myself should be ashamed to keep a moment longer were you to share it with me. But it will require only the slightest exercise of magic to make the exterior conform to the hoggish disposition. Assume your proper shapes, gormandisers, and begone to the sty!'

Uttering these last words, she waved her wand: and stamping her foot imperiously, each of the guests was struck aghast at beholding, instead of his comrades in human shape, one and twenty hogs sitting on the same number of golden thrones. Each man (as he still supposed himself to be) essayed to give a cry of surprise, but found that he could merely grunt, and that, in a word, he was just such another beast as his companions. It looked so intolerably absurd to see hogs on cushioned thrones, that they made haste to wallow down upon all-fours, like other swine. They tried to groan and beg for mercy, but forthwith emitted the most awful grunting and squealing that ever came out of swinish throats. They would have wrung their hands in despair, but, attempting to do so, grew all the more desperate for seeing themselves squatted on their hams, and pawing the air with their fore trotters. Dear me! what pendulous ears they had! what little red eyes, half buried in fat! and what long snouts, instead of Grecian noses!

But brutes as they certainly were, they yet had enough of human nature in them to be shocked at their own hideousness; and, still intending to groan, they uttered a viler grunt and squeal than before.

So harsh and ear-piercing it was, that you would have fancied a butcher was sticking his knife into each of their throats, or, at the very least, that somebody was pulling every hog by his funny little twist of a tail.

'Begone to your sty!' cried the enchantress, giving them some smart strokes with her wand; and then she turned to the serving-men – 'Drive out these swine, and throw down some acorns for them to eat.'

PETRONIUS
The Annals of Tacitus, circa AD 65

AT that time, it happened, the court had migrated to Campania; and Petronius had reached Cumae, when his detention was ordered. He disdained to await the lingering issue of hopes and fears: still, he would not take a brusque farewell of life. An incision was made in his veins: they were bound up under his directions, and opened again, while he conversed with his friends – not on the gravest of themes, nor in the key of the dying hero. He listened to no disquisitions on the immortality of the soul or the dogmas of philosophy, but to frivolous song and playful verses. Some of his slaves tasted of his bounty, others of the whip. He sat down to dinner, and then drowsed a little; so that death, if compulsory, should at least be natural. Even in his will, he broke through the routine of suicide, and flattered neither Nero nor Tigellinus nor any other of the mighty: instead, he described the emperor's enormities; added a list of his catamites, his women, and his innovations in lasciviousness; then sealed the document, sent it to Nero, and broke his signet-ring to prevent it from being used to endanger others.

FRANCIS ILES
Malice Aforethought, 1931

MRS Bickleigh had noticed their absence. She knew her husband, and contempt sharpened her voice. 'Oh, there you are, Edmund. I've been wanting you.'

'Yes, my dear?' To all appearances Dr Bickleigh was perfectly normal. The two little spots of red that burned on his cheek-bones were too tiny to be noticed.

'They're a ball short. Benjie hit one into the gooseberry-bushes again. Please go and find it at once.' She spoke with more than her usual peremptoriness, and her loud, grating voice could not have failed to reach every ear. The men looked most uncomfortable. Each of them had volunteered to look for the ball, and all had been told it was their host's task, and his only. The same thought was obvious now on all their faces: 'I'm hanged if I'd speak to a dog like that.' Dr Bickleigh felt his wife's tone and what lay behind it, and he felt his guests' reactions to it. The two tiny spots of colour on his cheek-bones spread a little.

And then – Gwynyfryd Rattery laughed.

It was, had Dr Bickleigh been able to recognise it, only the meaningless laughter of overwrought nerves. But he did not recognise it. What he heard was the mocking of the whole world, the traditional mocking at the insignificant, henpecked husband. And Gwynyfryd, whose respect he had so particularly wanted, whose understanding he had coveted so hungrily, had ranged herself with the mockers.

He turned on his heel, his whole face flaming; and every atom of his varied emotions leapt suddenly into overmastering hatred of his wife. 'My God,' he muttered to himself, as he strode round the end of the court, his small body taut with anger. 'My God, I can't stand this much longer. I wish she was *dead*. My God, I wish I could *kill* her.'

AGATHA CHRISTIE

The Mirror Cracked from Side to Side, 1962

SHE turned back to hear Heather Badcock's triumphant peroration.

'I've never forgotten how wonderful you were that day. It was a hundred times worth it.'

Marina's response was this time not so automatic. Her eyes which had wavered over Heather Badcock's shoulder, now seemed to be fixed on the wall midway up the stairs. She was staring and there was something so ghastly in her expression that Mrs Bantry half took a step forward. Was the woman going to faint? What on earth could she be seeing that gave her that basilisk look? But before she could reach Marina's side the latter had recovered herself. Her eyes, vague and unfocused, returned to Heather and the charm of manner was turned on once more, albeit a shade mechanically.

SOMERVILLE AND ROSS

Some Experiences of an Irish R.M., 1899

'YEATES!' he said, 'look up at the roof. Do you see anything up there by the kitchen chimney?'

He was pointing at a heavy stack of chimneys in a tower that stood up against the grey and pink of the morning sky. At the angle where one of them joined the roof smoke was oozing busily out, and, as I stared, a little wisp of flame stole through.

The next thing that I distinctly remember is being in the van of a rush through the kitchen passages, every one shouting 'Water! Water!' and not knowing where to find it, then up several flights of the narrowest and darkest stairs it has ever been my fate to ascend, with a bucket of water that I snatched from a woman, spilling as I ran. At the top of the stairs came a ladder leading to a trap-door, and up in the dark loft above was the roar and the wavering glare of flames.

'My God! That's sthrong fire!' shouted Denis, tumbling down the ladder with a brace of empty buckets; 'we'll never save it! The lake won't quinch it!'

The flames were squirting out through the bricks of the chimney, through the timbers, through the slates; it was barely possible to get through the trap-door, and the booming and crackling strengthened every instant.

'A chain to the lake!' gasped Flurry, coughing in the stifling heat as he slashed the water at the blazing rafters; 'the well's no good! Go on, Yeates!'

The organising of a double chain out of the mob that thronged and shouted and jammed in the passages and yard was no mean feat of generalship; but it got done somehow. Mrs Cadogan and Biddy Mahony rose magnificently to the occasion, cursing, thumping, shoving; and stable buckets, coal buckets, milk pails, and kettles were unearthed and sent swinging down the grass slope to the lake that lay in glittering unconcern in the morning sunshine. Men, women, and children worked in a way that only Irish people can work on an emergency. All their cleverness, all their good-heartedness, and all their love of a ruction came to the front; the screaming and the exhortations were incessant, but so were also the buckets that flew from hand to hand up to the loft. I hardly know how long we were at it, but there came a time when I looked up from the yard and saw that the billows of reddened smoke from the top of the tower were dying down, and I bethought me of old Mrs Knox.

I found her at the door of her room, engaged in tying up a bundle of old clothes in a sheet; she looked as white as a corpse, but she was not in any way quelled by the situation.

HONORÉ DE BALZAC
The Lily of the Valley, 1846

A LADY, deceived by my weakly appearance and taking me for a sleepy child waiting his mother's good pleasure, placed herself close to me with the movement of a bird lowering itself into its nest. And then I inhaled a feminine fragrance that burnt into my soul as Eastern poetry has since done. I looked at my neighbour, and was more dazzled by her than I had been by the fête; she became all my fête. If you have thoroughly grasped my preceding life, you will be able to imagine the feelings that welled up in my heart. My eyes were suddenly struck by the plump white shoulders upon which I should have liked to rest, slightly rosy shoulders that seemed to be blushing as if they were bared for the first time, chaste shoulders that had a soul, and whose satin skin shone in the light like some silken tissue. These shoulders were divided by a line along which ran my glance, bolder than my hand. I raised myself up, thrilling all over to see the bust, and was completely fascinated by a throat modestly covered with gauze, but whose azured, perfectly-rounded globes lay delicately reposing in clouds of lace. The slightest details of this head were attractions that awakened infinite delight within me; the glitter of the hair smoothed above a neck as velvety as a little girl's, the snowy lines traced by the comb and in which my imagination rambled as in fresh pathways, all combined to make me lose my senses. After having made sure that nobody was looking, I nestled into this back like a child throwing itself upon its mother's bosom, and covered those shoulders with kisses whilst burying my head in them.

The woman gave a piercing cry, which was drowned in the noise of the band, turned round, saw me, and said:

'Monsieur – !'

Ah! had she said: 'My little fellow, whatever possesses you?' I might perhaps have killed her; but at this *monsieur!* hot tears gushed from my eyes. I was petrified by a glance glowing with righteous anger, by a sublime head crowned with a diadem of pale-yellow hair, in keeping with that soft back. Her face was flaring with the purple of outraged modesty, already half disarmed by the forgiveness of the woman who understands frenzy when she is the cause of it, and recognizes boundless adoration in the tears of the penitent. She walked away with a queenly movement. I then became conscious of the ridiculousness of my position; then only, I understood that I was as absurdly dressed as a Savoyard's monkey. I was ashamed of myself. I remained, all stupefied, relishing the apple I had just stolen, my lips still retaining the warmth of the blood I had inhaled, following this Heaven-sent woman with my eyes.

'But now I had no pleasure from the spectacle'

* * *

MICHAEL ARLEN
The Romance of Iris Poole, 1921

BUT now I had no pleasure from the spectacle. I only wished, and heartily, that the room was empty of its music and people, empty of all but Iris . . . to whom, if miracles could happen at all, I would enter suddenly and brave her startled gaze with my love-making, and take her. But the most wonderful thing about miracles is that they never happen, so I could do nothing but stare at her as far as I could disjointedly see her among the moving crowd; a creature of green and gold that night, for her dress was of jade, and her hair, I thought, couldn't of course be but gold to ornament it fittingly; so that, I said, she will always be her own carnival, even in a desolate place. And once again, with that white face under hair which seemed that night more than ever barbaric in its splendour, she gave me that feeling of her as a strange thing from some wild legend, a woman of doubt and desire so consummately human as to be almost inhuman: tamed into life just for this moment, but only for this moment, without a why nor whence nor whither . . .

GEORGE AND WEEDON GROSSMITH
The Diary of a Nobody, 1892

WE had some music, and Lupin, who never left Daisy's side for a moment, raved over her singing of a song, called 'Some Day'. It seemed a pretty song, but she made such grimaces, and sang, to my mind, so out of tune, I would not have asked her to sing again; but Lupin made her sing four songs right off, one after the other.

At ten o'clock we went down to supper, and from the way Gowing and Cummings ate you would have thought they had not had a meal for a month. I told Carrie to keep something back in case Mr Perkupp should come by mere chance. Gowing annoyed me very much by filling a large tumbler of champagne, and drinking it straight off. He repeated his action, and made me fear our half-dozen of champagne would not last out. I tried to keep a bottle back, but Lupin got hold of it, and took it to the side-table with Daisy and Frank Mutlar.

We went upstairs, and the young fellows began sky-larking. Carrie put a stop to that at once. Stillbrook amused us with a song, 'What have you done with your Cousin John?' I did not notice that Lupin and Frank had disappeared. I asked Mr Watson, one of the Hollo-ways, where they were, and he said: 'It's a case of "Oh, what a surprise!"'

We were directed to form a circle – which we did. Watson then said: 'I have much pleasure in introducing the celebrated Blondin Donkey.' Frank and Lupin then bounded into the room. Lupin had whitened his face like a clown, and Frank had tied round his waist a large hearthrug. He was supposed to be the donkey, and he looked it. They indulged in a very noisy pantomime, and we were all shrieking with laughter.

I turned round suddenly, and then I saw Mr Perkupp standing half-way in the door, he having arrived without our knowing it. I beckoned to Carrie, and we went up to him at once. He would not come right into the room. I apologized for the foolery, but Mr Perkupp said: 'Oh, it seems amusing.' I could see he was not a bit amused.

Carrie and I took him downstairs, but the table was a wreck. There was not a glass of champagne left – not even a sandwich. Mr Perkupp said he required nothing, but would like a glass of seltzer or soda water. The last syphon was empty. Carrie said: 'We have plenty of port wine left.' Mr Perkupp said with a smile: 'No, thank you. I really require nothing, but I am most pleased to see you and your husband in your own home. Good night, Mrs Pooter – you will excuse my very short stay, I know.' I went with him to his carriage, and he said: 'Don't trouble to come to the office till twelve tomorrow.'

I felt despondent as I went back to the house, and I told Carrie I thought the party was a failure. Carrie said it was a great success, and I was only tired, and insisted on my having some port myself. I drank two glasses, and felt much better, and we went into the drawing-room, where they had commenced dancing. Carrie and I had a little dance, which I said reminded me of old days. She said I was a spooney old thing.

DAVID PLANTE

(unpublished)

GUESTS arrived at the drinks party when the sun was still up. Talking to them and making sure they had filled glasses, Howard, the host, didn't notice that the sun had set, and he became aware of the outside darkness only when he looked out a window at the back garden. Without his noticing, his wife Caroline must have lit the lights. He hadn't seen her in a while, and the odd desire to find her in the party came to him. When he asked a female friend of theirs, she said she might be downstairs in the kitchen. Howard went down, but there was no one there. The door to the garden was open, and he went out. A smell of fresh damp rose about him as he walked to the end of the garden, to where the ground was covered with apples beneath an old apple tree. When he looked back at the house, he saw his wife, in an illuminated window of an upstairs bedroom, facing their friend Carl. They were laughing, and Carl reached out and pinched the lobe of Caroline's ear. By Howard in the outside darkness was an old, rusting wash tub and a rotting mangle.

EDITH WHARTON

The Custom of the Country, 1939

THE dinner too was disappointing. Undine was too young to take note of culinary details, but she had expected to view the company through a bower of orchids and eat pretty-coloured *entrées* in ruffled papers. Instead, there was only a low centre-dish of ferns, and plain roasted and broiled meat that one could recognize – as if they'd been dyspeptics on a diet! With all the hints in the Sunday papers, she thought it dull of Mrs Fairford not to have picked up

something newer; and as the evening progressed she began to suspect
that it wasn't a real 'dinner party', and that they had just asked her
in to share what they had when they were alone.

But a glance about the table convinced her that Mrs Fairford
could not have meant to treat her other guests so lightly. They were
only eight in number, but one was no less a person than young Mrs
Peter Van Degen – the one who had been a Dagonet – and the
consideration which this young lady, herself one of the choicest
ornaments of the Society Column, displayed toward the rest of the
company, convinced Undine that they must be more important than
they looked. She liked Mrs Fairford, a small incisive woman, with a
big nose and good teeth revealed by frequent smiles. In her dowdy
black and antiquated ornaments she was not what Undine would
have called 'stylish'; but she had a droll kind way which reminded
the girl of her father's manner when he was not tired or worried
about money. One of the other ladies, having white hair, did not
long arrest Undine's attention; and the fourth, a girl like herself,
who was introduced as Miss Harriet Ray, she dismissed at a glance
as plain and wearing a last year's 'model'. The men, too, were less
striking than she had hoped. She had not expected much of Mr
Fairford, since married men were intrinsically uninteresting, and his
baldness and grey moustache seemed naturally to relegate him to the
background; but she had looked for some brilliant youths of her
own age – in her inmost heart she had looked for Mr Popple. He
was not there, however, and of the other men one, whom they called
Mr Bowen, was hopelessly elderly – she supposed he was the
husband of the white-haired lady – and the other two, who seemed
to be friends of young Marvell's, were both lacking in Claud
Walsingham's dash.

ALDOUS HUXLEY

Point Counter Point, 1928

'WHO'S that little woman in black,' he went on, 'rolling her
eyes and swaying her body like St Teresa in an ecstasy?'

'Fanny Logan,' Lady Edward whispered back. 'But do keep quiet.'

'People talk of the tribute vice pays to virtue,' John Bidlake went
on, incorrigibly. 'But everything's permitted nowadays – there's no
more need of moral hypocrisy. There's only intellectual hypocrisy

now. The tribute philistinism pays to art, what? Just look at them
all paying it – in pious grimaces and religious silence!'

'You can be thankful they pay *you* in guineas,' said Lady Edward.
'And now I absolutely insist that you should hold your tongue.'

Bidlake made a gesture of mock terror and put his hand over his
mouth. Tolley voluptuously waved his arms; Pongileoni blew, the
fiddlers scraped. And Bach, the poet, meditated of truth and beauty.

Fanny Logan felt the tears coming into her eyes. She was easily
moved, especially by music; and when she felt an emotion, she did
not try to repress it, but abandoned herself wholeheartedly to it.
How beautiful this music was, how sad, and yet how comforting!
She felt it within her as a current of exquisite feeling, running
smoothly but irresistibly through all the labyrinthine intricacies of
her being. Even her body shook and swayed in time with the pulse
and undulation of the melody. She thought of her husband; the
memory of him came to her on the current of the music, of darling,
darling Eric, dead now almost two years; dead, and still so young.
The tears came faster. She wiped them away. The music was
infinitely sad; and yet it consoled. It admitted everything, so to speak
– poor Eric's dying before his time, the pain of his illness, his
reluctance to go – it admitted everything. It expressed the whole
sadness of the world, and from the depths of that sadness it was able
to affirm – deliberately, quietly, without protesting too much – that
everything was in some way right, acceptable. It included the sadness
within some vaster, more comprehensive happiness. The tears kept
welling up into Mrs Logan's eyes; but they were somehow happy
tears, in spite of her sadness. She would have liked to tell Polly, her
daughter, what she was feeling. But Polly was sitting in another row.

BENJAMIN DISRAELI
Coningsby, 1844

IT was the hour for supper. The guests at a French ball are not
seen to advantage at this period. The custom of separating the
sexes for this refreshment, and arranging that the ladies should
partake of it by themselves, though originally founded in a feeling of
consideration and gallantry, and with the determination to secure,
under all circumstances, the convenience and comfort of the fair sex,
is really, in its appearance and its consequences, anything but

European, and produces a scene which rather reminds one of the harem of a sultan than a hall of chivalry. To judge from the countenances of the favoured fair, they are not themselves particularly pleased; and when their repast is over they necessarily return to empty halls, and are deprived of the dance at the very moment when they may feel most inclined to participate in its graceful excitement.

These somewhat ungracious circumstances, however, were not attendant on the festival of this night. There was opened in the Hotel of Sidonia for the first time a banqueting-room which could contain with convenience all the guests. It was a vast chamber of white marble, the golden panels of the walls containing festive sculptures by Schwanthaler, relieved by encaustic tinting. In its centre was a fountain, a group of Bacchantes encircling Dionysos; and from this fountain, as from a star, diverged the various tables from which sprang orange-trees in fruit and flower.

The banquet had but one fault; Coningsby was separated from Edith. The Duchess of Grand Cairo, the beautiful wife of the heir of one of the Imperial illustrations, had determined to appropriate Coningsby as her cavalier for the moment. Distracted, he made his escape; but his wandering eye could not find the object of its search; and he fell prisoner to the charming Princess de Petitpoix, a Carlist chieftain, whose witty words avenged the cause of fallen dynasties and a cashiered nobility.

LOUISA M. ALCOTT
Little Women, 1868

DOWN they went, feeling a trifle timid, for they seldom went to parties, and, informal as this little gathering was, it was an event to them. Mrs Gardiner, a stately old lady, greeted them kindly, and handed them over to the eldest of her six daughters. Meg knew Sallie, and was at her ease very soon; but Jo, who didn't care much for girls or girlish gossip, stood about with her back carefully against the wall, and felt as much out of place as a colt in a flower-garden. Half-a-dozen jovial lads were talking about skates in another part of the room, and she longed to go and join them, for skating was one of the joys of her life. She telegraphed her wish to Meg, but the eyebrows went up so alarmingly that she dared not stir. No one came to talk to her, and one by one the group near her dwindled away, till she was left alone. She could not roam about and amuse herself, for the burnt breadth would show, so she stared at people rather forlornly till the dancing began. Meg was asked at once, and the tight slippers tripped about so briskly that none would have guessed the pain their wearer suffered smilingly.

F. M. MAYOR
The Rector's Daughter, 1924

MARY found herself seated by a Mr Worsley of forty-five, the oldest person present. Feeling this disgrace, he was the most rebellious of the rebels, the youngest of the young. He took care to pay no attention to Mary, who was his nearest contemporary. He and his wife had discarded one another some years before. After different experiences he had now set up house with a girl of eighteen, and was trying to think and be just what she was. She was already beginning to find him 'mossy'.

On the other side of Mary was the fireplace, where once had been the grate and now was the radiator, not in full working order. If it was the place of honour, it had its dangers too, for all the ends of cigarettes were hurled at it. One missed, and hit Mary; another fell into a kitchen jug. There were four of them, filled with coffee, which was cooling on the hearth. Brynhilda introduced her to one or two people. They treated her as if she had not been there. On the whole she was grateful, though it was missing the only chance she was likely to get of coming into touch with the intellectual, young generation.

JANE AUSTEN
Northanger Abbey, 1818

IT was a splendid sight; and she began, for the first time that evening, to feel herself at a ball: she longed to dance, but she had not an acquaintance in the room. Mrs Allen did all that she could do in such a case, by saying very placidly, every now and then, 'I wish you could dance, my dear; I wish you could get a partner.' For some time her young friend felt obliged to her for these wishes, but they were repeated so often, and proved so totally ineffectual, that Catherine grew tired at last, and would thank her no more.

They were not long able, however, to enjoy the repose of the eminence they had so laboriously gained. Everybody was shortly in motion for tea, and they must squeeze out like the rest. Catherine began to feel something of disappointment: she was tired of being continually pressed against by people, the generality of whose faces possessed nothing to interest, and with all of whom she was so wholly unacquainted that she could not relieve the irksomeness of imprisonment by the exchange of a syllable with any of her fellow-captives; and when at last arrived in the Tea Room, she felt yet more the awkwardness of having no party to join, no acquaintance to claim, no gentleman to assist them. They saw nothing of Mr Allen; and after looking about them in vain for a more eligible situation, were obliged to sit down at the end of a table, at which a large party were already placed, without having anything to do there, or anybody to speak to, except each other.

Mrs Allen congratulated herself, as soon as they were seated, on having preserved her gown from injury. 'It would have been very shocking to have it torn,' said she, 'would not it? It is such a delicate muslin. For my part, I have not seen anything I like so well in the whole room, I assure you.'

'How uncomfortable it is,' whispered Catherine, 'not to have a single acquaintance here!'

'Yes, my dear,' replied Mrs Allen, with perfect serenity, 'it is very uncomfortable, indeed.'

'What shall we do? The gentlemen and ladies at this table look as if they wondered why we came here; we seem forcing ourselves into their party.'

'Aye, so we do. That is very disagreeable. I wish we had a large acquaintance here.'

'I wish we had *any*; it would be somebody to go to.'

'Very true, my dear; and if we knew anybody, we would join them directly. The Skinners were here last year; I wish they were here now.'

'Had not we better go away as it is? Here are no tea-things for us, you see.'

MOLLIE KEENE

Good Behaviour, 1981

NOT tears, but pain, seized on me, my insides griping and loosening. The absolute need of getting to the lavatory possessed me. Even my terrible distress had to find this absurd necessity. As I walked carefully down the long, warm room, I had the idea that the light had changed like a short winter afternoon, and the room and my life were both spread with sand and salt.

Back in the hall the fun of the party was blazing up now. I ploughed my way through the drinking, chattering, easy people to the foot of the staircase. The crowd was as impervious to interruption as the crowd at a race-meeting, where faces known and unknown float and pass one by, occupied and avoiding recognition. So I saw, without a nod or a smile, Mr Kiely standing with some of his friends. I didn't have to know he was there. I breasted on. Kenny Norton put a hand on my arm: 'Come and dance,' he said. The miracle was late.

'I'm sorry, nothing left,' I said. I felt his appalled stare following me as I flogged on up the stairs to the salvation of the lavatory. I had to get there; pain was twisting in me again, and above it the dreadful childish call: I'm going to be sick – sick in the basin. Partly in the plate holding the Bromo, partly over my dress, into my shoes, on the floor, I was sick. I must escape before it was found, get myself into my coat and run, with this taste in my mouth, and the smell under my coat going with me.

In the hall the crowd had thinned. Music was playing and those lucky ones who danced to it were distanced from me, far and foreign. I was at the hall door, almost on my way home, but the door was locked. I turned the handle violently. This was the last cruelty; I must get out. The studded door loomed. I shook the lock with both hands. A voice beside me said: 'I think Jody Kenny in the bar has the key.' I looked round and down at Mr Kiely, immaculate in his black tail coat, his white tie just too large. 'Are you on your own?' he said, when he had opened the door for me into the blessed frozen night.

'Yes. I was dining.'

'Ah. So you didn't enjoy the party?'

'Goodnight.' I kept my voice cold and steady against his familiarity and his helpfulness. 'Thank you so much.'

VIRGINIA WOOLF

'Dr Burney's Evening Party', from *The Common Reader*
(2nd Series), 1932

THE night arrived and the fire was lit. The chairs were placed and the company arrived. As Dr Burney had foreseen, the awkwardness was great. Things indeed seemed to go wrong from the start. Dr Johnson had come in his worsted wig, very clean and prepared evidently for enjoyment. But after one look at him, Mr Greville seemed to decide that there was something formidable about the old man; it would be better not to compete; it would be better to play the fine gentleman, and leave it to literature to make the first advances. Murmuring, apparently, something about having the toothache, Mr Greville 'assumed his most supercilious air of distant superiority and planted himself, immovable as a noble statue, upon the hearth.' He said nothing. Then Mrs Greville, though longing to distinguish herself, judged it proper for Dr Johnson to begin, so that she said nothing. Mrs Thrale, who might have been expected to break up the solemnity, felt, it seemed, that the party was not her party and, waiting for the principals to engage, resolved to say nothing either. Mrs Crewe, the Grevilles' daughter, lovely and vivacious as she was, had come to be entertained and instructed and therefore very naturally she, too, said nothing. Nobody said anything. Complete silence reigned. Here was the very moment for which Dr Burney in his wisdom had prepared. He nodded to Signor Piozzi; and Signor Piozzi stepped to the instrument and began to sing. Accompanying himself on the pianoforte, he sang an *aria parlante*. He sang beautifully, he sang his best. But far from breaking the awkwardness and loosing the tongues, the music increased the constraint. Nobody spoke. Everybody waited for Dr Johnson to begin. There, indeed, they showed their fatal ignorance, for if there was one thing that Dr Johnson never did, it was to begin. Somebody had always to start a topic before he consented to pursue it or to demolish it. Now he waited in silence to be challenged. But he waited in vain. Nobody spoke. Nobody interrupted. As he saw his chance of a pleasant evening's talk drowned in the rattle of a piano, Dr Johnson sank into silent abstraction and sat with his back to the piano gazing at the fire. The *aria parlante* continued uninterrupted. At last the strain became unendurable. At last Mrs Thrale could stand it no longer. It was the attitude of Mr Greville, apparently, that roused her resentment. There he stood on the hearth in front of the fire 'staring around him at the whole company in curious silence sardonically'. What right had he, even if he were the descendant of the friend of Sir Philip Sidney, to despise the company and absorb the fire? Her own pride of ancestry suddenly asserted itself. Did not the blood of Adam of Salzburg run in her veins? Was it not as blue as that of the Grevilles and far more sparkling? Giving rein to the spirit of recklessness which sometimes bubbled in her, she rose, and stole on tiptoe to the pianoforte. Signor Piozzi was still singing and accompanying himself dramatically as he sang. She began a ludicrous mimicry of his gestures: she shrugged her shoulders, she cast up her eyes, she reclined her head on one side just as he did. At this singular display the company began to titter – indeed, it was a scene that was to be described 'from coterie to coterie throughout London, with comments and sarcasms of endless variety'. People who saw Mrs Thrale at her mockery that night never forgot that this was the beginning of that criminal affair, the first scene of that 'most extraordinary drama' which lost Mrs Thrale the respect of friends and children, which drove her in ignominy from England, and scarcely allowed her to show herself in London again – this was the beginning of her most reprehensible, her most unnatural passion for one who was not only a musician but a foreigner. But all this still lay on the laps of the gods. Nobody yet knew of what iniquity the vivacious lady was capable. She was still the respected wife of a wealthy brewer. Happily, Dr Johnson was staring at the fire, and knew nothing of the scene at the piano. But Dr Burney put a stop to the laughter instantly. He was shocked that a guest, even if a foreigner and a musician, should be ridiculed behind his back, and stealing to Mrs Thrale he whispered kindly but with authority in her ear that if she had no taste for music herself she should consider the feelings of those who had. Mrs Thrale took the rebuke with admirable sweetness, nodded her acquiescence and returned to her chair. But she had done her part. After that nothing more could be expected from her. Let them now do what they chose – she washed her hands of it, and seated herself 'like a pretty little Miss', as she said afterwards, to endure what yet remained to be endured 'of one of the most humdrum evenings that she had ever passed'.

If no one had dared to tackle Dr Johnson in the beginning, it was scarcely likely that they would dare now. He had apparently decided that the evening was a failure so far as talk was concerned. If he had not come dressed in his best clothes he might have had a book in his pocket which he could have pulled out and read. As it was, nothing but the resources of his own mind were left him; but these were huge; and these he explored as he sat with his back to the piano looking the very image of gravity, dignity, and composure.

At last the *aria parlante* came to an end. Signor Piozzi indeed, finding nobody to talk to, fell asleep in his solitude. Even Dr Burney by this time must have been aware that music is not an infallible specific; but there was nothing for it now. Since people would not talk, the music must continue. He called upon his daughters to sing a duet. And then, when that was over, there was nothing for it but that they must sing another. Signor Piozzi still slept, or still feigned sleep. Dr Johnson explored still further the magnificent resources of his own mind. Mr Greville still stood superciliously upon the hearth-rug. And the night was cold.

But it was a grave mistake to suppose that because Dr Johnson was apparently lost in thought, and certainly almost blind, he was not aware of anything, particularly of anything reprehensible, that was taking place in the room. His 'starts of vision' were always astonishing and almost always painful. So it was on the present occasion. He suddenly woke up. He suddenly roused himself. He suddenly uttered the words for which the company had been waiting all the evening.

'If it were not for depriving the ladies of the fire,' he said, looking fixedly at Mr Greville, 'I should like to stand upon the hearth myself!' The effect of the outburst was prodigious. The Burney children said afterwards that it was as good as a comedy. The descendant of the friend of Sir Philip Sidney quailed before the Doctor's glance. All the blood of all the Brookes rallied itself to overcome the insult. The son of a bookseller should be taught his place. Greville did his best to smile — a faint, scoffing smile. He did his best to stand where he had stood the whole evening. He stood smiling, he stood trying to smile, for two or perhaps for three minutes more. But when he looked round the room and saw all eyes cast down, all faces twitching with amusement, all sympathies plainly on the side of the bookseller's son, he could stand there no longer. Fulke Greville slunk away, sloping even his proud shoulders, to a chair. But as he went, he rang the bell 'with force'. He demanded his carriage.

'The party then broke up; and no one from amongst it ever asked, or wished for its repetition.'

LADY MARY MONTAGU

from Letters 1709–1762

BUT one of the pleasantest adventures I ever met in my life was last night, and which will give you a just idea after what a delicate manner the *belles passions* are managed in this country. I was at the assembly of the Countess of ——, and the young Count of —— led me down stairs, and he asked me how long I intended to stay here? I made answer that my stay depended on the emperor, and it was not in my power to determine it. Well, madam, (said he,) whether your time here is to be long or short, I think you ought to pass it agreeably, and to that end you must engage in a little affair of the heart. – My heart (answered I gravely enough) does not engage very easily, and I have no design of parting with it. I see, madam, (said he sighing,) by the ill nature of that answer, that I am not to hope for it, which is a great mortification to me that am charmed with you. But, however, I am still devoted to your service; and since I am not worthy of entertaining you myself, do me the honour of letting me know whom you like best among us, and I'll engage to manage the affair entirely to your satisfaction. – You may judge in what manner I should have received this compliment in my own country, but I was well enough acquainted with the way of this, to know that he really intended me an obligation, and thanked him with a grave courtesy for his zeal to serve me, and only assured him that I had no occasion to make use of it.

HAROLD PINTER

'A View of the Party', 1958

THE thought that Goldberg was
A man she might have known
Never crossed Meg's words
That morning in the room.

The thought that Goldberg was
A man another knew
Never crossed her eyes
When, glad, she welcomed him.

The thought that Goldberg was
A man to dread and know
Jarred Stanley in the blood
When, still, he heard his name.

While Petey knew, not then,
But later, when the light
Full up upon their scene,
He looked into the room.

And by morning Petey saw
The light begin to dim
(That daylight full of sun)
Though nothing could be done.

Nat Goldberg, who arrived
With a smile on every face,
Accompanied by McCann,
Set a change upon the place.

The thought that Goldberg was
Sat in the centre of the room,
A man of weight and time,
To supervise the game.

The thought that was McCann
Walked in upon this feast,
A man of skin and bone,
With a green stain on his chest.

Allied in their theme,
They imposed upon the room
A dislocation and doom,
Though Meg saw nothing done.

The party they began,
To hail the birthday in,
Was generous and affable,
Though Stanley sat alone.

The toasts were said and sung,
All spoke of other years,
Lulu, on Goldberg's breast,
Looked up into his eyes.

And Stanley sat – alone,
A man he might have known,
Triumphant on his hearth,
Which never was his own.

For Stanley had no home,
Only where Goldberg was,
And his bloodhound McCann,
Did Stanley remember his name.

They played at blind man's buff,
Blindfold the game was run,
McCann tracked Stanley down,
The darkness down and gone

Found the game lost and won,
Meg, all memory gone,
Lulu's lovenight spent,
Petey impotent;

A man they never knew
In the centre of the room,
And Stanley's final eyes
Broken by McCann.

ANTON CHEKHOV

'The Party', 1888

HER arms and legs began to shake – the result, she supposed, of dejection, vexation, forced smiling and the discomfort that she felt all over her body. To conceal her trembling from the guests she tried to talk louder, to laugh, and to keep moving. 'If I suddenly burst into tears I'll say I have toothache,' she thought.

Well, they finally beached the boats at the 'Isle of Good Hope', this being a peninsula formed by a sharp bend in the river and overgrown with a coppice of old birch trees, willows and poplars. Under the trees stood tables with steaming samovars on them. Vasily and Gregory, in tail-coats and white knitted gloves, were busy with the tea things. On the far bank, opposite 'Good Hope', were the carriages that had brought the provisions and from them baskets and bundles of food were being ferried to the Isle in a skiff much like *Penderakliya*. The footmen, the coachmen, and even the peasant manning the skiff – all had the solemn, festive air seen only in children and servants.

While Olga made tea and poured the first glasses, the guests were busy with cordials and sweetmeats. There ensued the kind of tea-drinking chaos usual at picnics and so tiresome and exhausting for hostesses. Hardly had Gregory and Vasily had time to take the tea round when empty glasses were already being held out to Olga. One asked for it without sugar, another wanted it strong, a third wanted it weak, and a fourth was saying no more thank you. Olga had to remember all this and then shout, 'Were you the one without sugar, Ivan Petrovich?' or, 'I say, all of you, who wanted it weak?' But the person who had asked for it weak or without sugar had now forgotten which, being engrossed in agreeable conversation, and took the first glass that came to hand. A little way from the table drifted disconsolate ghostlike figures pretending to look for mush-rooms in the grass or read the labels on boxes. These were the ones for whom there were not enough glasses.

'Have you had tea?' Olga would ask, and the person in question would tell her not to worry, adding that he would have some later, though it would have suited her better if the guests didn't have some later; but got a move on.

Some of them were absorbed in conversation and drank their tea slowly, holding on to their glasses for half an hour, while others – especially those who had drunk a great deal at dinner – stayed close to the table drinking glass after glass, so that Olga hardly had time to fill them. One young wag sipped his tea through a lump of sugar, and kept saying: 'I love to pamper myself, sinner that I am, with the Chinese herb.' From time to time he sighed deeply, asking for 'the favour of another tiny dish'. He drank a lot and crunched the sugar aloud, thinking this all very funny and original – and a superb take-off of a typical Russian merchant. That these trivialities were all agony to the hostess no one realized, and it would have been hard for them to do so because Olga was all affable smiles and idle chit-chat.

She was not feeling well. She was irritated by the crowd, by the laughter, by the questions, by the funny young man, by the footmen – at their wits' end and run off their feet – by the children hanging round near the table. She was irked by Vata looking like Nata, and Kolya like Mitya, so that you couldn't tell which had had tea and which hadn't. She sensed her strained smile of welcome turning sour, and she felt ready to burst into tears at any moment.

HUGH WHITEMORE
Stevie (unpublished)

S TEVIE is waiting to collect the Queen's Gold Medal for Poetry at Buckingham Palace.

'I was met by a rather decorative young man in naval uniform, and he took me into an outer room, whatever it's called, a huge room, and there was this lady-in-waiting, a most agreeable girl, and we had a very giggly time. She asked me to do a poem, so I hissed a short one under my breath, the one about a poor debutante sitting alone at a grand ball. It seemed appropriate, I thought.

> I cannot imagine anything nicer
> Than to be struck by lightning and killed suddenly crossing a field
> As if somebody cared.
> Nobody cares whether I am alive or dead.

My word yes we had a very jolly time.

'The crowd was already thinning . . .'

―――――⊰∘∘∘⊱―――――

JAMES BALDWIN

Another Country, 1963

THE crowd was already thinning, most of the squares were beginning to drift away. Once they were gone, the party would change character and become very pleasant and quiet and private. The lights would go down, the music become softer, the talk more sporadic and more sincere. Somebody might sing or play the piano. They might swap stories of the laughs they'd had, gigs they'd played, riffs they remembered, or the trouble they'd seen. Somebody might break out with some pot and pass it slowly around, like the pipe of peace. Somebody, curled on a rug in a far corner of the room, would begin to snore. Whoever danced would dance more languorously, holding tight. The shadows of the room would be alive. Toward the very end, as morning and the brutal sounds of the city began their invasion through the wide French doors, somebody would go into the kitchen and break out with some coffee. Then they would raid the icebox and go home. The host and hostess would finally make it between their sheets and stay in bed all day.

TOM WOLFE

The Bonfire of the Vanities, 1987

BUT there was a yet more compelling reason for the hired car and driver. It would be perfectly *okay* for the two of them to arrive for dinner at a Good Building (the going term) on Fifth Avenue by taxi, and it would cost less than three dollars. But what would they do *after* the party? How could they walk *out* of the Bavardages' building and have all the world, *tout le monde*, see them standing out in the street, the McCoys, that game couple, their hands up in the air, bravely, desperately, pathetically trying to hail a taxi? The doormen would be no help, because they would be tied up ushering *tout le monde* to their limousines. So he had hired this car and this driver, this white-haired driver, who would drive them six blocks, wait three and a half or four hours, then drive them six blocks and depart. Including a 15 percent tip and the sales tax, the cost would be $197.20 or $246.50, depending on whether they were charged for four or five hours in all.

Hemorrhaging money! Did he even have a job left! Churning fear ... Lopwitz ... Surely, Lopwitz wouldn't *sack* him ... because of three miserable days ... *and $6 million, you ninny!* ... Must start cutting back ... tomorrow ... Tonight, of course, it was imperative to have a car and driver.

To make matters worse, the driver couldn't pull up to the sidewalk near the entrance, because so many limousines were in the way. He had to double-park. Sherman and Judy had to thread their way between the limousines ... Envy ... envy ... From the license plates Sherman could tell that these limousines were not hired. They were *owned* by those whose sleek hides were hauled here in them. A chauffeur, a good one willing to work long hours and late hours, cost $36,000 a year, minimum; garage space, maintenance, insurance, would cost another $14,000 at least; a total of $50,000, none of it deductible. *I make a million dollars a year – and yet I can't afford that!*

He reached the sidewalk. *Whuh?* Just to the left, in the gloaming, a figure – *a photographer* – right over there –

Sheer terror!

My picture in the paper!

The other boy, the big one, the brute, sees him and goes to the police!

The police! The two detectives! The fat one! The one with the lopsided face! McCoy – goes to parties at the Bavardages', does he! Now they truly smell blood!

Horrified, he stares at the photographer—

—and discovers that it's only a young man walking a dog.

MARTIN AMIS
Other People, 1981

NOW people started to leave. Mary thought at first that they were just going out somewhere; but then it became clear that they were going home, that they lived in other places . . . In confusion Mary announced that she was going home too. Jamie nodded abstractedly and said he might walk with her some of the way if he felt up to it. He would walk with her as far as he could.

Mary went to the lavatory. She felt strange, slipped, dangling. The flat was shadowy and vast, possibly endless. The high corridor had no light at the end, so any distances might be covered by the granulated air: anything might be happening down those distances. She went where she had been told to go. People were still leaving but by now she couldn't hear them. She had been heading for the fourth door on her right for quite a long time and still had a fair way to go!

ANNE BRONTË
The Tenant of Wildfell Hall, 1848

WE managed very well without them, however. With a single set of quadrilles, and several country dances, we carried it on to a pretty late hour; and at length, having called upon our musician to strike up a waltz, I was just about to whirl Eliza round in that delightful dance, accompanied by Lawrence and Jane Wilson, and Fergus and Rose, when Mr Millward interposed with—

'No, no, I don't allow that! Come, it's time to be going now.'

'Oh, no, papa!' pleaded Eliza.

'High time, my girl – high time! Moderation in all things, remember! That's the plan – Let your moderation be known unto all men!'

But in revenge, I followed Eliza into the dimly-lighted passage, where, under the pretence of helping her on with her shawl, I fear I must plead guilty to snatching a kiss behind her father's back, while he was enveloping his throat and chin in the folds of a night comforter. But alas! in turning round, there was my mother close beside me. The consequence was, that no sooner were the guests departed, than I was doomed to a very serious remonstrance, which unpleasantly checked the galloping course of my spirits, and made a disagreeable close to the evening.

'My dear Gilbert,' said she, 'I wish you wouldn't do so! You know how deeply I have your advantage at heart, how I love you and prize you above everything else in the world, and how much I long to see you well settled in life – and how bitterly it would grieve me to see you married to that girl – or any other in the neighbourhood. What you see in her I don't know. It isn't only the want of money that I think about – nothing of the kind – but there's neither beauty, nor cleverness, nor goodness, nor anything else that's desirable. If you knew your own value, as I do, you wouldn't dream of it. Do wait awhile and see! If you bind yourself to her, you'll repent it all your lifetime when you look round and see how many better there are. Take my word for it, you will.'

'Well, mother, do be quiet! – I hate to be lectured! – I'm not going to marry yet, I tell you; but – dear me! mayn't I enjoy myself at all?'

'Yes, my dear boy, but not in that way. Indeed, you shouldn't do such things. You would be wronging the girl, if she were what she ought to be; but I assure you she is as artful a little hussy as anybody need wish to see; and you'll get entangled in her snares before you know where you are. And if you marry her, Gilbert, you'll break my heart – so there's an end of it.'

'Well, don't cry about it, mother,' said I, for the tears were gushing from her eyes; 'there, let that kiss efface the one I gave Eliza; don't abuse her any more, and set your mind at rest; for I'll promise never – that is, I'll promise to think twice before I take any important step you seriously disapprove of.'

So saying, I lighted my candle, and went to bed, considerably quenched in spirit.

ANON

'Little Clothilda'

LITTLE Clothilda
   Well and hearty
Thought she'd like
To give a party

But as her friends were shy and wary
Nobody came
But her own canary.

WINTHROP MACKWORTH PRAED

'Goodnight to the Season!', 1848

GOOD-NIGHT to the Season! 'tis over!
  Gay dwellings no longer are gay;
The courtier, the gambler, the lover,
  Are scattered like swallows away:
There's nobody left to invite one,
  Except my good uncle and spouse;
My mistress is bathing at Brighton,
  My patron is sailing at Cowes:
For want of a better employment,
  Till Ponto and Don can get out,
I'll cultivate rural enjoyment,
  And angle immensely for trout.

Good-night to the Season! – the lobbies,
  Their changes, and rumours of change,
Which startled the rustic Sir Bobbies,
  And made all the Bishops look strange:
The breaches, and battles, and blunders,
  Performed by the Commons and Peers;
The Marquis's eloquent thunders,
  The Baronet's eloquent ears:
Denouncings of Papists and treasons,
  Of foreign dominion and oats;
Misrepresentations of reasons,
  And misunderstandings of notes.

Good-night to the Season! – the buildings
  Enough to make Inigo sick;
The paintings, and plasterings, and gildings
  Of stucco, and marble, and brick;
The orders deliciously blended,
  From love of effect, into one;
The club-houses only intended,

    The palaces only begun;
The hell where the fiend, in his glory,
    Sits staring at putty and stones,
And scrambles from story to story,
    To rattle at midnight his bones.

Good-night to the Season! the dances,
    The fillings of hot little rooms,
The glancings of rapturous glances,
    The fancyings of fancy costumes;
The pleasures which Fashion makes duties,
    The praisings of fiddles and flutes,
The luxury of looking at beauties,
    The tedium of talking to mutes;
The female diplomatists, planners
    Of matches for Laura and Jane,
The ice of her Ladyship's manners,
    The ice of his Lordship's champagne.

Good-night to the Season! the rages
    Led off by the chiefs of the throng,
The Lady Matilda's new pages,
    The Lady Eliza's new song;
Miss Fennel's macaw, which at Boodle's
    Is held to have something to say;
Mrs Splenetic's musical poodles,
    Which bark 'Batti Batti' all day;
The pony Sir Araby sported,
    As hot and as black as a coal,
And the Lion his mother imported,
    In bearskins and grease, from the Pole.

Good-night to the Season! the Toso,
    So very majestic and tall;
Miss Ayton, whose singing was so-so,
    And Pasta, divinest of all;
The labour in vain of the Ballet,
    So sadly deficient in stars;
The foreigners thronging the Alley,
    Exhaling the breath of cigars;
The 'loge' where some heiress, how killing,
    Environed with Exquisites sits,

The lovely one out of her drilling,
    The silly ones out of their wits.

Good-night to the Season! the splendour
    That beamed in the Spanish Bazaar;
Where I purchased – my heart was so tender –
    A card-case, – a pasteboard guitar, –
A bottle of perfume, – a girdle, –
    A lithographed Riego full-grown,
Whom Bigotry drew on a hurdle
    That artists might draw him on stone, –
A small panorama of Seville, –
    A trap for demolishing flies, –
A caricature of the Devil, –
    And a look from Miss Sheridan's eyes.

Good-night to the Season! the flowers
    Of the grand horticultural fête,
When boudoirs were quitted for bowers,
    And the fashion was not to be late;
When all who had money and leisure
    Grew rural o'er ices and wines,
All pleasantly toiling for pleasure,
    All hungrily pining for pines,
And making of beautiful speeches,
    And marring of beautiful shows,
And feeding on delicate peaches,
    And treading on delicate toes.

Good-night to the Season! another
    Will come with its trifles and toys,
And hurry away like its brother,
    In sunshine, and odour, and noise.
Will it come with a rose or a briar?
    Will it come with a blessing or curse?
Will its bonnets be lower or higher?
    Will its morals be better or worse?
Will it find me grown thinner or fatter,
    Or fonder of wrong or of right,
Or married, – or buried? – no matter,
    Good-night to the Season, Good-night!

EVELYN WAUGH
Brideshead Revisited, 1945

IT was a gruesome evening, and I was astonished to find, when at last the party broke up, that it was only a few minutes after eleven. My father helped himself to a glass of barley-water and said: 'What very dull friends I have! You know, without the spur of your presence I should never have roused myself to invite them. I have been very negligent about entertaining lately. Now that you are paying me such a long visit, I will have many such evenings. You liked Miss Gloria Orme-Herrick?'

'No.'

'No? Was it her little moustache you objected to or her very large feet? Do you think she enjoyed herself?'

'No.'

'That was my impression also. I doubt if any of our guests will count this as one of their happiest evenings. That young foreigner played atrociously, I thought. Where can I have met him? And Miss Constantia Smethwick – where can I have met *her*? But the obligations of hospitality must be observed. As long as you are here, you shall not be dull.'

RACHEL CUSK
Saving Agnes, 1993

THE house, like the party, was subsiding. It didn't lurch or tilt Titanically, crockery and silverware crashing to the floor, women in tight taffeta dresses flung screaming across the room; like the party, it wasn't a large-scale Hollywood affair. As yet the only evidence of its sinking was a crack, a long narrow wound in the sitting-room wall, and Agnes Day felt that it presaged a destiny altogether more menacing.

She stood at the foot of the stairs where a handful of stragglers, having not long ago heroically resisted the two o'clock exodus, now lingered with an air of having in some way been cheated. On the far side of the room, one or two people stood immobile in the landscape of bottles and ashtrays, overturned candles and shattered glass, of wine pools banked by little white hillocks of salt and fringed with

crumpled cigarette packets, like contorted statues in an abstract
sculpture park. She realised there was no one here she wanted to
talk to, no one she could even bear talking to.

'The condemned man ate a hearty breakfast,' said Merlin cheerfully, passing her by as he trawled the room with a large black
bin-liner.

Agnes headed for the stairs, where a candle was lying felled in a
pool of its own wax on the carpet. Merlin and Nina had, rightly she
now admitted, been opposed to her candle scheme; but the house
had looked so lovely by candlelight, so aglow with anticipation and
promise, that she had forced them to yield. Merlin had submitted
gratifyingly swiftly. Nina, less pliant but always with a ready
definition of democracy to hand, knew majority rule when she saw
it. They had seen it as a whim, Agnes knew; a flimsy, floating thing
which scientists might examine under a microscope. But if that were
what it was she was full of them, riddled with terminal caprice. She
toured her disease like a schizophrenic commuter, trudging back and
forth between how things were and how she wanted them to be. The
candles belonged to the latter world and it was a place she habitually
visited alone. Roaming through the gloaming, she had almost been
happy.

Agnes Day paused at the foot of the stairs. Her guests looked
wild-eyed and nocturnal, something seen in a nature documentary.
Some people in one corner were puncturing beer cans with ball-
point pens. A geyser of brown liquid foamed over the curtains. Nina
was lounging on a nearby sofa, engaged in conversation.

'Look,' she sighed impatiently. 'Women don't necessarily want
men to accept their hideous physical proclivities. We need a secret
life. It's part of our autonomy. In fact, I can't think of anything
worse than some post-feminist prat fawning over my body hair.'

'Not at all!' cried the recipient of this lecture, apparently unde-
terred by it. He had something on his upper lip which, on closer
inspection, Agnes saw to be a moustache. 'You shouldn't be embar-
rassed about it! In fact, I think there's nothing more beautiful than a
woman with hairy armpits.'

Nina rested her head on two fingers pointed at her temple like a
revolver and rolled her eyes at Agnes, who changed course with grim
determination and fled up the stairs.

JEROME K. JEROME

Three Men in a Boat, 1889

HE finished amid a perfect shriek of laughter. We said it was the funniest thing we had ever heard in all our lives. We said how strange it was that, in the face of things like these, there should be a popular notion that the Germans hadn't any sense of humour. And we asked the Professor why he didn't translate the song into English, so that the common people could understand it, and hear what a real comic song was like.

Then Herr Slossenn Boschen got up, and went on awful. He swore at us in German (which I should judge to be a singularly effective language, for that purpose), and he danced, and shook his fists, and called us all the English he knew. He said he had never been so insulted in all his life.

It appeared that the song was not a comic song at all. It was about a young girl who lived in the Hartz Mountains, and who had given up her life to save her lover's soul; and he died, and met her spirit in the air; and then, in the last verse, he jilted her spirit and went off with another spirit – I'm not quite sure of the details, but it was something very sad, I know. Herr Boschen said he had sung it once before the German Emperor, and he (the German Emperor) had sobbed like a little child. He (Herr Boschen) said it was generally acknowledged to be one of the most tragic and pathetic songs in the German language.

It was a trying situation for us – very trying. There seemed to be no answer. We looked round for the two young men who had done this thing, but they had left the house in an unostentatious manner immediately after the end of the song.

That was the end of that party. I never saw a party break up so quietly, and with so little fuss. We never said good night even to one another. We came downstairs one at a time, walking softly, and keeping the shady side. We asked the servant for our hats and coats in whispers, and opened the door for ourselves, and slipped out, and got round the corner quickly, avoiding each other as much as possible.

'The hideous aspect of departed pleasure'

KATHLEEN FERRIER

Marriage, 1818

MARY'S inexperienced mind expected to find, on her return to Beech Park, some vestige of the pleasures of the preceding night – some shadows, at least, of gaiety, to shew what happiness she had sacrificed – what delight her friends had enjoyed; but, for the first time, she beheld the hideous aspect of departed pleasure. Drooping evergreens, dying lamps, dim transparencies, and faded flowers, met her view as she crossed the hall; while the public rooms were covered with dust from the chalked floors, and wax from the droppings of the candles. Every thing, in short, looked tawdry and forlorn. Nothing was in its place – nothing looked as it used to do – and she stood amazed at the disagreeable metamorphose all things had undergone.

Hearing some one approach, she turned, and beheld Dr Redgill enter.

'So – it's only you, Miss Mary!' exclaimed he, in a tone of chagrin. 'I was in hopes it was some of the women-servants. 'Pon my soul, it's disgraceful to think that, in this house, there is not a woman stirring yet! I have sent five messages, by my man, to let Mrs Brown know that I have been waiting for my breakfast these two hours; but this confounded ball has turned every thing upside down! – You are come to a pretty scene,' continued he, looking round with a mixture of fury and contempt, – 'a very pretty scene! 'Pon my honour, I blush to see myself standing here! Just look at these rag!' kicking a festoon of artificial roses that had fallen to the ground. 'Can any thing be more despicable? – and to think that rational creatures in possession of their senses should take pleasure in the sight of such trumpery! – 'Pon my soul, I – I – declare it confounds me! I really used to think Lady Emily (for this is all her doing) had some sense – but such a display of folly as this!'

'Pshaw!' said Mary, 'it is not fair in us to stand here analysing the dregs of gaiety after the essence is gone. I daresay this was a very brilliant scene last night.'

'Brilliant scene, indeed!' repeated the Doctor, in a most wrathful accent: 'I really am amazed – I – yes – brilliant enough – if you mean, that there was a glare of light, enough to blind the devil. I thought my eyes would have been put out, the short time I staid; indeed, I don't think this one has recovered it yet,' advancing a fierce blood-shot eye almost close to Mary's. 'Don't you think it looks a *leetle* inflamed, Miss Mary?'

Mary gave it as her opinion that it did.

'Well, that's all I've got by this business; but I never was consulted about it. I thought it my duty, however, to give a *leetle* hint to the Earl, when the thing was proposed. "My Lord," says I, "your house is your own; you have a right to do what you please with it; burn it; pull it down; make a purgatory of it; but, for God's sake, don't give a ball in it!" The ball was given, and you see the consequences. A ball! and what's a ball, that a whole family should be thrown into disorder for it?'

'I daresay to those who are engaged in it, it is a very delightful amusement at the time.'

'Delightful fiddlestick! 'Pon my soul, I'm surprised at you, Miss Mary! I thought your staying away was a pretty strong proof of your good sense; but I – hem! Delightful amusement, indeed! to see human creatures twirling one another about all night like so many monkies – making perfect mountebanks of themselves. Really, I look upon dancing as a most degrading and a most immoral practice. 'Pon my soul, I – *I* couldn't have the face to waltz, I know; and it's all on account of this delightful amusement,' with a convulsive shake of his chin, 'that things are in this state – myself kept waiting for my breakfast two hours and a half beyond my natural time: not that I mind myself at all – that's neither here nor there – and if I was the only sufferer, I'm sure I should be the very last to complain – but I own it vexes – it distresses me – 'pon my honour, I can't stand seeing a whole family going to destruction!'

The Doctor's agitation was so great, that Mary really pitied him.

JOHN AUBREY
'Sir John Suckling', from *Brief Lives*, 1813

WHEN his *Aglaura* was put on, he bought all the Cloathes himselfe, which were very rich; no tinsell, all the lace pure gold and silver, which cost him . . . I have now forgott. He had some scaenes to it, which in those days were only used at Masques.

He went into France, where after sometime, being come to the bottome of his Found, reflecting on the miserable and despicable condition he should be reduced to, having nothing left to maintaine him, he (having a convenience for that purpose, lyeing at an apothecarie's house in Paris) tooke poyson, which killed him miserably with vomiting. He was buryed in the Protestants Churchyard. This was (to the best of my remembrance) 1646.

His Picture, which is like him, before his Poemes, says that he was about 28 yeares old when he dyed.

OSCAR WILDE
Lord Arthur Savile's Crime, 1887

TEN minutes later, with face blanched by terror, and eyes wild with grief, Lord Arthur Savile rushed from Bentinck House, crushing his way through the crowd of fur-coated footmen that stood round the large striped awning, and seeming not to see or hear anything. The night was bitter cold, and the gas-lamps round the square flared and flickered in the keen wind; but his hands were hot with fever, and his forehead burned like fire. On and on he went, almost with the gait of a drunken man. A policeman looked curiously at him as he passed, and a beggar, who slouched from an archway to ask for alms, grew frightened, seeing misery greater than his own. Once he stopped under a lamp, and looked at his hands. He thought he could detect the stain of blood already upon them, and a faint cry broke from his trembling lips.

Murder! that is what the chiromantist had seen there. Murder! The very night seemed to know it, and the desolate wind to howl it in his ear. The dark corners of the streets were full of it. It grinned at him from the roofs of the houses.

First he came to the Park, whose sombre woodland seemed to

fascinate him. He leaned wearily up against the railings, cooling his brow against the wet metal, and listening to the tremulous silence of the trees. 'Murder! murder!' he kept repeating, as though iteration could dim the horror of the word. The sound of his own voice made him shudder, yet he almost hoped that Echo might hear him, and wake the slumbering city from its dreams. He felt a mad desire to stop the casual passer-by, and tell him everything.

Then he wandered across Oxford Street into narrow, shameful alleys. Two women with painted faces mocked at him as he went by. From a dark courtyard came a sound of oaths and blows, followed by shrill screams, and, huddled upon a damp door-step, he saw the crooked-back forms of poverty and eld. A strange pity came over him. Were these children of sin and misery predestined to their end, as he to his? Were they, like him, merely the puppets of a monstrous show?

And yet it was not the mystery, but the comedy of suffering that struck him; its absolute uselessness, its grotesque want of meaning. How incoherent everything seemed! How lacking in all harmony! He was amazed at the discord between the shallow optimism of the day, and the real facts of existence. He was still very young.

After a time he found himself in front of Marylebone Church. The silent roadway looked like a long riband of polished silver, flecked here and there by the dark arabesques of waving shadows. Far into the distance curved the line of flickering gas-lamps, and outside a little walled-in house stood a solitary hansom, the driver asleep inside. He walked hastily in the direction of Portland Place, now and then looking round, as though he feared that he was being followed. At the corner of Rich Street stood two men, reading a small bill upon a hoarding. An odd feeling of curiosity stirred him, and he crossed over. As he came near, the word 'Murder', printed in black letters, met his eye. He started, and a deep flush came into his cheek. It was an advertisement offering a reward for any information leading to the arrest of a man of medium height, between thirty and forty years of age, wearing a billycock hat, a black coat, and check trousers, and with a scar upon his right cheek. He read it over and over again, and wondered if the wretched man would be caught, and how he had been scarred. Perhaps, some day, his own name might be placarded on the walls of London. Some day, perhaps, a price would be set on his head also.

The thought made him sick with horror. He turned on his heel, and hurried into the night.

Where he went he hardly knew. He had a dim memory of wandering through a labyrinth of sordid houses, and it was bright dawn when he found himself at last in Piccadilly Circus. As he strolled home towards Belgrave Square, he met the great waggons on their way to Covent Garden. The white-smocked carters, with their pleasant sunburnt faces and coarse curly hair, strode sturdily on, cracking their whips, and calling out now and then to each other; on the back of a huge grey horse, the leader of a jangling team, sat a chubby boy, with a bunch of primroses in his battered hat, keeping tight hold of the mane with his little hands, and laughing; and the great piles of vegetables looked like masses of jade against the morning sky, like masses of green jade against the pink petals of some marvellous rose. Lord Arthur felt curiously affected, he could not tell why. There was something in the dawn's delicate loveliness that seemed to him inexpressibly pathetic, and he thought of all the days that break in beauty, and that set in storm. These rustics, too, with their rough, good-humoured voices, and their nonchalant ways, what a strange London they saw! A London free from the sin of night and the smoke of day, a pallid, ghost-like city, a desolate town of tombs! He wondered what they thought of it, and whether they knew anything of its splendour and its shame, of its fierce, fiery-coloured joys, and its horrible hunger, of all it makes and mars from morn to eve. Probably it was to them merely a mart where they brought their fruit to sell, and where they tarried for a few hours at most, leaving the streets still silent, the houses still asleep. It gave him pleasure to watch them as they went by. Rude as they were, with their heavy, hob-nailed shoes, and their awkward gait, they brought a little of Arcady with them. He felt that they had lived with Nature, and that she had taught them peace. He envied them all that they did not know.

By the time he had reached Belgrave Square the sky was a faint blue, and the birds were beginning to twitter in the gardens.

MARY CHOLMONDELEY

Red Pottage, 1899

WHEN Hugh awoke the morning after Lady Newhaven's party the day was already far advanced. A hot day had succeeded to a hot night. For a few seconds he lay like one emerging from the influence of morphia, who feels his racked body still painlessly afloat on a sea of rest, but is conscious that it is drifting back to the bitter shores of pain, and who stirs neither hand nor foot for fear of hastening the touch of the encircling aching sands on which he is so soon to be cast in agony once more.

His mind cleared a little. Rachel's grave face stood out against a dark background – a background darker surely than that of the summer night. He remembered with self-contempt the extravagant emotion which she aroused in him.

'Absurd,' Hugh said to himself, with the distrust of all sudden springs of pure emotion which those who have misused them rarely escape. And then another remembrance, which only a sleeping draught had kept at bay, darted upon him like a panther on its prey.

He had drawn the short lighter.

He started violently, and then fell back trembling.

'Oh, my God!' he said involuntarily.

He lay still, telling himself that this dreadful nightmare would pass, would fade in the light of common day.

His servant came in noiselessly with a cup of coffee and a little sheaf of letters.

He pretended to be asleep; but when the man had gone he put out his shaking hand for the coffee and drank it.

The mist before his mind gradually listed. Gradually, too, the horror on his face whitened to despair, as a twilight meadow whitens beneath the evening frost. He had drawn the short lighter. Nothing in heaven or earth could alter that fact.

He did not stop to wonder how Lord Newhaven had become aware of his own dishonour, or at the strange weapon with which he had avenged himself. He went over every detail of his encounter with him in the study. His hand had been forced. He had been thrust into a vile position. He ought to have refused to draw. He did not agree to draw. Nevertheless he had drawn. And Hugh knew that if it had to be done again, he should again have been compelled to draw by the iron will before which his was as straw. He could not have met the scorn of those terrible half-closed eyes if he had refused.

'There was no help for it,' said Hugh, half aloud. And yet to die by his own hand within five months! It was incredible. It was preposterous.

'I never agreed to it,' he said, passionately.

Nevertheless he had drawn. The remembrance ever returned to lay its cold hand upon his heart, and with it came the grim conviction that if Lord Newhaven had drawn the short lighter he would have carried out the agreement to the letter. Whether it was extravagant, unchristian, whatever might have been truly said of that unholy compact, Lord Newhaven would have stood by it.

'I suppose I must stand by it, too,' said Hugh to himself, the cold sweat breaking on his forehead. 'I suppose I am bound in honour to stand by it, too.'

He suffered his mind to regard the alternative.

To wrong a man as deeply as he had wronged Lord Newhaven; to tacitly accept. – That was where his mistake had been. Another man, that mahogany-faced fellow with the colonial accent, would have refused to draw, and would have knocked Lord Newhaven down and half killed him, or would have been knocked down and half killed by him. But to tacitly accept a means by which the injured man risked his life to avenge his honour, and then afterwards to shirk the fate which a perfectly even chance had thrown upon him instead of on his antagonist! It was too mean, too despicable. Hugh's pale cheek burned.

'I am bound,' he said slowly to himself over and over again. There was no way of escape.

Yesterday evening, with some intuition of coming peril, he had said, 'I will get out.' The way of retreat had been open behind him. Now by one slight movement he was cut off from it for ever.

'I can't get out,' said the starling, the feathers on its breast worn away with beating against the bars.

'I can't get out,' said Hugh, coming for the first time in contact with the bars which he was to know so well, the bars of the prison he had made with his own hands.

He looked into the future with blank eyes. He had no future now.

ISAK DINESEN (KAREN BLIXEN)

Babette's Feast, 1958

WHEN Martine and Philippa locked the door they remembered Babette. A little wave of tenderness and pity swept through them: Babette alone had had no share in the bliss of the evening.

So they went out into the kitchen, and Martine said to Babette: 'It was quite a nice dinner, Babette.'

Their hearts suddenly filled with gratitude. They realized that none of their guests had said a single word about the food. Indeed, try as they might, they could not themselves remember any of the dishes which had been served. Martine bethought herself of the turtle. It had not appeared at all, and now seemed very vague and far away; it was quite possible that it had been nothing but a nightmare.

Babette sat on the chopping block, surrounded by more black and greasy pots and pans than her mistresses had ever seen in their life. She was as white and as deadly exhausted as on the night when she first appeared and had fainted on their doorstep.

After a long time she looked straight at them and said: 'I was once cook at the Café Anglais.'

Martine said again: 'They all thought that it was a nice dinner.' And when Babette did not answer a word she added: 'We will all remember this evening when you have gone back to Paris, Babette.'

Babette said: 'I am not going back to Paris.'

'You are not going back to Paris?' Martine exclaimed.

'No,' said Babette. 'What will I do in Paris? They have all gone. I have lost them all, Mesdames.'

The sisters' thoughts went to Monsieur Hersant and his son, and they said: 'Oh, my poor Babette.'

'Yes, they have all gone,' said Babette. 'The Duke of Morny, the Duke of Decazes, Prince Narishkine, General Galliffet, Aurélian Scholl, Paul Daru, the Princesse Pauline! All!'

The strange names and titles of people lost to Babette faintly confused the two ladies, but there was such an infinite perspective of tragedy in her announcement that in their responsive state of mind they felt her losses as their own, and their eyes filled with tears.

At the end of another long silence Babette suddenly smiled slightly at them and said: 'And how would I go back to Paris, Mesdames? I have no money.'

'No money?' the sisters cried as with one mouth.

'No,' said Babette.

'But the ten thousand francs?' the sisters asked in a horrified gasp.

'The ten thousand francs have been spent, Mesdames,' said Babette.

The sisters sat down. For a full minute they could not speak.

MRS HWFA WILLIAMS
It Was Such Fun!, 1935

B UT alas, the consequences of this party were rather unfortunate for me. I went down to supper with Lord Royston, and was just finishing my *consommé* when he said: 'You must not have any more; there is such an odd taste of copper.'

So I had no more *consommé*.

A little later I was eating my quail and had just taken my first mouthful, when he exclaimed: 'For heaven's sake don't swallow it! It has the same acid taste.'

I only laughed and said: 'I can't possibly get rid of it. I think you are mad on the subject.'

However, I did not eat much more supper.

The whole episode passed from my mind at the time, but at seven o'clock the next morning I woke with a terribly sore throat and raging fever. For seventeen weeks I was ill with ptomaine fever – seriously ill, for I had been badly poisoned. Several others who had been at the reception were, as I heard afterwards, also taken violently ill, but they had evidently not been so badly poisoned as I, and were able to shake off the effects quickly.

It appears that the chef had been obliged to hire some copper saucepans for the larger party of the second day; and when he came to *rechauffer* some of what had been left from the first night, he did not realize that those hired needed, as is so often the case in English kitchens, to be retinned. Hence the poisoning! It might have been much more serious, but as it was, I was the only really unlucky one.

JOSEPH MONCURE MARCH
'The Wild Party', 1928

T HE studio flickered with uneasy light.
Two sunken candles made a fight
Against grim, overwhelming night.
Their flames flared,
Whirled up gyrating;
And a crowd of shadows hovered,
Waiting.

The curtains shivered with a sudden chill:
They stirred a little on the window sill;
Then billowed, and flapped inward
Blown
By a wind that smelled of damp stone.

The room was filled with a stale reek.
It looked dishevelled:
Sordid:
Bleak.
Figures sprawled out
Flat on their backs:
Their faces were death-masks
In dirty-white wax.

The table was a wreck.
Bleared glasses stood
Half-empty, bottoms stuck to wood.

Cigarette stubs:
Ashes:
Bits of bread:
Bottles leaning,
Prostrate;
Dead.
A pink stocking: a corkscrew:
A powder puff: a French-heeled shoe:
Candle grease.
A dirty cup.
An agate saucepan, bottom up.
And a wet towel, with a stained border:
All stirred together in wild disorder.

Propped in a corner, two men stood giving
Each other a lecture on the high cost of living.
Horribly tight,
Equally polite,
Each insisted the other was right.
They stood there mumbling,
Gesturing, swaying:
Neither one knew what the other was saying.

The Victrola played steadily,
Beside it sat
A white-faced youth, with a battered hat
Aslant on his frowsy, dishevelled head,
Obviously, he wished he were dead.

He sat hunched over, staring at the wall
With eyes that saw no wall at all.
With half of one large foot he kept
The music's rhythm.
He wept.
The record played on.
Each time it ended,
He would look up startled: greatly offended.
He would then rise
With streaming eyes.
Carefully,
With a face of pain,
He would start the same tune over again.

The double bed was a tangled heap
Of figures interlocked; asleep.
Limp arms lay flung in all directions:
Legs made fantastic intersections:
White faces lay tossed back:
Mouths gaped; hideous, black.
Collars hung loose.
White bosoms lay bared.
One sleeper's eyes were open.
They stared
Up glassy; unfeeling;
At something beyond the ceiling.
A woman had taken off her gown.
She lay with drawn-up knees
In a heliotrope chemise.
Her flesh was tinted a delicate bronze-brown.

JAMES JOYCE
'The Dead', from *Dubliners*, 1914

S HE was fast asleep.

Gabriel, leaning on his elbow, looked for a few moments unresentfully on her tangled hair and half-open mouth, listening to her deep-drawn breath. So she had had that romance in her life: a man had died for her sake. It hardly pained him now to think how poor a part he, her husband, had played in her life. He watched her while she slept as though he and she had never lived together as man and wife. His curious eyes rested long upon her face and on her hair: and, as he thought of what she must have been then, in that time of her first girlish beauty, a strange friendly pity for her entered his soul. He did not like to say even to himself that her face was no longer beautiful but he knew that it was no longer the face for which Michael Furey had braved death.

Perhaps she had not told him all the story. His eyes moved to the chair over which she had thrown some of her clothes. A petticoat string dangled to the floor. One boot stood upright, its limp upper fallen down: the fellow of it lay upon its side. He wondered at his riot of emotions of an hour before. From what had it proceeded? From his aunt's supper, from his own foolish speech, from the wine and dancing, the merry-making when saying good-night in the hall, the pleasure of the walk along the river in the snow. Poor Aunt Julia! She, too, would soon be a shade with the shade of Patrick Morkan and his horse. He had caught that haggard look upon her face for a moment when she was singing *Arrayed for the Bridal*. Soon, perhaps, he would be sitting in that same drawing-room, dressed in black, his silk hat on his knees. The blinds would be drawn down and Aunt Kate would be sitting beside him, crying and blowing her nose and telling him how Julia had died. He would cast about in his mind for some words that might console her, and would find only lame and useless ones. Yes, yes: that would happen very soon.

EMILY DICKINSON

'This Quiet Dust was Gentlemen and Ladies', date unknown

THIS quiet Dust was Gentlemen and Ladies,
    And Lads and Girls;
Was laughter and ability and sighing,
    And frocks and curls.

This passive place a Summer's nimble mansion,
    Where Bloom and Bees
Fulfilled their Oriental Circuit,
    Then ceased like these.

ACKNOWLEDGEMENTS

Adler, Renata, from *Speedboat*, copyright Renata Adler 1977, reprinted by permission of Hamish Hamilton Ltd.

Allen, Hervey, from *Anthony Adverse*, copyright Hervey Allen 1934, reprinted by permission of Curtis Brown, London.

Amis, Kingsley, from *Take a Girl Like You*, copyright Kingsley Amis 1960, reprinted by permission of Victor Gollancz Ltd.

Amis, Martin, from *Other People*, copyright Martin Amis 1981, reprinted by permission of Jonathan Cape Ltd.

Anson, Lady Elizabeth, from *Party Planners Book*, copyright Lady Elizabeth Anson 1986, reprinted by permission of Weidenfeld & Nicolson.

Arlen, Michael, from *Hell Said the Duchess*, copyright Michael Arlen 1934, reprinted by permission of HarperCollins Publishers Ltd.

Arlen, Michael, from *The Romance of Iris Poole*, copyright Michael Arlen 1921, reprinted by permission of HarperCollins Publishers Ltd.

Atwood, Margaret, from *Cat's Eye*, copyright Margaret Atwood 1989, reprinted by permission of Bloomsbury Publishing Ltd.

Atwood, Margaret, from *Life Before Man*, copyright Margaret Atwood 1980, reprinted by permission of Jonathan Cape Ltd

Auchincloss, Louis, from *The Rector of Justin*, copyright Louis Auchincloss 1964, reprinted by permission of Curtis Brown, New York.

Auden, W. H. from 'At the Party', taken from *Collected Poems*, edited by Edward Mendelson, copyright W. H. Auden 1962, reprinted by permission of Faber and Faber Ltd.

Baldwin, James, from *Another Country*, copyright James Baldwin 1962, 1963, reprinted by permission of Michael Joseph Ltd.

Beaton, Cecil, from *Diaries: The Parting Years*, copyright Cecil Beaton 1978, reprinted by kind permission of the Literary Trustees of the late Sir Cecil Beaton.

Bedford, Sybille, from *A Legacy*, copyright Sybille Bedford 1956, reprinted by kind permission of Sybille Bedford.

Betjeman, John, from 'Indoor Games near Newbury' taken from *Collected Poems*, copyright John Betjeman 1958, reprinted by permission of John Murray Publishers Ltd.

Bowen, Elizabeth, from *The Death of the Heart*, copyright Elizabeth Bowen 1938, reprinted by permission of Curtis Brown, London for the Estate of E. Bowen.

Bradbury, Malcolm, from *The History Man*, copyright Malcolm Bradbury 1975, reprinted by permission of Martin Secker & Warburg.

Capote, Truman, from *Breakfast at Tiffany's*, copyright Hamish Hamilton 1958, copyright Truman Capote 1981, reprinted by permission of Hamish Hamilton Ltd.

Christie, Agatha, from *The Mirror Crack'd from Side to Side*, copyright Agatha Christie Limited 1962, reprinted by permission of Hughes Massie Ltd.

Colegate, Isabel, from *The Shooting Party*, copyright Isabel Colegate 1980, reprinted by permission of the Peters, Fraser & Dunlop Group Ltd.

Colette, from *My Mother's House*, copyright Colette 1922, reprinted by permission of Martin Secker & Warburg.

Connolly, Cyril, from *The Rock Pool*, copyright Cyril Connolly 1936, reprinted by permission of the Estate of Cyril Connolly c/o Rogers, Coleridge & White, 20 Powis Mews, London W11 1JN.

Cooper, Jilly, from *Octavia*, copyright Jilly Cooper 1977, reprinted by permission of Arlington Books (Publishers) Ltd.

Coward Noël, from *Marvellous Party*, copyright the Estate of Noël Coward 1929 by arrangement with Michael Imison Playwrights Ltd 28 Almeida Street, London N1 1TD.

Crompton, Richmal, from *William Carries On*, copyright Richmal Crompton 1942, copyright Richmal Ashbee reprinted by permission of Macmillan Children's Books Ltd.

Cusk, Rachel, from *Saving Agnes*, copyright Rachel Cusk 1993, reprinted by permission of Macmillan London Ltd.

Dinesen, Isak, from 'Babette's Feast', taken from *Anecdotes of Destiny*, copyright Isak Dinesen 1958 (Michael Joseph 1958, Penguin Books 1981), reprinted by permission of Penguin Books Ltd.

Drabble, Margaret, from *The Middle Ground*, copyright Margaret Drabble 1980, reprinted by permission of George Weidenfeld & Nicolson Ltd.

Du Maurier, Daphne, from *Rebecca*, copyright Daphne du Maurier Browning 1938, reprinted by permission of Curtis Brown Ltd., London, on behalf of the Estate of Daphne du Maurier.

Dunne, Dominick, from *People Like Us*, copyright Dominick Dunne 1988, reprinted by permission of Bantam Books, Inc., New York, all rights reserved.

Eliot, T. S., from *The Cocktail Party*, copyright T. S. Eliot 1950, reprinted by permission of Faber and Faber Ltd.

Fishlock, Trevor, from *Out of Red Darkness*, copyright Trevor Fishlock 1993, reprinted by permission of John Murray Publishers Ltd.

Freely, Maureen, from *The Life of the Party*, copyright Maureen Freely 1984, reprinted by permission of the Peters, Fraser & Dunlop Group Ltd.

Gerhardie, William, from *My Sinful Earth*, copyright William Gerhardie 1947, reprinted by permission of Curtis Brown, London.

Green, Henry, from *Party Going*, copyright Henry Green 1939, reprinted by permission of Hogarth Press, Random House UK Ltd.

Greene, Graham, from *Travels with my Aunt*, copyright Verdant SA 1969, reprinted by permission of The Bodley Head.

Hrabal, Bohumil, from *Too Loud a Solitude*, copyright Bohumil Hrabal 1976, reprinted by permission of Andre Deutsch Ltd.

Huth, Angela, from *Invitation to the Married Life*, copyright Angela Huth 1991, reprinted by permission of Sinclair-Stevenson, Reed International Books.

Huxley, Aldous, from *Point Counter Point*, copyright Aldous Huxley 1928, reprinted by permission of Chatto and Windus Ltd.

Iles, Francis, from *Malice Aforethought*, copyright The Society of Authors 1931, and published by Dent in their Mastercrime series, reprinted by permission of The Society of Authors.

Keane, Mollie, from *Good Behaviour*, copyright Mollie Keane 1981, reprinted by permission of Andre Deutsch Ltd.

Kee, Robert, from *Broadstrop in Season*, copyright Robert Kee 1959, reprinted by permission of Martin Secker & Warburg.

Lampedusa, Giuseppe di, from *The Leopard*, copyright Giuseppe di Lampedusa 1960, reprinted by permission of HarperCollins Publishers Ltd.

Larkin, Philip, from 'Vers de Société', taken from *High Windows*, copyright Philip Larkin 1971, reprinted by permission of Faber and Faber Ltd.

Lees Milne, James, from *People and Places*, copyright James Lees Milne 1992, reprinted by permission of John Murray Publishers Ltd.

Lehmann, Rosamond, from *Invitation to the Waltz*, copyright Rosamond Lehmann 1932, reprinted by permission of The Society of Authors as literary representative of the Estate of Rosamond Lehmann.

Leigh, Mike, from *Abigail's Party*, copyright Mike Leigh 1977, reprinted by permission of the Peters, Fraser & Dunlop Group Ltd.

Leigh-Fermor, Patrick, from *The Violins of St Jacques*, copyright Patrick Leigh-Fermor 1953, reprinted by permission of John Murray Publishers Ltd.

Mann, Thomas, from *Buddenbrooks*, copyright Thomas Mann 1901, reprinted by permission of Martin Secker & Warburg.

March, Joseph Moncure, from *The Wild Party*, copyright Joseph Moncure March 1928, reprinted by permission of Curtis Brown, London.

Mare, Walter de la, from 'The Feckless Dinner Party', copyright Walter de la Mare 1933, reprinted by permission of the Literary Trustees of Walter de la Mare and The Society of Authors as their representative.

Marsh, Ngaio, from *Final Curtain*, copyright Ngaio Marsh 1947, reprinted by permission of Aitken, Stone & Wylie.

Maugham, Somerset, from 'Before the Party', taken from *Collected Short Stories, Vol. 1*, copyright Somerset Maugham 1926, reprinted by permission of William Heinemann Ltd.

McWilliam, Candia, from *A Case of Knives*, copyright Candia McWilliam 1987, reprinted by permission of Bloomsbury Publishing Ltd.

Milford, Nancy, from *Zelda Fitzgerald*, copyright Nancy Milford 1970, reprinted by permission of The Bodley Head.

Mitchell, Margaret, from *Gone With the Wind*, copyright Margaret Mitchell 1936, reprinted by permission of The William Morris Agency, New York.

Mitford, Nancy, from *The Pursuit of Love*, copyright Nancy Mitford 1945, reprinted by permission of the Estate of Nancy Mitford and the Peters, Fraser & Dunlop Group Ltd.

Nabokov, Serge, from *Lolita*, copyright Serge Nabakov 1955, reprinted by permission of Weidenfeld & Nicolson Ltd.

Orczy, Baroness, from *The Scarlet Pimpernel*, copyright Baroness Orczy, reprinted by permission of Hodder & Stoughton.

Parker, Dorothy, from 'The Waltz' taken from *After Such Pleasures*, copyright Dorothy Parker 1934, reprinted by permission of Gerald Duckworth & Co. Ltd.

Pinter, Harold, from 'A View of the Party', taken from *Collected Poems and Prose*, copyright Harold Pinter 1958, reprinted by permission of Faber and Faber Ltd.

Plomer, William, from 'A Basuto Coming of Age' taken from *Collected Poems by William Plomer*, copyright William Plomer 1960, reprinted by permission of Jonathan Cape Ltd.

Sackville-West, Vita, from *The Edwardians*, copyright Vita Sackville-West 1930, reprinted by permission of Curtis Brown, London.

Shaw, George Bernard, from *Pygmalion*, copyright George Bernard Shaw 1912, reprinted by permission of The Society of Authors on behalf of the Bernard Shaw Estate.

Sitwell, Edith, from *English Eccentrics*, copyright Edith Sitwell 1933, reprinted by permission of David Higham Associates.

Smith, Martin Cruz, from *Gorky Park*, copyright Martin Cruz-Smith 1981, reprinted by permission of HarperCollins Publishers Ltd.

Spark, Muriel, from *The Batchelors*, copyright Muriel Spark 1960, reprinted by permission of Penguin Books Ltd.

Steinbeck, John, from *Cannery Row*, copyright John Steinbeck 1943, reprinted by permission of William Heinemann.,

Struther, Jan, from *Try Anything Twice*, copyright Jan Struther 1938, reprinted by permission of Curtis Brown, London.

Thomas, Dylan, from *Under Milk Wood*, copyright Dylan Thomas 1954, reprinted by permission of J. M. Dent.

Thurber, James, from 'The Ladies of Orlon', taken from *Alarms and Diversions*, copyright James Thurber 1957, copyright Helen Thurber and Rosemary A. Thurber 1985, reprinted by permission of HarperCollins Publishers Ltd.

Trefusis, Violet, from *Prelude to Misadventure*, copyright Violet Trefusis 1942, reprinted by permission of the authors estate.

Waugh, Evelyn, from *Brideshead Revisited*, copyright Evelyn Waugh 1945, reprinted by permission of the Peters, Fraser & Dunlop Group Ltd.

Waugh, Evelyn, from *Mr Loveday's Little Outing*, copyright Evelyn Waugh 1936, reprinted by permission of the Peters, Fraser & Dunlop Group Ltd.

Wells, H. G., from *The History of Mr Polly*, copyright H. G. Wells 1910, reprinted by permission of A. P. Watt Ltd on behalf of the Literary Executors of the Estate of H. G. Wells.

Wesley, Mary, from *A Dubious Legacy*, copyright Mary Wesley 1992, reprinted by permission of Bantam Press and all rights reserved.

White, Patrick, from *The Eye of the Storm*, copyright Patrick White 1973, reprinted by permission of the author's Estate and Jonathan Cape Ltd.

Williams, William Carlos, from *The Dance*, copyright William Carlos Williams 1944, reprinted by permission of Cambridge University Press.

Wilson, Angus, from *Anglo-Saxon Attitudes*, copyright Angus Wilson 1956, reprinted by permission of Martin Secker & Warburg.

Wolfe, Tom, from *The Bonfire of the Vanities*, copyright Tom Wolfe 1987, reprinted by permission of Jonathan Cape Ltd.

INDEX